GOTHAM GRAVES

VOLUME 1

FAMOUS GRAVES FOUND AROUND NEW YORK CITY

JOE FARRELL AND JOE FARLEY

Mechanicsburg, PA USA

Published by Sunbury Press, Inc.
Mechanicsburg, Pennsylvania

SUNBURY
PRESS
www.sunburypress.com

For information about special discounts for bulk purchases, please contact Sunbury Press Orders Dept. at (855) 338-8359 or orders@sunburypress.com.

To request one of our authors for speaking engagements or book signings, please contact Sunbury Press Publicity Dept. at publicity@sunburypress.com.

SECOND SUNBURY PRESS EDITION: January 2021

Set in Adobe Garamond | Interior design by Crystal Devine | Cover by Lawrence Knorr | Edited by Lawrence Knorr.

Publisher's Cataloging-in-Publication Data
Names: Farrell, Joe, author | Farley, Joe, author.
Title: Gotham graves : famous graves found around New York City / Joe Farrell and Joe Farley.
Description: Second trade paperback edition. | Mechanicsburg, PA : Sunbury Press, 2021. | Includes biographical references and index.
Summary: The Joes ventured to the Big Apple and its boroughs to visit the graves of the rich, famous, and infamous.
Identifiers: ISBN 978-1-620064-75-7 (softcover).
Subjects: BIOGRAPHY & AUTOBIOGRAPHY / Rich & Famous | HISTORY / US History / Mid-Atlantic.

Product of the United States of America
0 1 1 2 3 5 8 13 21 34 55

Continue the Enlightenment!

CONTENTS

Introduction

It was in 2011 when *Keystone Tombstones Volume One* first appeared in bookstores and on the Internet. The idea came to us about a year earlier at Nick's Café in New Cumberland, Pennsylvania, where we found ourselves surrounded by skeptics who now own multiple volumes of the series. During the writing and researching that resulted in *Volume One*, we discovered two things. One was that there were plenty of interesting stories to tell, too many to include in a single book. The other was that people we told of our project seemed to like the idea. As the publication date neared, we boldly decided to make it *Volume One*—hoping, planning, and believing that there would be a *Volume Two*. There are now eleven different volumes of Keystone Tombstones available, including four in the series and seven topical or regional volumes.

We have not exhausted the treasure trove of Pennsylvania stories, but while in a theater watching the movie *42*, I took out my phone and looked up where the subject of the film, baseball legend Jackie Robinson, was buried. I was pleased and not surprised to see that he was buried in Brooklyn. I was born and raised in Brooklyn and Queens. I grew up as a Brooklyn Dodgers fan and so thought it quite proper.

Shortly after seeing *42*, I introduced the idea of doing *Gotham Graves*, a book on people buried in New York, to the other Joe—my co-author for all ten Keystone Tombstones volumes, Joe Farley. He asked who else we would put in the book? I did some research and reported back with a list of exciting names. Joe, who grew up as a Yankees fan, asked, "Where's Babe Ruth? I thought the Babe was buried in New York." I explained that Ruth was buried in Westchester County, which, as anyone from "the City" will quickly point out, is not technically New York. "Then let's include Westchester County," he said, "We gotta have the Babe in the book." So, we included Westchester, which resulted in including Soupy Sales, Ed Sullivan, James Cagney, Ann Bancroft, and Jim Farley (no relation) in this volume and hopefully many more notables in a future volume. Researching and writing about some of the many interesting people who were laid to rest in the New York area was a pleasure. We hope you enjoy reading their stories and perhaps learning something new about them at the same time.

As with the Pennsylvania books, the first decision was who to include. This proved to be no easy task, and once again, when we were finished, we found that there were plenty of other stories left to tell. We hope to do so.

The next step was planning the trips to visit the burial sites. Anyone who has searched for a particular grave in a cemetery can attest that failing to prepare can make this difficult. In addition, because we were visiting multiple cemeteries in one visit, planning a route was necessary.

Our travels to and through New York's cemeteries were sometimes frustrating, sometimes stressful, but always interesting. We are grateful to Lou Sauers and "the other" Jim Farley (my co-author's brother who, rest assured, is very much alive) for helping us locate graves on one of our trips. We are also grateful to our publisher, Lawrence Knorr, for being our photographer on this book and booking us in a hotel we won't soon forget. We are also grateful to "the other OTHER" Jim Farley (my co-author's son), who helped us fill a photographic gap. A special thanks from both of us to my son, Marc Farrell, for his continuing interest as well as his technical support.

Finally, we are both smart enough and experienced enough to thank our wives, Mary Farrell and Sharon Farley. They have supported our every effort during this and all our other projects. They've offered solid advice and suggestions, rearranged their schedules to suit us, attended presentations, and multiple book signings. Without them, none of our books, including *Gotham Graves*, would have seen the light of day. We hope that someday they find the time to read one or two of them.

1

"What a Wonderful World"

Louis Armstrong

County: Queens • Town: Flushing
Buried at Flushing Cemetery
16306 46th Avenue

Louis Armstrong was a trumpeter, bandleader, singer, film star, and comedian. He is one of the most influential artists in jazz history. His genius and the power of his art transformed his life and continue to inspire us today. More than 40 years since his death, a larger number of his recordings from all periods of his career are available than at any time during his lifetime. His songs are broadcast and listened to every day throughout the world. His influence on the development of jazz is immeasurable.

Armstrong was born in one of the poorest sections of New Orleans on August 4, 1901. His father was a factory worker and abandoned the family soon after Louis' birth. His mother often worked as a prostitute and frequently left Louis and his younger sister Beatrice with his grandmother. Louis left school in the fifth grade to help support his family. He sang on street corners, sold newspapers, and delivered coal. On New Years' Eve in 1912, Armstrong fired his stepfather's gun in the air during a New Years' Eve celebration and was arrested and sent to the Colored Waifs Home for Boys. While there, he had his first formal music lessons and played in the home's brass band.

During these years at the home, Armstrong frequently worked for the Karnofsky family, who hired him for odd jobs. The Karnofskys treated Louis like family, feeding and nurturing him. He used to pass a local music store while working with Mr. Karnofsky and point to an old cornet in the window that he couldn't afford but longed to play. One day

Louis "Satchmo" Armstrong

Karnofsky stopped at the store, bought the cornet, and gave it to Louis. Armstrong wore a Star of David pendant for the rest of his life as a tribute to the Karnofskys.

In 1914, the home released Armstrong, and he immediately began dreaming of a life in music. He played in pick-up bands and small clubs.

He hauled coal by day and played his cornet at night. One of the best cornet players in New Orleans, Joe "King" Oliver, began acting as a mentor and occasionally used him as a substitute in his band. When Oliver decided to go north to Chicago, Armstrong replaced him in one of the most popular bands in New Orleans. His reputation grew, and soon he spent summers playing on riverboats, honing his music reading skills and meeting other jazz legends. He started to be featured in extended trumpet solos injecting his style into his solo turns and started singing and using patter in his performances. He was soon able to stop working manual labor jobs and concentrate on music.

In the summer of 1922, Armstrong received a call from King Oliver inviting him to come to Chicago and join his Creole Jazz Band. Oliver's band was the best and most influential jazz band in Chicago when it was the center of the jazz universe. He accepted and was soon taking Chicago by storm. He made his first recordings with Oliver on April 5, 1923. He soon began dating the female pianist in the band, Lillian Hardin. They married in 1924. It was his second marriage. His first, to Daisy Parker in 1918, had ended in divorce in 1923. Lil Hardin was a graduate of Fisk University and an excellent pianist who could read, write, and arrange music. She encouraged and enhanced Armstrong's career, encouraging him to cut ties with Oliver and join Fletcher Henderson's orchestra, the top African American dance band in New York City, which he did in 1924. Armstrong toured and recorded with Henderson's band, cut dozens of records as a sideman, and backed numerous blues singers, including Bessie Smith (See *Keystone Tombstones Volume 2*).

Armstrong returned to Chicago in 1925 to record with a band under his name for Okeh Records. For the next three years, he made more than 60 recordings with the Hot Five and later the Hot Seven. Today, these are generally regarded as the most important and influential recordings in jazz history. His solos on "Cornet Chop Suey" and "Potato Head Blues" changed jazz history. He also began singing on these recordings, popularizing wordless "scat singing" with his hugely popular vocal on "Heebie Jeebies." Armstrong's popularity continued to grow in Chicago, and he and a young pianist from Pittsburgh, Earl Hines, formed a potent team.

The two of them made some of the greatest recordings in jazz history, including "West End Blues."

The year 1929 was a breakthrough one for Louis Armstrong. Headlining in the popular Broadway musical *Hot Chocolates*, Armstrong had a crossover hit record with "Ain't Misbehavin'," written by Fats Waller and Andy Razaf. The recording introduced the use of a pop song as material for jazz interpretation. For the first time, Armstrong's genius touched audiences outside the jazz world, and he developed a following among white fans.

He started to work at Connie's Inn in Harlem, chief rival to the Cotton Club and a front for gangster Dutch Schultz. He found himself caught between rival mob bosses who controlled the nightclub scene in New York and Chicago and spent a lot of time on the road to avoid being forced to play for some mobster. He continued recording. Instead of doing strictly jazz numbers, Okeh Records began allowing Armstrong to record popular songs, including "I Can't Give You Anything but Love," "Stardust," In 1931, he recorded "When It's Sleepy Time Down South," which would become his theme song.

Armstrong moved to Los Angeles in 1930, seeking new opportunities and hoping to get away from the mob. He returned to Chicago in late 1931, but mob trouble still pursued him, and he went to Europe. At first, he created a sensation, but things fell apart starting in 1933. He and his second wife split up. His manager, Johnny Collins, had him in trouble financially and with the mob. Armstrong found himself being sued for breach of contract. Years of exhausting tours were taking a toll on his fingers and lips. He split with Collins and spent most of 1934 resting in Europe.

Armstrong returned to Chicago in 1935. He had no band, no engagements, and no recording contract. His lips were still sore. He still had mob troubles, and his wife, Lil Hardin, was suing him. He turned to a man with mob ties named Joe Glaser, and within months he had a new big band and was recording for Decca Records. In 1936, he became the first African American to get featured billing in a major Hollywood movie, *Pennies from Heaven,* starring Bing Crosby. In 1937, he substituted

The beautiful final resting place of the man whose influence is felt by musicians and entertainers to this day.

for Rudy Vallee on the CBS radio network and became the first African American to host a sponsored national broadcast.

In 1938, Armstrong divorced Lil Hardin and married Alpha Smith, whom he had been dating for over a decade. They divorced in 1942. That same year, he married Lucille Wilson, a Cotton Club dancer, and they settled in Corona, Queens, where they would live for the rest of their lives.

In 1947, Armstrong formed a small ensemble called the All-Stars, a group of extraordinary players whose success revitalized mainstream jazz. He was the first jazz musician to appear on *Time* magazine's cover on February 21, 1949.

Throughout the 1950s and '60s, Armstrong appeared in popular films and made numerous international tours, earning him the title "Ambassador Satch." The nicknames "Satchmo" and "Satch" are short for "Satchel Mouth." The name has many possible origins, the most popular of which is that when he would dance and sing for coins as a kid, he would scoop them up and put them in his mouth to avoid having them stolen by bigger boys. He spread goodwill for America worldwide, including State Department-sponsored tours and broadcasts in the '50s and '60s. One such concert in Ghana in 1956 drew over 100,000 fans. Legendary CBS newsman Edward R. Murrow followed Armstrong with a camera crew on some of his worldwide excursions and turned the footage into a theatrical documentary called *Satchmo the Great*. It was released in 1957.

Armstrong suffered a heart attack in 1959 while traveling in Italy. He took a few weeks off and resumed performing 300 nights a year into the 1960s. In the '60s, he continued to record, including two albums with Duke Ellington and the hit "Hello Dolly," his biggest-selling record. "Hello Dolly" went to number one on the pop chart, dislodged The Beatles from the top spot in the process, and won Armstrong a Grammy in 1964.

Although "Hello Dolly" was his biggest hit in this country, his most lasting song was a ballad recorded in 1967, which featured no trumpet; instead, it placed Louis' gravelly voice in the middle of strings and angelic

Stone that marks Armstrong's burial site.

voices. "What a Wonderful World" became a number one hit in Europe and South Africa but did not chart at all in America. The song garnered greater popularity when it was used in the 1987 movie *Good Morning Vietnam* and topped charts around the world.

Armstrong's grueling lifestyle started to take a toll on him. He stopped performing in 1969 for most of the year because of heart and kidney problems. He began performing again in 1970, but a heart attack sidelined him for two months. He died in his sleep on July 6, 1971, a month before his 70th birthday, at his home in Queens. He is buried in Flushing, New York. His pallbearers were Bing Crosby, Ella Fitzgerald, Dizzy Gillespie, Pearl Bailey, Count Basie, Harry James, Frank Sinatra, Ed Sullivan, Earl Wilson, Alan King, Johnny Carson, and David Frost.

The house where Armstrong and his wife Lucille Wilson lived from 1943 until his death was declared a National Historic Landmark in 1976. It is located at 34-56 107th Street in Corona, Queens. It is now a museum that presents concerts and educational programs. The Louis Armstrong Educational Foundation was founded and funded by Armstrong in 1969 and still operates today. Armstrong started the Foundation to give back to the world, "some of the goodness he received."

These grave goods left behind by visitors show that the great musician hasn't been forgotten.

In 1972, Armstrong was posthumously awarded the Grammy Lifetime Achievement Award. Over the years, 11 of his recordings have been inducted into the Grammy Hall of Fame. In 1960 he was given a star on the Hollywood Walk of Fame. In 1995, the U.S. Postal Service issued a commemorative postage stamp. In 2001—in commemoration of his birth centennial—New Orleans' main airport was renamed Louis Armstrong New Orleans International Airport.

If You Go:

Many graves of notable people are in Flushing Cemetery, including one of Louis Armstrong's friends and pallbearers, **Dizzy Gillespie** (1917–1993). Gillespie was himself one of the significant contributors to the development of American bebop and modern jazz. He began his career in the 1930s as a member of Cab Calloway's orchestra and then led his own bands for the next 60 years. Many critics say he was the best trumpeter of all time. He played with all the greats and in 1960 was inducted into the Jazz Hall of Fame. In 1989, he received the Grammy Lifetime Achievement Award and the National Medal of Arts from President George Bush. He died of cancer at the age of 75.

Ironically, another jazz great is also buried in Flushing Cemetery. **Johnny Hodges** (1906–1970) was an alto saxophonist and featured soloist in Duke Ellington's orchestra from 1928 until he died in 1970.

Also buried here is **Vincent Sardi** (1885–1961), the famous Sardi's restaurant founder and owner. In its heyday, Sardi's was the watering hole for all of Broadway. Stars dined there after opening night performances. Producers and reporters held court there, while tourists and theatergoers gawked at famous faces. The restaurant was featured in many films, and television shows (including a recent episode of *Mad Men*) were filmed at Sardi's. Vincent Sardi died in 1969 at the age of 91.

Others buried in Flushing Cemetery:

George Hicks (1905–1965), a noted war correspondent and journalist, was one of the few reporters to witness the June 6, 1944, Allied invasion of Normandy and broadcast it live from the USS *Ancon*. He has a star on the Hollywood Walk of Fame.

Bernard Baruch (1870–1965) was a famous financier, statesman, and political consultant. He left Wall Street in 1916 to advise President Woodrow Wilson on national defense, served on the War Industries Board, and was a staff member at the Paris Peace Conference. He remained a prominent government adviser during Franklin D. Roosevelt's administration and served as Chairman of the War Industries Board. In 1946, Truman appointed Baruch to prepare a nuclear weapons disarmament plan, where he reportedly coined the term "Cold War." Baruch graced the cover of *Time* magazine on three occasions.

2

"And Here's to You Mrs. Robinson"

Anne Bancroft

County: Westchester • Town: Valhalla
Buried at Kensico Cemetery
273 Lakeview Avenue

Her father dismissed her childhood ambition to become an actress as the product of a young girl's dreams. Yet before her career was over, she would become a noted star of both the stage and big and little screens. She would win an Academy Award for best actress and be nominated for her work in four other films. She would also place two Golden Globes, two Tony Awards, two Emmy Awards, and three British Academy of Film and Television Awards on her crowded mantel. She portrayed everything from a ballet dancer to a medieval nun in her extraordinary career but remains best known for the role she said came to cast a shadow on her other work, the alcoholic seductress Mrs. Robinson in *The Graduate.* She is best known by her stage and screen name Anne Bancroft.

She was born on September 17, 1931, in the Bronx, and christened Anna Maria Louisa Italiano. Her grandparents on both sides of the family were Italian immigrants. Her father was a pattern maker, and her mother worked for Macy's as a switchboard operator. Bancroft had two sisters, and age-wise, she was the middle child.

By the time she reached the age of five, Bancroft was already taking singing and dancing lessons. Never shy, she would showcase her talents to visiting family members and construction workers during their lunch breaks. Bancroft was raised in a Catholic family and graduated from Christopher Columbus High School in 1948. She then enrolled at the American Academy for Dramatic Arts located in Manhattan. Live

Anne Bancroft

television drama was very big at the time in New York, and she quickly found work in that genre. During this period, she appeared under the name Anne Marno.

In 1951, she agreed to help another actor who was scheduled to do a screen test. After seeing her perform, 20th Century Fox signed her to a contract. The company urged her to change her name, and after reviewing several possibilities, she decided on Bancroft. The studio relegated her to some B-movies, most of which are forgettable. As soon as her contract expired, she headed back to New York City to seek work on the stage.

During this period in 1954, Bancroft married a law student, Martin May. The marriage was short-lived. By 1956 the two had separated, and they were divorced in 1957. Meanwhile, Bancroft had come to the attention of the director Arthur Penn who arranged a meeting with the young actress. The first thing Bancroft asked Penn was, "Where's the john?" Penn, expecting that the actress would be battling her nerves, found himself taken by her sense of calm and honesty. From that beginning, the two would form quite a partnership.

Penn cast her in a Broadway play titled *Two for the Seesaw*. It was a romantic comedy/drama, and Bancroft appeared opposite Henry Fonda. Her Broadway debut was wildly successful. She won a Tony award for Best Performance by a Featured Actress in a Play. *Seesaw* launched her career, and she would never look back.

In 1959, Penn chose Bancroft to play the role of Annie Sullivan, Helen Keller's tutor, in *The Miracle Worker*. The Penn-Bancroft combination struck gold again as the play was an instant hit. In what at the time many believed would come to be her signature role, her performance earned her another Tony, this one for Best Performance by a Leading Actress in a Play. On June 27, 1960, Bancroft met Helen Keller at the latter's 80th birthday party. When the two shook hands, Keller told Bancroft that her handshake was like Sullivan's.

In 1962, United Artists hired Penn to transfer *The Miracle Worker* to the big screen. The studio wanted Elizabeth Taylor to play the part of Sullivan and agreed to budget 5 million dollars to make the film if Taylor was cast. Even though the studio cut his budget considerably, Penn decided to stick with Bancroft. It turned out to be the right choice as the film opened to positive critical reviews, and Bancroft won the Academy Award for Best Actress. To this day, she remains among the few in her profession to have taken home both a Tony and an Academy Award for the same role.

Penn went on to direct such films as *Bonnie and Clyde*, *Alice's Restaurant*, and *Little Big Man*, but he never forgot Bancroft. Recalling her later in his life, Penn said, "Annie changed my life not only because she brought both of us success, but because she taught me the importance of always being hungry, of always trying harder, of always defying expectations."

In Bancroft's next significant movie, she starred with Peter Finch in the British film *The Pumpkin Eater.* The movie revolves around her role as an unusually fertile woman who becomes depressed and withdrawn due to her third husband's marital affairs. *Time* magazine said that "the ironing out of a well-kept wife's unkempt psyche is portrayed with harrowing perception by Anne Bancroft." Her performance would earn her a second Academy Award nomination though she would lose to Julie Andrews for her role in *Mary Poppins.*

In 1964, Bancroft married Mel Brooks. The two had met in 1961, at a rehearsal for the *Perry Como* television show. They would stay together for the rest of her life, and she would appear in a few of his films, most notably *To Be or Not to Be,* in which they co-starred. In other Brooks's films, she made cameo appearances. The couple had one child: Maximillian Brooks, born in 1972.

After *The Pumpkin Eater,* Bancroft appeared in a couple of movies before she landed the part for which, somewhat to her chagrin, she will always be remembered. On December 21, 1967, *The Graduate* was released. Bancroft was by far the most well-known cast member in the production, and the *New York Times* described her performance as "contemptuous and voracious." As the story goes, Bancroft wasn't the first choice to play Mrs. Robinson. Some say that director Mike Nichols initially wanted Doris Day to play the part. Other actresses mentioned as interested in playing Mrs. Robinson included Lauren Bacall, Audrey Hepburn, and Ava Gardner. While Nichols confirmed that other actresses were discussed, he insisted that only Bancroft was offered the role. According to Nichols, Bancroft received quite a bit of advice telling her to turn the part down. Many felt that it was too much of a stretch and too risky to go from playing Annie Sullivan to a character like Mrs. Robinson. Mel Brooks, who had created the television series *Get Smart* with Buck Henry (who happened to write the script for *The Graduate*), disagreed and urged her to make the movie.

The film was a surprise hit, making instant stars of Dustin Hoffman and Katherine Ross. Film critic Roger Ebert called it the "funniest American comedy of the year." To this day, the film continues to be praised for both the performances and the music provided by Simon and Garfunkel. Indeed, the duo's hit single "Mrs. Robinson" (which was initially titled "Mrs. Roosevelt") may be their best-known recording. For Bancroft, the role became the one for which she was and will be most remembered. For years afterward, men would tell Bancroft that she had been their first sexual fantasy in their younger years. The praise caused her more than a little irritation in that she came to see the role as one which made it seem as if she had done little if anything else.

However, there is no denying that Bancroft was brilliant in the film, and the role earned her another Academy Award nomination for best actress. The award went to Katherine Hepburn, who starred in *Guess Who's Coming to Dinner*. This author recently rewatched both films and can only conclude that Hepburn's win had more to do with the politics of the time and the civil rights movement than the performance. The Hepburn film seems very dated when compared to *The Graduate,* and Bancroft's portrayal of Mrs. Robinson has lost none of its impact over time.

Having conquered the big screen, Bancroft now turned to the small screen to display her many talents. In 1970, she hosted her television special *Annie: The Women in the Life of a Man* and promptly won an Emmy Award for her acting and singing. With that award, she became one of the few entertainers to take home an Oscar, an Emmy, and a Tony Award. In 1974, she hosted another successful TV special *Annie and the Hoods,* and in that same year, she made a cameo appearance in her husband's comedy film classic *Blazing Saddles*.

In 1977, she starred with Shirley MacLaine in the critically acclaimed movie *The Turning Point*. The film was nominated for eleven Academy Awards, and Bancroft once again received a Best Actress nomination. *The Turning Point* set a record, at the time, for being the most nominated film to fail to win a single Oscar. Diane Keaton beat out Bancroft that year for her performance as the title character in *Annie Hall.*

Bancroft with Dustin Hoffman in a scene from The Graduate.

In that same year, Bancroft found herself back on Broadway, starring in the play *Golda*. Back onstage, where she had risen to stardom, her work earned her another Tony nomination for Best Performance by a Leading Actress in a Play.

It appears that, at this point in her life, Bancroft was ready to try something new and different. So, she wrote, directed, and co-starred in the 1980 film *Fatso*. In the film, Dom DeLuise plays what is, in effect, the title character battling his weight. Bancroft plays his supportive sister. Film critic Peter Wu described the movie as "A very humorous and yet serious movie about obesity." Not all the reviewers were as kind. Roger Ebert, for example, gave the film one star out of four.

During this period, Bancroft was thought to be a leading candidate to get the role of Aurora Greenway (for which Shirley MacLaine took home an Oscar) in the smash hit *Terms of Endearment*. She took herself out of the running for that part by choosing to make a film with her husband, *To Be or Not to Be*. The Mel Brooks comedy was released in 1983 to positive reviews though it performed modestly at the box office.

An angel weeps atop Bancroft's tombstone.

The New York Times said, "It's no news that Mr. Brooks is one of our national treasures. The revelation for film audiences is that Ms. Bancroft is such a wildly gifted comedienne. She is not a foil, but an equal partner, who never fails to meet Mr. Brook's comic challenges and who, I suspect, provides him with the sort of solid presence that allows him to reach the heights he does. Performing singly or in tandem, they are terrific." The latter description certainly holds for the first scene in the film, with Brooks and Bancroft performing a song and dance number. The song is "Sweet Georgia Brown," and they deliver it in Polish.

Bancroft followed this film with a starring role in the movie *Garbo Talks*. For her role, in this underrated film, as a dying mother whose final wish to her son is to meet and talk to Garbo, she was nominated for a Golden Globe award for Best Actress in a Musical or Comedy. Then in 1985, she played a nun, Mother Miriam Ruth, in *Agnes of God.* Her performance would result in a fifth and final Oscar nomination for best actress. However, the Academy chose to honor Geraldine Page for her work in *The Trip to Bountiful.*

For the remainder of her career on the silver screen, she was cast in supporting roles in which she shared billing with major stars. Examples include *Love Potion No. 9,* which featured Sandra Bullock, *G. I. Jane* with Demi Moore, and *Keeping the Faith,* which had Ben Stiller and Ed Norton in the lead roles. She also continued to work in television, appearing as a shrink in a 1994 episode of *The Simpsons* and starring in the Showtime production of *The Roman Spring of Mrs. Stone.* Her role in the latter resulted in her last Emmy nomination.

On June 6, 2005, Bancroft's death came as a surprise to many, even those who counted themselves as being among her friends. She was a private person and had kept her battle with uterine cancer just that, private. She was laid to rest near her parents in Kensico Cemetery. Her tomb features a weeping angel. Her husband has never forgotten her. In 2010, Brooks gave Bancroft credit for being the guiding force behind his work, developing both *The Producers* and *Young Frankenstein* as musicals.

If You Go:

Kensico is a large cemetery that offers many sites you might want to visit. It contains a National Vaudeville Association section where several luminaries were laid to rest. Also, **Florenz Ziegfeld** and his wife **Billie**

Burke are buried here. Burke is best remembered for her role as Glinda the Good Witch of the North in the classic film *The Wizard of Oz.*

The well-known musician and big band leader **Tommy Dorsey** was laid to rest here as well. The Fabulous Dorsey Brothers Orchestra was one of the biggest bands around. Dorsey's brother and fellow musician Jimmy was buried in Shenandoah, Pennsylvania, and is a chapter in *Keystone Tombstones Volume Three*.

Yankee fans may want to stop by and visit the grave of **Harry H. Frazee,** a theatrical producer and owner of the Boston Red Sox. Frazee decided to sell **Babe Ruth** (See Chapter 19) to the Bronx Bombers.

For further information on Kensico's famous graves, see Chapter 20 on **Soupy Sales**.

3

"Lonely Orphan Girl"

Nellie Bly

County: Bronx • Town: New York
Buried at Woodlawn Cemetery
517 East 233rd Street

Nellie Bly was an American journalist known for her investigative and undercover reporting. She was a pioneer in her field and launched a new kind of investigative journalism, earning acclaim in 1887 for her exposé of patients' treatment in an insane asylum and her trip around the world in 1889.

She was born Elizabeth Jane Cochran on May 5, 1864, in Cochran's Mills, Pennsylvania. Her father, Michael Cochran, founded the town. He was a judge and mill owner, whose first marriage produced ten children. After his first wife's death, Michael Cochran met and married a woman named Mary Jane, and together they had five kids of their own, the third of which was Elizabeth. Michael died suddenly when Elizabeth was six. His death was a terrible financial blow as he left no will to protect his second family's interests. Within a year of his death, Mary Jane had to auction off their home, and the family faced what can only be described as challenging times. She remarried three years later to a man who turned out to be abusive, and it ended in a tortuous divorce.

Elizabeth went to the Indiana Normal School (now Indiana University of Pennsylvania) in Indiana, Pennsylvania, at the age of 15, to train to become a teacher, one of the few professions open to women. She was forced to drop out because of a lack of funds for tuition. She then moved with her mother to Pittsburgh and helped run their house, which they opened to boarders.

Nellie Bly

In January 1885, Elizabeth read an article in the *Pittsburgh Dispatch* by Erasmus Wilson, Pittsburgh's most popular columnist. The article was entitled "What Girls Are Good For." Wilson wrote that women belonged in the home doing domestic tasks such as serving, cooking, and raising children. He called the working woman, "a monstrosity." The article admonished women for even attempting to gain an education or embark on a career. Elizabeth, familiar with the many young women who had to work to survive in industrial Pittsburgh, read the column with anger and wrote a fiery rebuttal which she signed "Lonely Orphan Girl." The paper's editor, George Madden, was so impressed with the anonymous writer's passion that he ran an ad asking her to identify herself.

When Elizabeth went to the newspaper's office and introduced herself, Madden offered her the chance to write a rebuttal piece for publication. She wrote an article called "The Girl Puzzle," and Madden was so impressed he offered her a full-time job. At the time, it was customary for female writers to use pennames. Madden gave Elizabeth hers: Nellie Bly, after a popular song by Stephen Foster, one of Pittsburgh's favorite songs. "Nellie" began her career as a reporter by writing about social issues, including labor laws and divorce law. She became known for her investigative and undercover reporting. She posed as a sweatshop worker to expose poor working conditions and wrote a series of articles about female factory workers. These exposés brought a lot of pressure on the paper from the business community to stop her.

She convinced the editors to allow her to visit Mexico and report on her experience. She spent nearly six months reporting on the lives and customs of the Mexican people. She uncovered political corruption, which she then revealed in her articles. In one, she protested a local journalist's imprisonment for criticizing the Mexican government (a dictatorship under Porfirio Diaz). She soon found herself threatened with arrest and left the country. Her accounts were later collected in the book *Six Months in Mexico.*

Despite her love of and success in investigative reporting, Bly's editors at the *Dispatch* relegated her to the paper's "women's pages." Frustrated with doing stories about fashion and flowers, she quit and moved to New York City in hopes of a more meaningful opportunity. She hoped to land a job at a major newspaper, but she was near broke after four months with no offers. She talked her way into the editor's office at Joseph Pulitzer's paper, the *New York World*, and got hired. The first assignment for the 23-year-old was to feign insanity to investigate reports of brutality and neglect at the Women's Lunatic Asylum on Blackwell Island (now Roosevelt Island).

Photo of the great female investigative reporter.

She began by checking into a boardinghouse and refusing to go to bed, claiming to be afraid of the other boarders. In the morning, the owners called the police, and when taken in front of a judge, Bly faked amnesia. (Ironically, a rival newspaper, the *New York Sun*, ran an article in its September 25, 1887, issue detailing her arrest, beneath the headline "Who Is This Insane Girl?") She was examined by several doctors who all declared her to be insane. The head of the Insane Unit at Bellevue Hospital pronounced her "undoubtedly insane," and she was committed to the asylum where she joined 1,600 other women. She experienced horrible food and undrinkable water, ice-cold baths, flimsy garments, and abusive treatment by the staff. Dangerous patients were tied together with rope. "What, excepting torture, would produce insanity quicker than this treatment?" she asked.

After ten days, a *World* agent rescued her. On October 9, 1887, Nellie wrote the first of a two-part article detailing her experience, published in the Sunday edition of *The World* under the headline "Behind Asylum Bars." A week later, *The World* published part two, entitled "Inside the Mad House." The articles created a tremendous uproar. A grand jury launched an investigation into conditions at the asylum and invited Bly to assist. It turned out that many of the women were not mentally ill at all; some were immigrants who simply didn't know English and had trouble communicating. As a result, more money and needed reforms were instituted by the city. Her entire experience was published in book form in 1887 as *Ten Days in a Madhouse*.

Bly would spend the next several years writing articles for *The World*. She pioneered the field of investigative journalism. After going undercover, she exposed crooked lobbyists in government, tracked the plight of unwanted babies, reported on the conditions for factory workers, and arranged to be thrown into jail to expose female inmates' treatment. In 1894, she went to Chicago to cover the Pullman railroad strike and was the only reporter to tell the story from the strikers' perspective. Nellie Bly became so popular that *The World* would often use her name in the actual headline itself. People could not wait to see what she was up to next. Her fame also opened up doors of the rich and famous. She profiled boxer John L. Sullivan, suffragist Susan B. Anthony, and anarchist Emma Goldman.

This is Bly's story of a trip that is still being writtten about to this day.

Her most famous exploit, however, was more like a stunt. In 1888, she proposed to her bosses at *The World* that she take a trip around the world, attempting to turn the fictional *Around the World in 80 Days* into fact for the first time. She wanted to beat Phileas Fogg's time, the hero of Jules Verne's massively popular 1873 novel. Her editor liked the idea, but the paper's business manager wanted to send a man.

"Very well," Bly said, "start the man, and I'll start the same day for some other newspaper and beat him."

The next year, a few months after her 25th birthday, the paper said "yes." She set sail on November 14, 1889, on the steamer *Augusta Victoria* heading east. Her journey took her to England, Egypt, Ceylon, Singapore, Hong Kong, and Japan. During a stop in France, she met Jules Verne, who encouraged her to beat the fictional record. *The World* promoted a hugely popular guessing contest to predict how many weeks/

days/hours/minutes it would take her to complete the journey, offering a trip to Europe as first prize.

A new magazine called *Cosmopolitan* sent its reporter, Elizabeth Bisland, in the opposite direction to try to beat Bly around the globe, creating an actual race for all to follow. Bly sent short progress reports to the paper by cable and telegraph and more comprehensive reports by regular post, which ran weeks behind. Millions of people followed her journey, and it resulted in significantly increased newspaper readership. She traveled by ship, horse, rickshaw, sampan, burro, balloon, and more. When she reached Hong Kong, she learned that Bisland was ahead of her. Undaunted, Bly reached American soil in San Francisco on January 21, 1890, and boarded a private train chartered by Joseph Pulitzer. All along her journey eastward, she was met with cheering crowds.

Meanwhile, Bisland had missed her ship across the Atlantic and was still sailing westward from Europe on a different, slower ship when Bly's train pulled into New Jersey. When she stepped off the train at her official finish line in Jersey City, cannons boomed from the southern tip of Manhattan's Battery Park, and a large crowd roared. She had traveled around the world in 72 days, six hours, and 11 minutes. It would be four and a half more days before Bisland arrived.

Bly had earned international stardom for her months-long stunt. She turned her adventure into the 1890 book, *Nellie Bly's Book: Around the World in Seventy-Two Days.*

In 1895, Bly married millionaire manufacturer Robert Seaman. He was the owner of Iron Clad Manufacturing Company and 42 years her senior. As the marriage progressed, Nellie became more involved with the company and even patented a milk can of her design. When Seaman died in 1904, Nellie took over the company and became the world's leading female industrialist until employees' embezzlement led her into bankruptcy in 1914.

When World War I broke out, she returned to journalism and became America's first female war correspondent for the *New York Evening Journal.* She returned to New York in 1919 and regularly wrote for the *Evening Journal.*

Gravesite of newspapers grand lady.

Nellie Bly died of pneumonia at St. Mark's Hospital in New York City on January 27, 1922, at age 57. She continued to write her column up until her death. She was buried in a modest grave in Woodlawn Cemetery in the Bronx. In 1978, the New York Press Club formally recognized Nellie and erected a monument at her grave.

If You Go:

Woodlawn Cemetery is itself a National Historic Landmark and contains over 300,000 interments. Its monuments, including over 1,300 mausoleums, were designed by legendary American architects, landscape designers, and sculptors. It contains the graves of many notables from all walks of life.

One such person is **David Farragut** (1801–1870), a Navy Admiral who received great acclaim for his service to the Union during the Civil

War. He commanded the Union blockade of Southern ports, helped capture the Confederate city of New Orleans, and provided support for General Grant's Vicksburg siege. He is best known for his victory at the Battle of Mobile Bay in August 1864. The bay was heavily mined (mines were called torpedoes in those days), and Farragut ordered his fleet to enter the bay. When one ship struck a mine, the others began to pull back, but Farragut rose to the occasion and famously proclaimed to "Damn the torpedoes, full speed ahead!" The fleet succeeded, and the heroic quote became famous. He was the first rear admiral, vice admiral, and admiral in the United States Navy.

Farragut died from a heart attack at 69 in Portsmouth, New Hampshire, on August 14, 1870. His grave is listed on the National Historic Register of Historic Places. Many destroyers have since been named USS *Farragut* in his honor, and he has been depicted on U.S. postage stamps three times.

For more information on notables buried in Woodlawn Cemetery, see the "If You Go" section in Chapter 13 (**Bat Masterson**).

4

"You Dirty Rat"

James Cagney

County: Westchester • Town: Hawthorne
Buried at Gate of Heaven Cemetery
10 West Stevens Avenue

He was a star on both stage and screen. He initially made his mark playing tough guys in movies, including *The Public Enemy* and *Angels with Dirty Faces*. He always considered himself to be a song and dance man, and he won his only Oscar portraying another song and dance man, George M. Cohan (see Chapter 5), in the movie *Yankee Doodle Dandy*. The American Film Institute ranked him eighth when selecting the 50 greatest American screen legends. Orson Welles said that he may have been the greatest actor who ever appeared in front of a camera. His name was James Cagney.

Cagney was born on July 17, 1899, in New York City. He grew up on the Lower East Side of Manhattan. His father was of Irish descent and was a bartender and an amateur boxer. In his autobiography, Cagney recalled that his dad was quite a baseball player and that he earned the nickname "Jimmy Steam" because of his fastball. His mother was of both Norwegian and Irish descent. Cagney was the second of seven children, though two of his siblings died within months of their birth. As a young child, he was sickly to the point that his mother feared he would die before he could be baptized.

Cagney graduated from Stuyvesant High School in 1918. He then attended Columbia College of Columbia University, where he planned to study art. However, when his father died during the flu pandemic in 1918, he dropped out of school to help out at home.

James Cagney

Cagney would later recall that he couldn't remember a time when he wasn't working. At the age of 14, he began working as an office boy at the *New York Sun* newspaper. A year later, he began working at the New York Public Library, and he would also work nights as a doorman. On Sundays, he would sell tickets on the Hudson River Day Line. He was doing all this while going to school. Cagney was a very busy young man.

By 1919 Cagney was working at the Wanamaker's Department Store. There he met a fellow who had an interest in show business and told Cagney that if he could dance a little, he could get a job with a vaudeville act at Keith's Eighty-First Street Theatre. The play was called *Every Sailor*, and Cagney got the part. It was a female impersonation act with six guys in skirts serving as the chorus line. Cagney was one of the six, and for his work, he received thirty-five dollars a week, which he described as a mountain of money at the time. It was here that Cagney began to learn to dance. So, the man who became America's quintessential tough guy got his start in show business as a female impersonator.

Cagney as George M. Cohan.

Cagney's mother didn't want him to make a career in show business, so when *Every Sailor* closed, he got a job as a brokerage house runner. Cagney found this job to be dull and boring. He later said that he hated it with great intensity.

While he was working, he kept looking for jobs on the stage. He successfully auditioned for a chorus part in a play called *Pitter Patter*. He supplemented his salary by becoming the dresser for the plays leading man and taking charge of the touring company's baggage. He was paid fifty-five dollars a week, and every week he sent forty dollars home to his mother. While doing the play, he met a chorus line performer Frances Willard "Billie" Vernon. Cagney said the two of them hit it off from the start, and they were married in 1922.

The Cagneys struggled to make ends meet in the early years of their marriage. In 1924 they moved to Hawthorne, California, to see about breaking into the movies. They failed in garnering any interest from the studios and had to borrow money to get back to New York City.

Cagney went back to doing specialty dancing jobs. He eventually replaced a man by the name of Archie Leach in a three-man vaudeville act. Leach is better known today by the name Cary Grant. Cagney, eager for work, went to all kinds of auditions, even those outside his realm of expertise. He later noted that this provided him with valuable experience; it also helped him develop a healthy resilience when facing tough times in a demanding profession.

Cagney landed his first real significant non-dancing role in the play *Outside Looking In* in 1925. The part of Little Red called for an actor with red hair. Cagney maintained that the only reason he got the part was that his hair was redder than that of another New York actor named Alan Bunce. The play ran for four months, and both the play and Cagney received excellent reviews.

After the show closed, it was back to vaudeville for Cagney. During this period, he met George M. Cohan, whom he would later portray in what he said is his favorite movie. Next, Cagney landed the lead role in a play called *Broadway* in the show's London Company. The show's management told Cagney that they wanted him to copy Lee Tracey's performance, who had previously played the part. Although Cagney considered Tracey to be a fine actor, he wasn't happy copying his performance. The day before the company was to sail to England, there was a dress rehearsal, which Cagney described as uncomfortable. After the performance, management decided to replace him. This was a terrible turn of events for the Cagneys as they had already given up their apartment. Cagney gave serious thought to quitting show business after losing the part, but his wife wouldn't allow it.

Cagney's next acting job came in a play called *Women Go on Forever*. At the same time, he opened a dancing school in Elizabeth, New Jersey. He would work at the dancing school and then head to New York to do the play. The play ran for four months, and by the time it closed, Cagney was exhausted.

Cagney's reputation as a teacher helped him land the lead role in the *Grand Street Follies of 1928*. Also, he choreographed the show. The musical received excellent reviews and led to the *Grand Street Follies of 1929*, in which Cagney played a dancing traffic cop. He was then cast in the play *Maggie the Magnificent,* where he met the playwright and director George Kelly. Cagney would recall that Kelly taught him what a director was for and what a director could do. He considered working with Kelly to be a privilege.

Cagney was then teamed with the actress Joan Blondell to star in the play called *Penny Arcade.* The critics hated the play but gave both Cagney and Blondell good reviews. One person who saw the play and liked it was Al Jolson, who bought the film rights. Based on Jolson's recommendation, Warner Brothers hired both Cagney and Blondell to play their original roles. Cagney went to Hollywood with a contract that gave him a three-week guarantee; he would stay for thirty-one years.

Cagney's three-week contract paid him five hundred dollars a week. It appears that the studio liked what they saw because they gave him a three-week extension followed by a seven-year contract at four hundred dollars per week. However, this contract allowed the studio to drop him at the end of any forty weeks.

Penny Arcade was retitled *Sinners Holiday* and was shot in about three weeks. Cagney plays a tough thug who becomes a killer. However, the character gets sympathy because of his rough childhood. Cagney would play similar roles throughout his career.

In 1931 Cagney starred in the film *Public Enemy.* This was the film that made him a star. The critics loved his portrayal of a petty killer. Many critics believe that the scene where he shoves a grapefruit into Mae Clark's face is a great moment in movie history. According to Warner Classic Movies, Cagney and Clark decided to play a joke on the crew, but the director liked it so much he left it in the film. Cagney said that for years he couldn't go into a restaurant without being offered a grapefruit. The movie took 26 days to make and cost $151,000, but it became one of the first low budget films to gross one million dollars.

Next, Cagney made his only film with Edward G. Robinson. It was called *Smart Money,* and Robinson was cast as a gangster while Cagney played his pal. According to Cagney, he was playing a lot of pals in those days. This was in 1931, the year that Cagney's brother Bill came to

California for a visit. Bill made a few pictures himself and then became Cagney's business manager. Bill's first job was to get Cagney a pay raise, and after the success of *Public Enemy*, Warner Brothers offered him one thousand dollars per week.

In1932, Cagney starred in the film *Taxi* with George Raft. It was the first film Cagney danced in, and it was the last time he allowed himself to be shot at with live ammunition after he was almost hit. The film was another hit, and it was where he uttered the line, "Come out and take it, you dirty yellow-bellied rat, or I'll give it to you through the door." Cagney impressionists commonly used this line, which they changed to "Mmmm, you dirty rat."

Although Cagney's career was going well, he was having trouble with the studio. Warner Brothers pushed a 100 percent participation charity drive that had been organized by Douglas Fairbanks Jr. Cagney refused to contribute for the sole reason that the company was making it mandatory. Jack Warner nicknamed Cagney the "Againster" and vowed that Cagney's failure to contribute would be remembered. Finally, still upset over his salary, Cagney walked. Cagney noted that he had walked several times over the years, saying that when studio heads failed to live up to their promises, his only option was to deny them his services. He sued Warner Brothers for violating his contract by billing another name over his at the Warner Theatre in Hollywood. Cagney won the suit.

Cagney wanted more money for the successful films he was making, and he offered to take less for those that didn't make it. Warner turned him down, so Cagney walked again. Warner's response was to suspend him. Cagney then offered three films for free if Warner would cancel the remaining five years on his contract. After six months, a deal was reached, and Cagney's salary was increased to three thousand dollars per week, he was guaranteed top billing, and the number of films he would make a year was limited to four.

Returning to the studio in 1933, Cagney went back to work. One of the films he made was *Footlight Parade,* which allowed him to sing and dance once more. The film included scenes choreographed by the legendary Busby Berkeley. In 1934 Cagney appeared in *Here Comes the*

Navy. It was the first of many films he would make with Pat O'Brien, and the two became lifelong friends.

By 1935, Cagney was one of Hollywood's top ten moneymakers. Also, he was being cast in movies where he wasn't always playing a gangster. In *G-Men*, he was cast as a lawyer who joins the FBI. He also played the part of Nick Bottom in Shakespeare's *A Midsummer Night's Dream,* which starred Mickey Rooney as Puck. During the making of this film, Rooney decided to go for a toboggan ride, and during the descent, he stuck a leg out to slow himself down. He broke the leg, and when he was well enough to film, his leg was in a cast, so all the shots of him were from the waist up.

The last movie Cagney made in 1935 was called *Ceiling Zero,* which starred Pat O'Brien, who received top billing despite Cagney's contract, which called for him to get it. Also, he had made five movies in 1934, which violated his contract. Cagney still felt that the studio was paying him a small percentage of the money that was made by his movies, so he again filed suit against Warner and walked. He spent the next year back east on a farm he had purchased.

It was then that Cagney received an offer from Grand National Films, a newly established and relatively small studio. Grand National agreed to pay him $100,000 per film plus ten percent of the profits. Cagney made two films for this studio, *Great Guy* and *Something to Sing About*. While he received good reviews, the production quality was not up to snuff, and the films did poorly.

The Warner Brothers lawsuit was decided in Cagney's favor. He won, and the studio took him back for a five-year $150,000-a-film deal. The contract also stated that he would make no more than two pictures per year, and his brother Bill was guaranteed to be an assistant producer for the films in which Cagney starred.

One of the films Cagney had wanted to do at Grand National was *Angels with Dirty Faces*. Now back at Warner, he got the chance. He based his character, Rocky Sullivan, on a man he had observed when he was a boy. Cagney said the man would stand on a corner all day long hitching up his trousers, moving his necktie, lifting his shoulders, snapping his fingers, and finally bringing his hands together in a soft smack. In the film, Sullivan is a gangster who is admired by a group of boys known as the Dead End Kids. One of Sullivan's old pals is a priest, played by Pat O'Brien, concerned for the kids' welfare. After a shootout, Sullivan is taken by the police and sentenced to death in the electric chair. The priest visits Sullivan before the execution and urges him to turn yellow on his way to the chair so the kids would lose respect for him. Sullivan says there is no way he is going to do that. However, on his way to the chair, he does break down and beg for his life. You can't tell, and Cagney never told, whether Sullivan acted out of cowardice or if he did it to help the kids. Cagney was nominated for Best Actor, but he lost the Academy Award to Spencer Tracy. Cagney did receive the Best Actor award from the New York Film Critics.

During the filming of *Angels with Dirty Faces,* Cagney was once again asked to do a scene involving live ammunition. He refused, and it proved to be a wise move. One of the bullets fired from a machine gun hit the steel edge of a window and was deflected through the wall where Cagney's head had been. Cagney said the experience convinced him that flirting with real bullets was ridiculous.

In 1939 Cagney made his first western, *The Oklahoma Kid.* Cagney had hoped to make a historically accurate movie, but the studio heads had other ideas, and according to Cagney, the film became a predictable horse opera. Cagney said the script was so predictable that the actors ad-libbed to liven it up.

Cagney wrapped up his first decade of movie-making when he co-starred in *The Roaring Twenties,* which turned out to be the last film he made with Humphrey Bogart. It would be another ten years before Cagney made another gangster film. Cagney was the second-highest-paid actor in the land, earning $368,333 per year.

On Pearl Harbor Day, December 7, 1941, Cagney began filming what he would later call his favorite movie, *Yankee Doodle Dandy.* Cagney said he needed no preparation to play the role of George M. Cohan. He didn't have to pretend to be a song and dance man. He was one. The producer of the film, Hal Willis, said he never considered anybody but

Cagney for the role, but in his autobiography, Cagney says the role was first offered to Fred Astaire, who turned it down. According to Cagney, his brother Bill was looking for a story with American flavor at the time. When he came upon the Cohan story, it was just what he had in mind.

Cohan himself was trying to sell his story, and he checked out Cagney's vaudeville credentials before taking the idea to Warner Brothers with the requirement that Cagney play him. When Cagney read the original script, he didn't like it. In his view, it was too serious and needed lightening up. He told his brother Bill he would do it provided Julius and Phil Epstein were brought in to liven the script up and inject some humor. Also, he had Warner Brothers hire Johnny Boyle to help him prepare for the role. Boyle had appeared in *The Cohan Revue of 1916* and knew Cohan's dancing style firsthand. Cagney and Boyle worked hard together, learning Cohan's stiff-legged dancing technique.

When the film was completed, Cohan was given a private screening. After viewing it, he thanked Cagney for doing an excellent job. Several critics have said that it's Cagney's best film. It was nominated for eight Academy Awards and won three. Cagney took home the Oscar for Best Actor. In accepting the award, Cagney said, "I've always maintained that in this business, you're only as good as the other fellow thinks you are. It's nice to know that you people thought I did a good job. And don't forget that it was a good part, too."

The year 1942 was busy for Cagney. He became president of the Screen Actors Guild, and he was chairman of the Actors Committee of the National Victory Committee. He was also part of the Victory Caravan that went cross-country selling war bonds. The group included Cary Grant, Pat O'Brien, Frank McHugh, Laurel and Hardy, Bert Lahr, and Groucho Marx. Starlets were represented by Claudette Colbert, Joan Bennett, Joan Blondell, and Olivia de Havilland. Bob Hope acted as the emcee.

It was around this time that Cagney ran into trouble with Warner Brothers yet again. His contract called for him to get a percentage of the gate, and Cagney felt the studio was doing funny things with the books. He walked again, and he and his brother Bill formed a company to make their films.

The first movie released by Cagney Productions was *Johnny Come Lately* in 1943. The movie got mixed reviews, but according to Cagney did turn a profit. In 1945 he starred in *Blood on the Sun*. It did worse at the box office than *Johnny Come Lately*. Next, Cagney was eager to adapt William Saroyan's Broadway play *The Time of Your Life*. While Saroyan liked the film, Cagney Productions lost half a million dollars on the movie. The poor returns from the films they had made left Cagney Productions in financial trouble. Cagney returned to Warner Brothers, where he signed a deal making Cagney Productions a unit of Warner Brothers.

The first film Cagney made upon his return to Warner was *White Heat*. Cagney portrayed Cody Jarrett as a raving lunatic, an idea he came up with himself. Jarrett is psychotically tied to his mother, and while serving time in prison, he is informed of her death. His explosion of rage and anger upon receiving this information has been hailed as one of Cagney's most memorable performances. In the film, his final line, "Made it Ma! Top of the world!" was selected as the 18th greatest movie line by the American Film Institute.

Cagney returned to musicals with his next film, *The West Point Story*. He played opposite Doris Day in the movie. Cagney would later claim a scene in the film where he dances with Virginia Mayo was some of the best dancing the two ever did.

In his next movie, *Kiss Tomorrow Goodbye*, it was back to playing a gangster. While it didn't receive *White Heat*'s critical acclaim, it did well at the box office. Also, Cagney had worked out a deal where Warner Brothers would pay the banks the $500,000 owed to them by Cagney Productions resulting from the losses incurred in producing *The Time of Your Life*. In 1953 William Cagney produced his last film, *A Lion in the Streets,* and Cagney Productions came to an end.

In 1954 Cagney received a call from the director John Ford who was planning on making *Mister Roberts*. Ford offered Cagney the role of the ship's captain. According to Cagney, Ford said it would take but a few weeks of filming in Honolulu and that Spencer Tracy would play the role of Doc. To Cagney, it sounded like a vacation, so he accepted. As it turned out, Tracy had no intention of being in the film, and the role of Doc went to that fine actor Bill Powell. The film turned out to be a success earning three Oscar nominations, including one for best picture.

While he was filming *Mister Roberts,* Cagney received the script for *Love Me or Leave Me.* Cagney described it as that extremely rare thing, the perfect script. Cagney accepted the role, and he teamed once again with Doris Day, an actress he admired. It appears the feeling was mutual as Day said Cagney was "the most professional actor I've ever known." It also appears that Cagney was right in accepting the role of Martin "Moe the Gimp" Snyder, a Jewish-American gangster. His performance earned him another Academy Award nomination for best actor.

In 1957 Cagney portrayed the actor Lon Chaney in the film *Man of a Thousand Faces.* Cagney found the role to be challenging. However, he received excellent reviews for his performance. The *New York Journal American* rated it as one of his best roles. Also, the film was a box office smash.

That same year a friend approached Cagney and asked him if he would direct the Paramount production of *Short Cut to Hell.* Cagney said he was moved to do it out of friendship, and he agreed to do it for free. The film was shot in twenty days, which Cagney said was long enough for him. He described directing as a bore, and this would be his first and final time behind the camera.

In 1959 Cagney appeared in the film *Never Steal Anything Small.* This would be his final musical. He played a labor leader, and the movie features a comical song and dance scene with Cara Williams playing the part of his girlfriend.

That same year Cagney traveled to Ireland to make *Shake Hands with the Devil.* Cagney believed it to be the best movie he made overseas, and the critics agreed. Some view his performance as an Irish Republican Army commander during the Troubles of 1921 to be one of the best in his later career.

In 1960 with his career winding down, Cagney made one film. He described *The Gallant Hours* as a labor of love. The film was a tribute to Admiral William F. "Bull" Halsey. The film did well, and Cagney was singled out for praise in a review that appeared in *The New York Times,* calling it one of the quietest, most reflective, subtlest jobs that Mr. Cagney has ever done.

The next year Cagney appeared in the film *One, Two, Three.* The director, Billy Wilder, picked Cagney to play a Coca-Cola executive in this fast-paced comedy. Cagney said making the film was backbreaking work. One scene required 50 takes, which was something Cagney wasn't used to. Also, for the first time, he had trouble with another actor. Cagney said that Horst Buchholz tried all kinds of scene-stealing didoes and that he had to depend on Billy Wilder to step in and correct the kid. According to Cagney, if Billy hadn't, he was going to knock Buchholz on his ass. After he completed the film, Cagney decided to retire.

In 1974 the American Film Institute presented Cagney with a Lifetime Achievement Award. Charlton Heston opened the show, and Frank Sinatra introduced Cagney. During his acceptance speech, Cagney addressed the impressionist Frank Gorshin (See *Keystone Tombstones Volume One*), saying, "Oh, Frankie, just in passing, I never said MMMmmm, you dirty rat."

In 1981 Cagney came out of retirement to play the role of Police Commissioner Rhinelander Waldo in *Ragtime.* The film was primarily

Modest tomb of the great actor who never said "You dirty rat."

shot in Surrey, England. When Cagney arrived in Southampton, he was greeted by hundreds of fans. The officials responsible for security at the dock said they had never experienced anything like it before. Harold Robbins, who starred in the film and was nominated for an Oscar for Best Supporting Actor, said, "I was frightened to meet Mr. Cagney. I asked him how to die in front of the camera. He said, just die." This was Cagney's final film role though he did appear in a TV movie in 1984 called *Terrible Joe Moran*.

Cagney died at his farm in New York of a heart attack on March 30, 1986, at 86. President Ronald Reagan delivered his eulogy. His pallbearers included Floyd Patterson, Mikhail Baryshnikov, Ralph Bellamy, and Milos Forman. He was laid to rest in the Gate of Heaven Cemetery in Hawthorne, New York.

If You Go:

There are several other graves worth visiting at Gate of Heaven Cemetery. The legendary New York Yankee slugger **George Herman "Babe" Ruth** (See Chapter 19) is buried here. So is another baseball player and manager who made his name with the Yankees, **Billy Martin**.

The columnist, radio, and television personality **Dorothy Kilgallen** was laid to rest here. Kilgallen was a regular on the show *What's My Line*. She was also an outspoken critic of the Warren Commission. Her death was the result of a self-induced drug overdose, but Kennedy assassination conspiracy theorists believe that foul play was involved.

Two-time Oscar nominee **Sal Mineo** is buried here. Mineo is best remembered for his roles in *Rebel Without a Cause*, *Giant*, *Exodus*, and *The Longest Day*.

5

"Yankee Doodle Dandy"

George M. Cohan

County: Bronx • Town: New York
Buried at Woodlawn Cemetery
517 East 233rd Street

George M. Cohan was often referred to as the most significant single figure the American theater has ever produced. He is a Broadway legend and the Father of American Musical Comedy. He was a man of many skills, an actor, singer, dancer, songwriter, playwright, and producer. He is a fiercely patriotic man, probably best known for his World War I songs "Over There" and "You're a Grand Old Flag," for which he received the Congressional Gold Medal from President Franklin D. Roosevelt in 1936.

George Michael Cohan was born in 1878 in Providence, Rhode Island, to Irish Catholic parents. His parents, Helen and Jeremiah, were traveling vaudeville performers who lived out of a trunk and, for the most part, never had a home. The family apparently couldn't resist the publicity value of claiming George was born on the fourth of July, but records indicate that he was born on the third. George and his sister Josephine, who was two years older, were carried along on this nomadic existence and were used in the act. George was used as a prop at first and learned to dance and sing soon after walking and talking. In 1890, George and "Josie" were integrated officially into the act, and the group became The Four Cohans. They would typically tour most of the year and spend summer vacations at his grandmother's home in North Brookfield, Massachusetts. During one of those vacations, George befriended baseball great Connie Mack. He played sandlot baseball, rode his bike, and had many happy summers enjoying ordinary childhood

George Cohan

experiences. These experiences inspired his 1907 musical *50 Miles from Boston*, set in North Brookfield and contains one of his most famous songs, "Harrigan."

Cohan began writing original skits and songs for the family act while in his teens. An important part of Cohan's output of popular songs came from the many stage shows he wrote. As the Four Cohans became increasingly popular, George took on more of the responsibilities for the act, including control of the sketches, songs, and management of the troupe's affairs. The senior Cohan (Jerry) insisted that the Four Cohans were a road act and could never please the hard-nosed critics in New York City. The act traveled to every corner of the United States but bypassed Manhattan year after year. George was frustrated by this, and at age 14, he decided to run off on his own and try to make it on Broadway. Jerry decided to give in and make his debut with his family in the fall of 1893.

They made their Manhattan debut at B.F. Keith's new Union Square Theater, where George's dream turned into a nightmare. Keith was a major vaudeville theater owner, and he needed to fill out the opening bill of his show. To do so, he ordered that the Cohans perform separately. George put up such a fuss that the theater manager almost fired them but instead relegated him to open the show. Audiences typically ignored the first act as they settled in, and George's song and dance were no exception. Josie, however, was a smash hit and became the "toast of New York." George had difficulty finding bookings while Josie was in demand, but he used his time to write songs. Soon he had a string of minor hits, and performers searching for fresh material were seeking out George to write for them. These successful tunes' momentum led Josie to give up solo performing, and the family act was reunited.

George's songs and skits made them more popular than ever, and soon they were earning $1,000 a week. It was around this time that George began ending the shows with what became his trademark: "Ladies and gentlemen, my mother thanks you, my father thanks you, my sister thanks you, and I thank you."

George continued to have a conflict with B.F. Keith, who controlled most of the vaudeville theaters. After one argument, George swore that no Cohan would ever work for Keith again. Thus, the Cohans had no choice but to make the jump to the stage.

While on tour with the family, George met and fell in love with a talented vaudeville singer and comedienne, Ethel Levey. They married in

Cohan showcasing a small bit of his amazing talent.

1899, and although she continued to perform on her own, she frequently joined the Cohans in their shows.

In 1901, George wrote, composed, directed, and produced *The Governor's Son*, his first Broadway production. It was not the hit he hoped for, and poor reviews sent the show packing after 32 performances. Once the show left Broadway, it was a hit, and the Cohans performed it for two profitable years. The same fate awaited his second attempt, *Running for Office*, in 1903.

Record cover of the Music of George M. Cohan.

In 1904, George was introduced to Sam Harris, a gambler and boxing promoter who loved the theater and had a sound business mind. They formed a partnership that took Broadway by storm. Together they put on *Little Johnny Jones*, a patriotic and sentimental production that was the breakout hit for which George had long hoped. George wrote the script and the songs, produced and directed the performance, and starred in the title role. The show introduced two of Cohan's most lasting songs, "Give My Regards to Broadway" and "The Yankee Doodle Boy." The show went on a year-long tour, which included two return trips to New York. Audiences loved him.

In 1906, Cohan wrote a hit show for musical comedy star Fay Templeton called *45 Minutes from Broadway*, and one for the Cohan family called *George Washington, Jr.*, which boasted the wildly popular song "You're a Grand Old Flag," one of the most popular marching band pieces of all-time. George M. Cohan was one of Broadway's top stars, a distinction he relished for the rest of his life.

In 1907, Ethel Levey obtained a divorce from George on the grounds of adultery. She was enormously talented and went on to be one of Broadway's most popular headliners while raising their daughter Georgette on her own. In 1908, George married Agnes Nolan, a chorus girl who had been in some of his shows. The couple would remain married until his death. They had two girls and a boy, all of whom went into show business. Sam Harris married Agnes's sister, and the partners became in-laws.

The Cohan and Harris partnership lasted for 15 years, during which they produced more than 50 shows. At one time, they controlled five theaters in New York and one in Chicago. Cohan's abrasive, demanding business style covered tremendous empathy and generosity to anyone in the theater. He and Harris were unfailingly fair to actors and authors. He was so popular with fellow actors that they made him the "Abbot" of the Friars Club for two terms, a unique honor.

Cohan possessed tremendous energy. He would go on the road as the star of one play, take the cast of another with him, write a script late at night, and rehearse the second cast in the morning. He did most of his writing between midnight and dawn with a pencil on yellow paper. His shows ran simultaneously in as many as five theaters. No one else in the American performing arts has worn so many hats so successfully. An actor and longtime friend William Collier put it this way:

> George is not the best actor or author or composer or dancer or playwright. But he can dance better than any author, compose better than any manager, and manage better than any playwright. And that makes him a very great man.

In 1908, Josie went off on a solo career, and that year *The Yankee Prince* was the last joint appearance by the Four Cohans. In 1916, George suffered the loss of Josie, who died of heart failure, and of his father. He was devastated and threw himself into his work. The next year when the United States entered World War I, Cohan wrote the stirring "Over There," which many say was his greatest hit. It captured the whole nation's attention, and President Woodrow Wilson's secretary sent him a note saying, "The President considers your song 'Over There' a genuine inspiration to all American manhood." In 1918, he toured in a war play called *Out There*, which raised $600,000 for the Red Cross. As the war ended, Cohan seemed to be secure as the King of Broadway, admired by actors, writers, producers, and the general public.

Just after the war, a group of actors banded together to form The Actors' Equity Association. Most producers treated actors very poorly. They often went unpaid, had tours extended or cut without notice, were fired, were forced to rehearse to exhaustion, and even supply their costumes. When producers refused to negotiate with Equity, they called a strike in 1919. Cohan, who was always fair with his actors, surprisingly opposed the strike. He lashed out at Equity in speeches and print and seemed quite surprised when his fellow actors labeled him a traitor. He felt actors were professionals and above unionization. At one point, Cohan proclaimed he would quit acting and run an elevator before giving in to Equity. Comedian Eddie Cantor publicly pointed out that elevator operators were unionized.

With producers losing money and the fall season in jeopardy, Sam Harris led a delegation of producers that agreed to meet Equity's demands. The actors were jubilant. Cohan ended his partnership with Harris, disbanded his production company, quit several theater-centered organizations such as the Friars, and retired for several years. Cohan refused to join the union as an actor, which hampered his ability to appear in his productions. Neither Harris nor Cohan would ever publicly discuss their dispute.

The union granted Cohan a dues-free lifetime membership, but he refused to accept it. Equity actors were allowed to appear with him under an amnesty granted to some members of Equity. For the rest of his life, Cohan was the only actor on Broadway who worked under a non-Equity contract.

In the 1920s, Cohan wrote and produced several successes, such as *The Tavern* and *Little Nellie Kelly*. He continued to announce his retirement every few years but always got drawn back. He had little use for Hollywood and resisted all efforts to get him into films until 1915, when he signed a contract that resulted in three silent films. He did not return to Hollywood until 1932 when he was asked to star in his first talkie, *The Phantom President*. It was a musical and also starred Claudette Colbert and Jimmy Durante. The film got good reviews, but there was friction between Cohan and the producers and directors. He returned to New York, claiming it was his last movie.

He returned to Broadway the next year in Eugene O'Neill's *Ah, Wilderness!* It was in this play that Cohan gave his finest performance as a serious actor. Many were surprised to see the song-and-dance legend in a play by America's most acclaimed modern dramatist, but his performance was so moving that the critics hailed him like never before.

On June 29, 1936, by an act of Congress, Cohan was awarded the Congressional Gold Medal for his contributions to morale during World War I, particularly for the songs "You're a Grand Old Flag" and "Over There." Cohan was the first person in any artistic field selected for this honor. He would keep President Roosevelt waiting to present it until 1940.

In 1937, Cohan played Roosevelt in *I'd Rather Be Right*, which ran for nearly two years. The show was produced by Sam Harris, who remained a close friend and in-law. The show opened amid much hoopla. The critics raved, Roosevelt (a longtime fan) expressed his approval, and the show was a smash.

In 1940, Cohan made one last attempt to produce a Broadway play with *The Return of the Vagabond*. The show closed after only seven performances, and Cohan announced yet another retirement. It was expected that this retirement would prove to be as brief as the others, but Cohan had been diagnosed with terminal stomach cancer, which he kept a secret but never performed again.

In 1941, Warner Brothers produced a film based on Cohan's life. Despite his failing health, he served as a consultant during the production. He approved the choice of James Cagney (see Chapter 4), a song and dance man himself early in his career, and was delighted when longtime friend Walter Huston was cast as Jerry Cohan. He lived to see *Yankee Doodle Dandy* become a phenomenal success. The New York premiere on May 20, 1942, raised $5,750,000 worth of war bonds. Mayor Fiorello La Guardia proclaimed July 3, 1942, as "George M. Cohan Day" in New York. Against doctor's orders, Cohan snuck out of his Fifth Avenue apartment in a wheelchair to watch a few minutes of the film at the Hollywood Theater. After hearing the audience cheer his old songs, he had his nurse take him home. It was his last visit to his beloved Broadway.

The film was nominated for eight Academy Awards and won three, including Best Actor for a phenomenal performance by Cagney. In 1993, the film was selected for preservation in the United States National Film

The remains of the man who gave his regards to Broadway lay within this mausoleum.

Registry by the Library of Congress as "culturally, historically or aesthetically significant."

George M. Cohan died peacefully in his bedroom on the morning of November 5, 1942, at 64. President Roosevelt telegrammed Mrs. Cohan, saying "a beloved figure is lost to our national life. . . ." After a large funeral at St. Patrick's Cathedral, Cohan was buried at Woodlawn Cemetery in the Bronx, in a private mausoleum he had erected a quarter-century earlier for his sister and his parents. Cohan was always predominantly

Cohan's final resting place.

the artist rather than the businessman. He had an office but rarely went to it. He considered his office to be in his hat and transacted much of his business from public telephone booths.

Cohan is remembered in many ways. In 1968, the Broadway musical *George M!* was based on his life. He was inducted into the Songwriters Hall of Fame in 1970, and he received a star on the renowned Hollywood Walk of Fame at 6734 Hollywood Boulevard. The United States Postal Service issued a 15-cent commemorative stamp honoring Cohan on the centenary of his birth, July 3, 1978. There is a bronze bust of him in Providence a few blocks from his birthplace. The city renamed the location the "George M. Cohan Plaza."

In 1956, a memorial committee announced plans for a statue in Cohan's honor to be erected in Times Square. The chairman of the committee was noted songwriter and producer Oscar Hammerstein II. Hammerstein solicited a donation from Actors' Equity for the statue, and the union contributed the cost of lifetime membership, $240. Hammerstein returned the check, claiming he refused to cooperate with pinpricking Cohan's ghost. On September 11, 1959, the statue was unveiled and accepted on behalf of the city by Mayor Robert Wagner at 46th Street and Broadway. The base has an inscription which reads: "Give My Regards to Broadway."

If You Go:

Information about Woodlawn Cemetery can be found in the chapters on **Bat Masterson** (Chapter 13) and **Nellie Bly** (Chapter 3). The grave of **James Cagney** (Chapter 4), who won an Academy Award playing Cohan in *Yankee Doodle Dandy* and played Cohan again in the 1955 film *The Seven Little Foys*, is located 18 miles from Woodlawn in Gate of Heaven Cemetery in Hawthorne, Westchester County.

6

"As Maine Goes, So Goes Vermont"

Jim Farley

County: Westchester • Town: Hawthorne
Buried at Gate of Heaven Cemetery
10 West Stevens Avenue

He was the grandson of Irish Catholic immigrants, and his formal public education ended when he graduated from high school. At an early age, he developed a keen interest in politics. He grew up a Democrat in Rockland County, a part of New York's solidly Republican upstate bastion. He would come to be the most powerful non-elected Democrat in his home state and then in the nation. He was often referred to as a political kingmaker, and many credit him with being primarily responsible for Franklin D. Roosevelt's election as President in 1932. Indeed, on the evening of his election, FDR himself referred to him as one of the two most responsible for the election results. He would serve as a member of Roosevelt's cabinet and as the National Chairman of the Democratic Party for eight years before breaking with the President over Roosevelt's decision to seek an unprecedented third term. After leaving government service, he led Coca-Cola International for more than thirty years and is considered the driving force behind its global expansion during World War II and the post-war years. He was born James Aloysius Farley, but everyone knew him as Jim.

Farley was born on May 30, 1888, in Grassy Point, New York. He was one of five sons born to James and Ellen Farley. Grassy Point was a small, predominately Irish American community that stood on the Hudson River banks just forty miles away from New York City. Farley's father worked in the brick-making business. Just a few months before his

Jim Farley

namesake's tenth birthday, the elder Farley was kicked in the chest by a horse as he was hitching the animal to a carriage. The blow proved to be fatal, and Farley's mother was left on her own to raise her five sons.

Using the money that came to her through her husband's life insurance policy, Ellen Farley purchased a combination grocery store and saloon. Though he was only twelve years old, Farley helped out behind the bar. Listening to the locals, Farley learned that alcohol and loose talk seemed to be companions. He decided that if he were going to succeed, it would be best to avoid the demon rum.

After graduating from high school in 1905, Farley studied bookkeeping at a commercial school in New York City. In 1906, he took a job as a bookkeeper that paid eight dollars a week. Two years later, he took a position with the United States Gypsum Company, for whom he performed several tasks. Farley was nothing if not a hard worker. He was still living in Grassy Point, so he would catch an early morning train into the city and not arrive back home until twelve hours later. This didn't mean his day was over since he would head to meetings to discuss matters with local politicians on a nightly basis.

Farley was a success both in the business world and in the world of politics. Much of this was due to his personality. He was easy to talk to, able to hold his temper, exhibited confidence, and had what came to be known as a legendary memory when it came to the many people with whom he came into contact. Many stories attest to the strength of Farley's memory. One is recounted in the book, *Mr. Democrat: Jim Farley The New Deal and the Making of Modern American Politics,* written by Daniel Scroop. According to Scroop, Farley had a brief meeting with an Iowa man who was part of a reception committee that greeted the then postmaster general on a campaign stop. Three years later, the same man turns up in Washington and bets Farley that he doesn't remember him. Farley then called the man by his first name, mentioned the other reception committee members, named the hotel where they had eaten lunch, reviewed the menu, recalled the luncheon discussion, and followed that by asking the man how his children were while naming each one. Eleanor Roosevelt summed it up when she said of Farley that he had a "marvelous gift with people."

In 1911, Farley officially began his political career when he was elected town clerk of the town of Stony Point. Farley used this unsalaried position to make himself known in the area as an honest man and one on whom you could count. He didn't charge the fees he was entitled to collect from citizens who needed hunting, fishing, or marriage licenses. The people appreciated it and elected him to four two-year terms.

Bob Dylan wrote a song with a line that went, "to live outside the law, you must be honest." In many ways, Farley adopted the rule to live and strive inside both the business world and the political world; the same held true. Farley believed that rules were to be followed in the political game, and those who decided to go their way had no business playing.

In 1918, Farley was elected chairman of the Rockland County Democratic Party. In that capacity, Farley urged Al Smith (See Chapter 21) to run for governor. Farley tried to convince Smith that upstate New York was changing and that a Democrat could make inroads in the solidly Republican region. Smith knew that his support came from New York City, and he sent Farley to see the boss of Tammany Hall, Charles Murphy. As it turned out, Smith was right. He was elected governor, but he did so by piling up huge margins in Manhattan and Brooklyn, which overcame the losses he suffered in upstate New York.

In April of 1920, Farley married Elizabeth Finnegan. The union would produce three children: two daughters and a son. Starting a family didn't curtail his political ambitions as in 1922, he was elected to the New York State Assembly as a representative from Rockland County, long considered a Republican stronghold. He served but one term in Albany, but he utilized that time in building up friendships with other upstate Democrats.

In 1923, Al Smith appointed Farley to the New York State Athletic Commission. Within a short time, he was selected to be the Chairman of the Commission. Though traditionally, the chairmanship was rotated among the three Commission members regularly, Farley would hold the title until 1933, when he left New York to join Franklin Roosevelt in Washington.

Before Farley became a member, the commission had issued a ruling that the heavyweight champion, Jack Dempsey, would be required to defend his title against a Black American fighter named Harry Wills. Wills, a superb boxer, was the number one challenger for the championship but had always been denied the opportunity to win it because of the "color line" that had existed ever since the reign of the first black champion Jack Johnson. The well-known boxing promoter Tex Richard was opposed to the match as he wanted to set up a fight between Dempsey and the up-and-coming Irish fighter Gene Tunney. Despite public pressure,

FDR with James Farley in 1937.

Farley refused to budge when it came to reversing the ruling made by his predecessors. Some believe that Farley's stance had little to do with standing up for the little guy but was motivated by his long-held belief that you don't break a precedent and you don't go back on a promise once it's been made. Whatever the reason, Richard was forced to move the Dempsey-Tunney match to Philadelphia, and Farley deserves recognition for his stance regardless of his motivation. As for Wills, though he never got a chance to fight for the title, *Ring Magazine* would name him one of the 100 greatest punchers of all time.

Another important event occurred in Farley's life in 1924. He was elected a delegate to that year's Democratic Party convention held in New York. Farley was a strong supporter of Al Smith, and at the convention, he met another Smith supporter, Franklin D. Roosevelt. That meeting resulted in a partnership that would have a profound effect on the lives of both men.

Despite Farley's keen political mind and his rising position in the ranks of New York's Democratic Party, he could never join Governor Smith's inner circle. There are many explanations for this, including the fact that Smith had already formed his political team when Farley arrived on the scene. Add to this that Farley's political ties were largely in the upstate that didn't impress Smith, who saw New York City as his power base. Then, Farley, like Smith, was an Irish Catholic, and Smith saw little to gain by adding another Irishman to his team. These things that lessened Farley's attraction to Smith bolstered his appeal to the Protestant Franklin D. Roosevelt.

In 1928, Smith won the Democratic nomination for President. Roosevelt, with Farley's support, became the party's nominee to replace Smith as governor. Smith took a beating in the election, even losing New York, but Roosevelt bucked the tide and narrowly won the governorship. Farley, who had managed the Roosevelt campaign's New York office, was named secretary of the New York State Democratic Committee.

At that time in New York State, the governor's term was two years. Farley and Roosevelt shared a goal of building a strong Democratic Party throughout the state, and during Roosevelt's first term, Farley directed his energies. With his eyes squarely set on reviving the party in the upstate, Farley toured every one of the 57 upstate counties. He collected information on local leaders and made many friends on his visits, which often included speeches to loyal party workers. One of Farley's conclusions communicated to Roosevelt was that local Democratic leaders had received little if any encouragement by way of patronage. Throughout his political life, Farley was a strong proponent of patronage and made the point that these leaders could be spurned to put out more effort if they thought their labors were appreciated. In 1930, Roosevelt took a big step in taking over the party's leadership role (from Al Smith) when pro-Roosevelt supporters elected Farley to the state chairman.

During Roosevelt's reelection campaign, Farley served as campaign manager. At the same time, he was changing the face of the state's party. For instance, in 1930 alone, 16 new county chairmen began their duties. In particular, Farley had replaced men who were known to have cooperated with Republicans in past elections. On Election Day, Roosevelt scored a magnificent victory winning by 725,001 votes and carrying 42 upstate counties. Not only did the overwhelming victory cement

Roosevelt as a leading contender for his party's presidential nomination, but it also established Farley as a significant political force in the affairs of the nation. Roosevelt saw this as well when in a letter thanking Farley for his work, he said, "I have an idea that you and I make a combination which has not existed since Cleveland and Lamont, and that is so long ago that neither you and I know anything about it except from history books." The day after the results were counted, Farley stated that he did see how anybody but Roosevelt could be the party's standard-bearer for president in 1932.

Despite Farley's prediction, Roosevelt's nomination in 1932 was hardly a sure thing. Al Smith was still around, and the Roosevelt supporters knew that if Smith entered the race, they would receive stiff competition in securing the votes of delegates from the important northeastern states. With this in mind, Farley turned his attention to the western states. In the early summer of 1931, Farley visited 18 western states in 19 days. The Elks (a group that included Farley as a member) were holding their convention in Seattle. Farley's thinly disguised trip was said to be to attend this convention. As detailed in Scroop's book, Farley traveled to Seattle, taking what could hardly be called a direct route. Not to mention the fact that it seemed that every stop along the way included get-togethers with influential Democratic Party leaders. Farley even claimed to be "embarrassed by the overwhelming response of western Democrats who have seemed to be under the impression I was in the west to represent some particular candidacy."

The Democrats met in Chicago the next year to choose their nominee. Smith, who had caught the presidential bug, entered the race as did scores of favorite son candidates. Many believed that Roosevelt would be stopped and that the convention would be forced to turn to a compromise candidate. After three ballots, Roosevelt remained the front runner, but his failure to have secured the nomination fueled his opponents' hopes of stopping him.

Farley would later maintain that even before the balloting began, he had assurances from the Texas delegation that they would turn to Roosevelt after a few rounds of voting. At the end of the third ballot, Farley was convinced that now was the time for the switch. He proposed that a Texan, John Nance Garner, round out the ticket as the vice-presidential candidate. Farley used his connections with Sam Rayburn to contact Garner and seal the deal. When the fourth ballot began, California's turn came early, and it told the final tale. California votes that had previously gone to Garner as part of the stop Roosevelt strategy were now delivered to the New York governor. William McAdoo, who blamed his failure to secure the 1924 nomination on Al Smith, took to the microphone to deliver the news. Writing of McAdoo's announcement, H. L. Mencken said, "If revenge is really sweet, he (McAdoo) was sucking a colossal sugar teat . . ." Texas too fell into line, and Franklin Delano Roosevelt was the Democratic nominee for president.

Farley became Roosevelt's campaign manager, and he was also elected chairman of the Democratic National Committee. He immediately began an unprecedented national correspondence effort aimed at solidifying new contacts he had made within the party and cementing old ones. As was his habit and trademark, he would sign each letter in green ink. To give you an idea of this campaign's scope, letters went out to over 100,000 party workers. In his book, Mr. Scroop estimates that during the 1932 campaign, Farley sent 1.7 million pieces of correspondence. Farley also had a very distinct view of his role in the campaign, delivering the vote. He told one intellectual who had been invited to join the Roosevelt team as an advisor, "Issues aren't my business. They're yours and his. You keep out of mine, and I'll keep out of yours."

Farley was sure of a Roosevelt victory but come election night; he did not expect what amounted to a landslide. Roosevelt carried all but six states, and Democrats secured large majorities in both the House and Senate. After Hoover conceded, the president-elect addressed his supporters, saying, "There are two people in the United States more than anybody else who are responsible for this great victory. One is my old friend and associate, Colonel Louis McHenry Howe, and the other is that splendid American, Jim Farley." The new president named Farley to a cabinet position, Postmaster General. In addition to his new position, Farley remained as chairman of both the national and the New York

State Democratic Party. While it was unusual to have a cabinet member concurrently serving as the head of a political party, Roosevelt would make a habit of breaking precedents. In Farley's book, *Jim Farley's Story*, one finds the claim that no president shattered tradition nor set as many precedents as did Roosevelt. In 1932, Farley had no problem with this, but eight years later, Roosevelt would break a tradition that ultimately broke up the Roosevelt-Farley team.

As the head of the victorious Democrats, Farley was bombarded with pleas from jobseekers. As he described it, they flooded his office, they would come up to him on the street, they would interrupt his meals at restaurants, and he had to deal with mountains of mail and telegrams. The burdens came with the job he had as the chief disperser of government positions in the new administration. It should be pointed out that Farley self admittedly had no problem with the spoils system. He always felt that it was as easy finding a good Democrat to fill a position as it was to find a good Republican. He also felt that it was his duty as the head of the party to reward the faithful. While, in the first term, at least, most major appointees had to be acceptable to Farley, Roosevelt had no problem appointing men and women with Republican backgrounds. The Democrats were the minority party, and Roosevelt was looking to create a new coalition and broaden the base behind him.

One example of the pressures brought to bear on Farley is cited in the Scroop biography. Roosevelt had named Henry Wallace to the post of Secretary of Agriculture. Farley grew to admire the work Wallace did as a cabinet member but was often frustrated by Wallace's appointments of Republicans to positions in the Agriculture Department. In August of 1933, Molly Dewson, the head of the Democrat's Women's Division, wrote to Farley complaining about the appointment of Iris Calderhead Walker, the daughter of a former Republican congressman, to an Agricultural Department post. Dewson described Walker as "one of the rankest Republicans I ever knew," adding that Walker had bitterly opposed Roosevelt's election. In his response, Farley said that his powers were limited and that this was one of those "highbrow" appointments made by the administration. He promised to look into the matter but added, "... I doubt if it will make any difference." It is a testament to Farley's political skills that during these times, he was able to balance the demands of the Democratic Party powers with the president's desire to grow the party by including progressive and independent thinkers that Roosevelt felt could push the country forward.

In 1936, Farley directed his political and organizational skills toward one goal: reelecting Roosevelt. He courted the nation's press, doting on them and holding press conferences twice a day. He invited numerous state leaders to the national headquarters to mirror the national organization on the state level. He regularly corresponded with local leaders, using the information he received from them to gauge how things were going state by state. He pressured party workers to get out the Democratic vote that he viewed as essential to a convincing victory come Election Day.

As the election neared, Roosevelt told Farley that he expected to win the electoral vote 360 to 171. The pollster Emil Hurja predicted a Roosevelt win 376 to 155. Some prognostications were dire. *The Literary Digest* was predicting a Republican win, and the columnist Arthur Krock, writing in the *New York Times,* said that the Republicans would do much better than they had in 1932. Farley told Roosevelt and others that the president would carry every state but Maine and Vermont and prevail 523 to 8. At the time, Maine was viewed as a bellwether state when predicting winners in presidential contests. Hence the saying popular at the time and first introduced in 1888, "As Maine Goes, so Goes the Nation." On the morning after the election, Farley stood before the press, after nailing his election prediction, and commented, "As Maine Goes, so Goes Vermont." Roosevelt himself joined in the fun, saying, "I knew I should have gone to Maine and Vermont, but Jim (Farley) wouldn't let me."

In the 1920s Will Rogers had quipped, "I don't belong to an organized political party. I'm a Democrat." By the time of the 1936 election, the joke could only be told in the past tense. Farley had built and presided over what came to be called the New Deal Coalition. It brought together under one tent big-city political machines, labor unions, liberals, farmers, Catholics, Jews, African Americans, and Southern whites. From 1932 to 1964, the coalition would provide the Democratic Party with seven wins out of nine presidential contests. The coalition broke up in the 1960s over civil rights issues, the War in Vietnam, and abortion.

During Roosevelt's first term, Farley was indispensable in bringing groups who had differing political interests together to work toward compromise. However, whether Farley saw it or not, his efforts in constructing the New Deal coalition resulted in politicians like himself losing influence to the growing bureaucracy. For example, the massive relief programs that the New Deal began to combat the Great Depression took power away from the political machines. They placed it in the hands of local administrators and the new executive agencies which controlled the purse strings by which federal aid would be disbursed. As a result, savvy party bosses, such as Pennsylvania's David Lawrence (see *Keystone Tombstones Volume 1*), began to work directly through the new agencies rather than the traditional party machinery.

It is impossible to precisely determine the cause of the split between Roosevelt and Farley in the second term. In his autobiography, Farley maintained that the president had surrounded himself with advisors that had no loyalty to the party. This led to Roosevelt's misguided attempts to pack the Supreme Court and purge the party of elected Democratic representatives in the 1938 elections because they failed to adequately support New Deal policies. In Farley's view, the court-packing plan, which was sprung on him by surprise, was a political mistake. As the head of the Democratic Party, he made it clear that he could not offer assistance to those who would challenge incumbent Democrats in the coming off-year elections.

While there is little doubt the actions detailed above contributed to the eventual split, the proverbial straw had to be the 1940 Presidential election. After the off-year elections, where Roosevelt's purge plans failed, the press began speculating on the next election and who the presidential candidates might be. Roosevelt kept his cards close to the vest when the talk turned to the possibility of a third term. If Roosevelt chose not to run, Farley was among the names mentioned in the press that might be nominated to succeed him. It is a fact that as 1940 approached, and Roosevelt refused to declare his intentions publicly, Farley began seeking support for his candidacy. Farley believed that if Roosevelt stayed out of the race, the advantages he had due to the years of work he had put into building the party would result in his nomination.

To help build his credentials in foreign policy, Farley toured Europe for five weeks in 1939. On one of his stops in Italy, he was granted an audience with Pope Pius XII. Farley and the Pope began to talk politics, and Farley observed that Roosevelt would violate what had become an unwritten American law by running for a third term. The Pope, pointing out that there is a first time for everything, said he was the first Italian papal Secretary of State to be elected to his present office. After seeing what had happened to Al Smith, many believe that the Catholic Church was not anxious to have another Catholic presidential candidate. Further evidence of this comes from a meeting Farley had with Cardinal Mundelein, who told him that a Catholic could not be elected president.

It appears that Roosevelt shared the views of those who believed that the time had not yet come when Americans were willing to elect a Catholic leader. Roosevelt believed that a Catholic on the ticket as the vice-presidential candidate would cost the Democrats votes. Despite this, during a meeting with Farley on January 31, 1940, Roosevelt told Farley that he had no objections to Farley entering the New Hampshire and Massachusetts primaries as a candidate for president. Farley did not view this as an endorsement from Roosevelt, but he did believe that it was an indication that Roosevelt would not seek a third term. By February 12th, the *New York World-Telegram* reported that Farley had received "what he considers assurances" that Roosevelt would not be a candidate. The article also noted Farley's entrance into the Massachusetts primary.

Possessing the political instincts at his disposal, it is unlikely that Farley was convinced that Roosevelt had made a firm decision not to run. It was a public secret that Farley was opposed to a third term. Still, as the months passed and the 1940 Democratic Convention drew nearer, it became apparent the Roosevelt was more than willing to accept his party's nomination for the third time. According to Farley, considerable pressure was brought to bear on him to drop out of the race. Despite the pressures, Farley decided that he would have his name placed in nomination at the convention to demonstrate his opposition to a third term. He had also decided to resign both his cabinet position and chairman of the national party. In keeping with the loyalty he had always shown the party, he was determined that whatever action he took would not hurt the Democrats.

On July 7th, the day before Farley was scheduled to leave for the convention in Chicago, he met with Roosevelt for two hours. According to Farley, Roosevelt admitted that he had told Farley that he would not run for a third term and would make those intentions known by letter. The President went on to say that the situation in Europe had made it impossible for him to issue such a declaration, but he added that he still had no desire to run and that he was going to make his feelings known to the convention. Farley said that he then told the president that the Democratic Party had always opposed the third term and that if we couldn't put forth another candidate who could run and be elected on the accomplishments of the past eight years, then "we deserved to lose." At this point, Roosevelt said that he could not issue a Sherman-like statement that he would not run if called upon by his party, saying, "I could not in these times refuse to take the inaugural oath." Farley then responded that while he knew who had the votes, he would have his name placed in nomination.

Roosevelt did indeed have a statement read on his behalf at the convention declaring that he had no desire to be the Democratic nominee and that the delegates were free to vote for the candidate of their choice. After the announcement was read, a voice came over the loudspeakers in the convention hall, proclaiming, "We want Roosevelt." Followed by "Chicago wants Roosevelt." "The World needs Roosevelt." "Everybody wants Roosevelt." A Roosevelt demonstration began that went on for 45 minutes as the voice on the loudspeaker continued the chant. The balloting was a mere formality; Roosevelt received 946 and 1/2 votes to Farley's 72 and 1/2. After the ballot, Farley went to the podium and moved that the nomination be made unanimous. Eleanor Roosevelt flew into Chicago to heal the Farley-Roosevelt split, but she was unsuccessful, and Farley refused to join Roosevelt's 1940 campaign team. He did announce his intention to vote a straight Democratic ticket.

Grave of the man many credit with making Franklin Delano Roosevelt President of the United States.

After the convention, Farley resigned from the cabinet and as national party chairman though he retained the chairman of the New York State party. He also was named Chairman of the Board of the Coca-Cola Export Corporation. He would hold that position until he retired in 1973. As chairman of the New York Democratic Party, Farley had one last tussle with Roosevelt during the 1942 race for the party's nomination for governor. The two favored different candidates, and when the smoke cleared, Farley's choice emerged victoriously. In Farley's view, this victory affirmed his belief that the party rewards those who have proved their loyalty. This, like all victories, had its cost as the Democratic candidate received little support from Roosevelt and was soundly defeated in the general election.

In 1947, President Truman appointed Farley to serve on the Commission on the Organization of the Executive Branch of the Government. Farley's work led to the development and ratification of the 22nd Amendment to the Constitution that established presidential term limits. Some viewed this as vindication for Farley's opposition to Roosevelt's third term. Indeed, on its passage, Farley issued a public statement saying it was "only natural that I should be gratified."

Six days before he died, Farley was notified that he would be chairman emeritus at the Democrats' national convention scheduled for the following month. Farley never made it to that convention as he suffered a heart attack and passed away on June 9, 1976. He was laid to rest next to his wife, Bess, in Gate of Heaven Cemetery in Hawthorne, New York.

If You Go:

There are several famous people buried in the Gate of Heaven cemetery. **Bess Houdini**, the wife of the famous magician and escape artist **Harry Houdini** (See Chapter 10), was laid to rest here. Her remains were interned at Gate of Heaven as a result of her family's wishes.

The National Football League franchise owner and Hall of Famer **Tim Mara** is here. Mara owned the New York Giants football team and is considered an NFL pioneer.

You can also find New York City's flamboyant mayor from the '20s at Gate of Heaven. **Jimmy Walker,** who was forced to resign from office in 1932 due to corruption charges, was buried here in 1946.

For more information, see the "If You Go" section in Chapter 4 on **James Cagney**.

7

"Uncle Sam"

Ulysses Grant

County: Manhattan • Town: New York
Buried at General Grant National Memorial
West 122nd Street and Riverside Drive

Ulysses S. Grant is best known as the Union general who led the United States to victory over the Confederate States during the American Civil War. He also served two terms as President of the United States. His life was filled with ups and downs and contradictions, and his reputation has fluctuated almost as much as his life did.

He was born Hiram Ulysses Grant on April 27, 1822, in Point Pleasant, Ohio. He was the first of six children born to Jesse and Hannah Grant. A year after his birth, his family moved to Georgetown, Ohio, and Grant had what he described as an "uneventful" childhood.

Grant's father owned a tannery, and his son hated the family business's horrible stench and filth. Jesse acknowledged that his son would never make it as a businessman and arranged for him to be appointed by Congressman Thomas Hamer to the United States Military Academy at West Point, New York. The Congressman mistakenly wrote the boy's name down as "Ulysses S. Grant." When he arrived at West Point, he just adopted the name. His nickname became "Sam" among the cadets since the initials "U.S." also stood for "Uncle Sam."

Grant received average grades and graduated in 1843, ranking 21st out of 39. He was glad to be out of the academy and planned to resign from the military after serving his mandatory four years of duty.

After graduation, Grant was stationed in St. Louis, Missouri, where he met and courted Julia Dent. She accepted his marriage proposal in

Ulysses Grant

1844, but he was called for duty in the Mexican War before they could marry. From 1846 to 1848, Grant fought in the Mexican War and was twice cited for bravery. He served under General Zachary Taylor and General Winfield Scott, closely observing their military tactics and leadership skills. He also developed strong feelings that the war was wrong and that it was being waged only to spread slavery.

After the war, Grant moved to various Army postings in Detroit and New York. He married Julia on August 22, 1848, and they had four children. In 1852, he was transferred to Fort Vancouver in what is now

Washington State, and trouble began. He missed his family, tried and failed at several business ventures, and then, despondent, began to drink. In the summer of 1853, he was promoted to captain and assigned to Fort Humboldt in California. His drinking got him in trouble there, and on April 11, 1854, against his father's strenuous objections, Grant resigned from the Army.

The next seven years were difficult for the Grant family. He tried farming, insurance sales, real estate, and bill collecting but failed at all of them. Finally, he humbled himself and moved his family to Galena, Illinois, where he worked as a clerk in his father's leather goods shop.

When the Civil War began in 1861, experienced officers like Grant were in short supply. Grant helped recruit a company of volunteers and accompanied the regiment to the state capital of Springfield. Governor Richard Yates offered Grant a position recruiting and training volunteers, which he accepted but still sought a field command in the regular army. He made several efforts through contacts, but Major General George McClellan refused to meet with him (remembering Grant's reputation for drinking). He was finally promoted to colonel on June 14, 1861, thanks to Congressman Elihu Washburne's assistance, and put in charge of the unruly 21st Illinois Volunteer Infantry Regiment. Grant drilled the men and instituted badly needed discipline, which won him the respect of his troops. The Army noted his efforts, and he was promoted to brigadier general.

In February 1862, in a joint operation with the U.S. Navy on the Tennessee River, Grant's forces took Tennessee's Forts Henry and Donelson. At Fort Donelson, Grant demanded "unconditional and immediate surrender." These battles are credited as the earliest significant Union victories of the war. Lincoln promoted Grant to major general of volunteers, and the Northern press treated Grant as a hero. Playing off his initials, they dubbed him "Unconditional Surrender Grant."

Two months later, in April, Grant fended off a surprise attack at Shiloh and defeated the Confederate troops in one of the Civil War's bloodiest battles. Grant, however, was criticized for failing to entrench and for high casualties, and as a result, he was removed from command of his army. Discouraged and disappointed, Grant considered resigning his commission, but Lincoln fended off demands that Grant be removed by saying, "I can't spare this man; he fights." He reinstated Grant as field commander of the Army of the Tennessee.

Shortly after Lincoln's preliminary Emancipation Proclamation in September 1862, Grant ordered his units to incorporate African American slaves into the Union war effort, giving them clothes, shelter, and wages for their services.

In December 1862, Grant moved overland to take Vicksburg, Mississippi—a key fortress city of the Confederacy. Taking Vicksburg proved difficult, and after several bloody assaults, Grant's army settled in for a siege. Vicksburg fell on July 4, 1863, and the Union gained control of the Mississippi River, splitting the Confederacy in two.

Although the success at Vicksburg was a significant morale boost for the war effort, Grant received criticism for his decisions and his reported drunkenness. Some historians claim that Grant suffered from migraine headaches brought on by stress. Because of his reputation as a drinker, it was assumed he was drunk or hungover when he was suffering an attack, thus exaggerating the perception of the frequency and effects of his drinking. Lincoln defended Grant, and in a famous story that appeared in the *New York Herald* on September 18, 1863 (and was repeated in the *New York Times* and many other papers), Lincoln reportedly asked where Grant got his whiskey. When no one knew the answer, they asked why he desired to know. Lincoln said, "because, if I can only find out, I will send a barrel of this wonderful whiskey to every general in the army."

Lincoln commissioned Grant a major general in the regular army, and assigned him command of the newly formed Division of the Mississippi in October 1863. The following month, Union forces under Grant routed Confederate troops in Tennessee at Lookout Mountain and Missionary Ridge, known collectively as the Battle of Chattanooga. This gave the Union control of Tennessee and opened Georgia to invasion. In March 1864, a grateful Lincoln appointed Grant commander of all the U.S. Armies, with the rank of lieutenant general. No soldier since George Washington had held that rank.

Grant proved to be the general for whom Lincoln had been looking. Historian David Coffey wrote:

> Throughout the war, Lincoln had placed his faith and the armies of the United States in the hands of dozens of men—George McClellan, John Pope, Ambrose Burnside, Joseph Hooker, Henry Halleck, Don Carlos Buell, and William S. Rosecrans, to name but a few—all of whom he found wanting in drive and, most important, in success. Even George Meade, who commanded at Gettysburg, had ultimately disappointed. By the end of 1863, Lincoln knew of only one man who had delivered consistently the kind of performance the president needed so desperately to see—Ulysses S. Grant.

Grant biographer Jean Edward Smith observed:

> Lincoln, who had dealt with Napoleonic figures like Fremont and McClellan, blustery show-offs like Hooker and Pope, and academic strategists like Halleck, was relieved to find a plain, direct, unassuming commander who eschewed the trappings of command, who never raised his voice, and who shared his view that the quickest way to end the war was to defeat the Confederate army.

Historian James McPherson wrote:

> Shy with strangers, uncomfortable in the limelight, notoriously taciturn, Grant earned a reputation as 'the American Sphinx.' Yet wherever he went, things got done—quietly, efficiently, quickly, with no wasted motion. In crisis situations during combat, Grant remained calm. He did not panic. He persevered, and he never accepted defeat even when he appeared to be beaten.

Photo of the man who would lead the Union Army to victory in the Civil War.

One Union officer famously wrote that Grant "habitually wears an expression as if he had determined to drive his head through a brick wall and was about to do it." Another described him as "a man who could remain silent in several languages."

From March 1864 until April 1865, Grant doggedly hunted for General Robert E. Lee's army in Virginia's forests, all the while inflicting unsustainable casualties. Finally, on April 9, 1865, Lee surrendered at

Lee surrenders to Grant ending the War between the States.

Appomattox Court House, and in a magnanimous gesture, Grant allowed Lee's men to keep their horses and return to their homes, taking none of them as prisoners of war.

After the war, Grant led the Army's supervision of Reconstruction in the former Confederate states. In 1868, with the nation still struggling to heal the wounds of war, Grant accepted the Republican presidential nomination. Running under the slogan "Let Us Have Peace," Grant defeated Democratic Horatio Seymour by an Electoral College landslide of 214 to 80. He was, at the time, the youngest president ever elected at 46 years of age. He won a second term in 1872, running against Horace Greeley and getting 56 percent of the popular vote and another Electoral College landslide (286 to 66).

During two terms in office, Grant worked hard to bring the North and South together again. He pushed for the passage of the 15th Amendment giving male African Americans the right to vote, supported expanding federal authority in civil rights matters, and sent federal troops to enforce the law against the Ku Klux Klan's activities. He met with Native American leaders, including Red Cloud, to develop a peace policy in the West. During the Great Sioux War, fueled by the discovery of gold in the Black

Hills, Grant came into conflict with Colonel George Armstrong Custer. Custer was a witness in an 1876 Congressional investigation about corruption in the War Department. Custer testified on hearsay evidence that President Grant's brother, Orvil, was involved in the Trader Post Scandal. This infuriated the president, who in retaliation stripped Custer of his command in the campaign against the Sioux. Custer lobbied hard, and Grant relented and let Custer fight under Brigadier General Alfred Terry. Sioux warriors, led by Sitting Bull and Crazy Horse, killed Custer at the Battle of Little Big Horn. Two months later, Grant criticized Custer in the press, saying, "I regard Custer's massacre as a sacrifice of troops, brought on by Custer himself, that was wholly unnecessary—wholly unnecessary."

Though scrupulously honest, Grant became known for appointing people who were not of good character. Scandals rocked both of his terms in office. There were charges of misconduct in nearly all federal departments, especially in the Treasury and Interior. Although Grant was never personally implicated in any of the scandals, he did not disassociate himself from those who were guilty. His inability to clean up his administration tarnished his reputation and led many in the Republican Party to repudiate him and oppose a third term. Grant decided not to seek a third term. In his farewell address, Grant said, "It was my fortune, or misfortune, to be called to the office of Chief Executive without previous political training . . . Mistakes have been made, as all can see, and I admit." He told a reporter, "I was never as happy in my life as the day I left the White House."

After leaving the White House in 1877, Grant traveled with Julia on a round-the-world tour. He was the most famous American of his time. In city after city, he was welcomed by cheering mobs and world leaders, including Queen Victoria and the Emperor of Japan. After two years, the Grants returned to the U.S. and landed in San Francisco, greeted by cheering crowds, a parade, and fireworks. In Philadelphia, in December 1879, about 350,000 people honored him with a parade. This renewed popularity gave rise to a movement to nominate Grant for the presidency in 1880. Grant said nothing publicly, but privately he wanted the job. When the convention convened in Chicago in June, more delegates pledged to Grant than any other candidate. He received 304 votes for the nomination on the first ballot, with 370 needed to win. After 36 ballots, a compromise candidate, James A. Garfield, was nominated.

Grant moved to New York, where he concentrated on making a living, but his lack of success in civilian life returned. He wound up becoming a partner in the financial firm of Grant & Ward, only to have his partner Ferdinand Ward embezzle investors' money. The firm went bankrupt in 1884, and so did Grant.

Desperate for money, Grant turned to write his wartime memoirs as a way to support his family. He began by selling short magazine articles to *Century Magazine* and then negotiated a book contract with a publishing company owned by his friend, the novelist Mark Twain. The book, titled *Personal Memoirs of Ulysses S. Grant*, was a two-volume set and a huge success. It sold over 300,000 copies and has been highly regarded by the public, military historians, and literary critics. Grant never saw any of the profits.

Shortly after he had begun to write, Grant was diagnosed with throat cancer. He died at his cottage on Mt. McGregor in New York on July 23, 1885, just two months after the book went to press. He was 63 years old. After private services, Grant's body was placed on a funeral train, which traveled to West Point and then New York City. Grant's funeral was one of the most extraordinary outpourings of public grief in history. A large funeral procession, led by General Winfield S. Hancock, marched through New York City from City Hall to Riverside Park. The column of mourners was seven miles long. Among them were President Grover Cleveland and two ex-presidents, Rutherford B. Hayes and Chester A. Arthur.

His pallbearers included General William T. Sherman, General Philip H. Sheridan, and Admiral David Porter, as well as former Confederate generals Joseph Johnston and Simon Buckner. Attendance topped 1.5 million. Grant's body was laid to rest in Riverside Park, first in a temporary tomb, and finally in a sarcophagus in a circular atrium at the General Grant National Memorial ("Grant's Tomb"), the largest mausoleum in North America.

Throughout the 20th Century, historians ranked his presidency near the bottom. In reviewing 12 historical rankings by academic historians

Outside view of Gran'ts tomb.

and political scientists since 1948, Grant is ranked near the bottom. His best ranking is 33rd of 41 in 1999.

In addition to his mausoleum in New York City, Grant is memorialized in Washington, D.C., at the foot of Capitol Hill with one of the largest equestrian statues in the world set on a platform 250 feet wide. Grant Park in Chicago is named after him, and there are smaller memorials that honor his life in Chicago's Lincoln Park, Philadelphia's Fairmount Park, the Ulysses S. Grant National Historic Site near St. Louis, and other sites in Ohio and Illinois. Grant has appeared on several stamps. The Ulysses S. Grant Presidential Library is located at Mississippi State University.

If You Go:

Grant's Tomb is located in Riverside Park near Riverside Drive and 122nd Street in Manhattan. Admission is free. We suggest you check the

View inside the impressive tomb where Grant and his wife lay side by side.

website before visiting since the hours of operation seem somewhat fluid. http://www.nps.gov/gegr.

At this writing, the Visitor Center and the Memorial are closed on Monday and Tuesday and certain holidays. Grant's wife, Julia's remains, are also there. His first choice for his final resting place would have been at the U.S. Military Academy at West Point. However, he stipulated that his wife be buried next to him, thereby eliminating West Point because of academy regulations.

Groucho Marx popularized the question "Who is buried in Grant's Tomb?" on his TV game show *You Bet Your Life.* The correct answer is "no one" since Grant and his wife are entombed, not buried there.

The cottage where Grant spent the last weeks of his life completing his memoirs is also preserved as a state historic site. It is located on Mt. McGregor near Saratoga Springs, New York. For specific information, we suggest a visit to Grant's Cottage State Historical website: http://nysparks.com/historic-sites/9/details.aspx.

8

"America's Financial Founder"

Alexander Hamilton

County: Manhattan • City: New York City
Buried at Trinity Churchyard
74 Trinity Place – Broadway and Wall Street

During the Revolution, this founding father was on the staff of General George Washington. He was one of the principal authors of the *Federalist Papers* and a signer of the Constitution. He was the first United States Secretary of the Treasury. He is considered the founder of the nation's financial system and the country's first political party. He was killed fighting a duel with the nation's sitting Vice President. His name was Alexander Hamilton.

There is controversy about Hamilton's date of birth. Some historians believe he was born in 1755, others favor 1757, and there is evidence to support both dates. We do know that Hamilton celebrated his birthday on January 11th.

Of all the founders, Hamilton had to be considered the longest shot to achieve success. Most of the founders were born and raised in the families of America's elite. Hamilton was born to an out of wedlock mother and raised in the West Indies. He was orphaned at age 11. After his mother passed away, some of the islanders saw that he learned to read and write. He became a clerk for a mercantile firm, Beekman and Cruger, a company that carried out trade with the New England colonies. A cousin, Peter Lytton, adopted him and his brother James, but after Lytton committed suicide, they were separated. A merchant by the name of Thomas Stevens adopted Hamilton. Some believe that Stevens was Hamilton's biological father. Stevens had another son named

Alexander Hamilton

Edward, who was said to very much resemble Hamilton. Both boys were fluent in French and had similar interests.

Stevens recognized that Hamilton was brilliant. He sent his adopted son to America to continue his education. In 1772, Hamilton enrolled at Elizabethtown Academy in Elizabethtown, New Jersey. He met and was influenced by William Livingston, a leading intellectual who was also a patriot who favored revolution. In 1773, Hamilton continued his education at King's College (now Columbia University) in New York. His first public appearance, where he addressed the day's issues, was at the liberty pole on the college campus. Robert Troup praised Hamilton's ability to clearly explain the rights and reasons that patriots had in making their case against the British.

During this time frame in New York, the debate over independence versus loyalty to the King reached a crescendo. Debates at the time were generally waged in written form. Hamilton got involved in a pamphlet battle with a loyalist who wrote under the name "The Farmer." Hamilton answered his arguments by writing under the name "Friend to America." It was clear that Hamilton favored the patriot side, and, in his writings, he did not shrink from blasting English Parliament.

In addition to being involved in the debate over independence, Hamilton was also preparing for war. He began studying artillery warfare. His studies paid off in 1775 when he joined a volunteer militia company called the Hearts of Oak. His study of military tactics resulted in him achieving the rank of lieutenant. He led a successful raid to capture British cannon, which resulted in the Hearts of Oak becoming an artillery company. In 1776, he raised and led the New York Provincial Company of Artillery, which took part in both the Battle of White Plains and the Battle of Trenton. His skill as an artillery officer caught George Washington's eye, who offered Hamilton a position on his staff. He had previously received similar offers from Generals Nathanael Greene and Henry Knox, which he had turned down. He didn't feel he could refuse Washington's invitation, so he accepted the position and was made a Lieutenant Colonel.

For the next four years, Hamilton served as Washington's chief aide. He handled Washington's correspondence and drafted the general's orders. His duties included intelligence, diplomacy, and negotiation with senior army officers on Washington's behalf. His performance won Washington's confidence and support.

In 1780, Hamilton married Elizabeth Schuyler, the daughter of Philip Schuyler, an influential and wealthy landowner from New York. They were married at the Schuyler Mansion in Albany, New York.

Though he was on Washington's staff, Hamilton desired a command of his own. This desire led to a short-lived falling out between the two.

In February of 1781, Hamilton resigned from his staff position. He continued to ask Washington for a field command as he sensed the war was drawing to a close and with it his opportunity for military glory. Washington finally relented, and Hamilton was given his command. During the siege of Yorktown, he, with General Peter Muhlenberg, led the Americans in the final attack on British positions. Hamilton fought bravely and successfully. His actions contributed to the American victory and the surrender of the entire British army, effectively ending the war. After the battle, Hamilton ended his military career and returned to New York to study law.

In July of 1782, Hamilton was appointed to the Congress of the Confederation as a representative from New York. Under the Articles of Confederation, Congress had no power to collect taxes or demand money from the states. In 1781, an amendment to the Articles had been proposed to give Congress the authority to collect 5 percent duty on all imports. To implement such law required that all the states ratify it. This proved to be impossible after Rhode Island rejected the proposal in November 1782. Hamilton and James Madison persuaded Congress to send a delegation to Rhode Island to get the state to reverse its position. This effort failed when Virginia rescinded its ratification. Frustrated after a year in Congress, Hamilton resigned his position and returned to New York to practice law.

In 1784, Hamilton founded the Bank of New York. It is now the oldest operating bank in the country. He also contributed to the restoration of King's College (it had been suspended in 1776) as Columbia College. He had always been dissatisfied with the Articles of Confederation, and as a result, he played a significant role in the Annapolis Convention of 1786. It was Hamilton who drafted a resolution that eventually resulted in the Constitutional Convention. In the book *Miracle at Philadelphia*, Catherine Drinker Bowen states that evidence points to Hamilton as the most potent single influence toward calling the Constitutional Convention of 1787.

The state of New York named Hamilton as one of its delegates to the Convention. Unfortunately for Hamilton, New York's other two delegates, John Lansing and Robert Yates, opposed Hamilton's goal of creating a strong national government. As a result, Hamilton's influence at the convention was limited since Lansing and Yates controlled New York's vote. Even after the two left the Convention in protest, Hamilton was left without a vote because at least two representatives were required for any state to cast a vote.

Although Hamilton was not satisfied with the constitution the convention produced, he signed it because he saw it as an improvement over the present state of affairs. Since Lansing and Yates had left the convention, Hamilton was the only New York signer of the document. He was also very active in working for the Constitution's ratification in New York, a crucial state in national ratification.

Hamilton's role in the actual ratification of the Constitution was vital. He convinced James Madison and John Jay to join him in writing a series of essays championing the proposal. These essays are now known as *The Federalist Papers*, and Hamilton did the bulk of the work writing 51 of the 85 that were published. Those essays are now cited by jurists, lawyers, and historians as the Constitution's primary contemporary interpretation.

After George Washington was elected the first president, he appointed Hamilton to United States Secretary of the Treasury in 1789. It was in this position that Hamilton put his brand on the young nation's economy. He often butted heads with his old friend James Madison and the Secretary of State Thomas Jefferson. In 1790, Hamilton proposed that the federal government assume state debts incurred during the Revolution. This would greatly enhance the federal government's power by placing the country's most serious financial obligation in its hands rather than that of the states. Both Jefferson and Madison strongly objected to the proposal. They also opposed other proposals that Hamilton made to Congress. Both thought that Hamilton's plans went beyond what was allowed by the Constitution. Madison said that Hamilton was trying to make the government into what he thought it should be. In the end, the assumption plan passed when Hamilton made a deal with Jefferson and Madison to secure their support. To get their backing,

Hamilton agreed to support a plan to put the country's permanent capital on the banks of the Potomac River. By 1792, Jefferson changed his tune and complained to President Washington that he had been fooled by Hamilton and "made a tool for forwarding his schemes, not then sufficiently understood." During this time, political parties were born in America, with Hamilton's supporters becoming known as Federalists and Jefferson's Democratic-Republicans.

Meanwhile, back in New York, Hamilton had begun to bump political heads with a man that he would grow to despise, Aaron Burr. George Clinton was the governor of New York, where he was running for a fifth consecutive term in 1789. Burr and Hamilton found themselves on the same side in this election. They both supported Robert Yates as opposed to Clinton who won the election and holding no grudges. He brought the popular young attorney into his administration by making Burr the state's attorney general. Simultaneously, the powerful Livingston family broke their ties with Hamilton because they believed he had denied them some expected patronage. In 1790 Hamilton's father-in-law Philip Schuyler was running for reelection to the United States Senate. In those days, senators were chosen in the state legislature, and Clinton arranged for Burr to be the choice over Schuyler. After the election, he replaced Burr as attorney general with a member of the Livingston family. Hamilton was outraged over how his father-in-law had been dumped. As pointed out by Bernard A. Weisberger in his book *America Afire*, from that time on, Hamilton's hostility toward Burr "would fester and swell to neurotic proportions."

As stated previously, Hamilton believed in a strong federal government. He believed that the Constitution allowed the government to fund the national debt, assume state debts, and create its own bank. Also, he proposed that a tariff on imports and a tax on whiskey fund these programs. His views on the role of the federal government were nothing if not controversial.

However, it was not his controversial views that effectively ended his public service career but a lapse in judgment. Hamilton was involved in what would become the country's first political sex scandal. In 1791,

Hamilton began an affair with a woman by the name of Maria Lewis Reynolds. Her husband, James Reynolds, discovered what was going on and began blackmailing Hamilton by threatening to inform Hamilton's wife. After being arrested for counterfeiting, Reynolds contacted James Monroe, saying he could expose a high government official for corruption. Monroe was convinced that Reynolds was talking about Hamilton. Monroe and Frederick Muhlenberg interviewed Hamilton and told him of their suspicions as part of a congressional investigation. Hamilton admitted to the affair but denied any misconduct in public office. Hamilton's confession convinced them of his innocence, and they agreed not to make the story public. However, two years after Hamilton had left office in1797, a newspaperman named James Callender published the affair's details. Hamilton went into a rage and accused Monroe of leaking the information. Monroe denied it but the confrontation between the two nearly ended in a duel. A duel was avoided when the man Monroe had chosen to be his second was able to smooth the matter over. That man's name was Aaron Burr. Hamilton answered the charges by publishing a detailed confession of the affair. This confession damaged his reputation for the rest of his life.

In 1795, Hamilton resigned from the cabinet to resume his law practice. He remained a close friend and advisor to President Washington. Washington and the cabinet members continued to consult him, and he assisted Washington in writing his farewell address.

Hamilton also attempted to influence the presidential election of 1796. He did so in a manner that certainly upset John Adams, who later called Hamilton a "bastard brat of a Scotch pedlar." Back in 1796, each of the presidential electors had two votes cast for different men. The man who received the most votes became the president, and the runner-up became vice president. The Federalist plan was to have all their electors vote for John Adams and all but a few vote for Thomas Pinckney. The opposition party was headed by Thomas Jefferson, who chose Aaron Burr as a running mate.

Adams disliked Hamilton and resented the influence he had with President Washington. Likewise, Hamilton felt that John Adams was too emotionally unstable to be President. Hamilton devised a plan that would have all the northern electors vote for Adams and Pinckney but have South Carolina's vote for Pinckney and Jefferson. If it worked out as planned, Pinckney would be president, and Adams would remain the vice president. The plan failed. Northern Federalists found out about it and voted for Adams but not Pinckney, and as a result, Adams became the president and Jefferson became the vice president.

From 1798 to 1800, the United States was involved in a "quasi-war" with France. At this time, no politician could ignore a request from George Washington. Because of Washington's backing, Adams (against his wishes) was forced to appoint Hamilton a major general in the Army. Hamilton was hoping a full-scale war would break out so that he could lead his troops against the North American colonies of France's ally Spain. Adams thwarted Hamilton's hopes by opening negotiations with France. Hamilton served as a major general until June 15, 1800.

Adams had kept Washington's cabinet intact, and he suspected that Hamilton was influencing them. In 1800, after Washington died, he fired several of them for that very reason. As detailed in the book *America Afire,* the firings infuriated Hamilton. He wrote to Massachusetts representative Theodore Sedgwick saying that nothing, even losing the election, could be worse than another four years of Adams. In the letter, he said, "I will never more be responsible for him by my direct support, even if the consequence should be the election of Jefferson . . . If we must have an enemy at the head of the government, let it be one . . . For whom we are not responsible."

In the election of 1800, Hamilton was up to his old tricks. The Democratic-Republican candidates were once again Jefferson and Burr. The Federalists went with Adams and Charles Cotesworth Pinckney of South Carolina. Once more, Hamilton plotted to have Pinckney selected over Adams. That September, Hamilton wrote a pamphlet titled *Letter from Alexander Hamilton Concerning the Public Conduct of John Adams, Esq. President of the United States.* It contained a list of presidential blunders, all aimed at proving that Adams lacked the stature to be president due to the "great and intrinsic defects in his character" including

Plaque at the site of America's most famous duel.

"disgusting egotism . . . and an ungovernable indiscretion of temper." Against the advice of those who had seen the pamphlet, Hamilton mailed it to two hundred leading Federalists. A Republican postmaster opened a copy, and it found its way into the hands of Aaron Burr. In late October, it appeared in Republican papers. Even Hamilton's Federalist friends criticized him. One told him that "some very worthy and sensible men say you have exhibited the same vanity . . . which you charge as a dangerous weakness in Mr. Adams."

The election itself remains one of the most controversial in the nation's history. Jefferson was favored in the South and West, while Adams was expected to sweep New England. Thus New York, Pennsylvania, and New Jersey became key battlegrounds. In New York, Burr put together a slate of candidates filled with well-known names. Meanwhile, Hamilton was working the state hard on behalf of the Federalists. When the smoke cleared, Burr and the Republicans prevailed. In what was not one of his finer moments, Hamilton approached New York Governor John Jay with a plan to nullify the result. He suggested that Jay call an emergency session of the current expiring legislature to rewrite the election statute to award electors by district rather than give them all to Jefferson. Jay responded that Hamilton was proposing a measure for party purposes, "which it would not become me to adopt."

The loss in New York did not end Hamilton's role in the election. The Democratic-Republicans had planned to have one of their electors abstain from casting a second vote for Burr. Something went wrong, and each elector that voted for Jefferson also voted for Burr, resulting in an electoral vote tie. Per the Constitution, the matter would be settled by the outgoing House of Representatives.

Jefferson was worried that to thwart him, the Federalists might support Burr making him president. He would have been surprised to discover that he had a Federalist ally working to see that that did not happen. That ally was Jefferson's old enemy, Hamilton. Hamilton wrote, "Jefferson is to be preferred . . . As to Burr, there is nothing in his favor . . . He is bankrupt beyond redemption except by the plunder of his country . . . He is truly the Catiline of America." How much influence Hamilton had is not known, but Jefferson was elected president on the 36th ballot.

Jefferson believed that Burr plotted to steal the presidency from him. The available evidence doesn't support this. Instead, it appears that Burr stayed out of the fray and simply let events run their course. At any rate, it became apparent to Burr that he would be replaced on the ticket in 1804. Indeed, when the Republican caucus met on February 25, 1804, Burr didn't receive a single vote. Governor George Clinton of New York was chosen to run with Jefferson. Therefore, Burr decided to run for the governorship of New York.

With George Clinton out of the governor's race, the Clintonians backed Chancellor John Lansing. On February 16th, Lansing accepted the nomination. Two days later, Burr supporters made it public that Burr intended to run for governor. That very day, Lansing withdrew from the race as he didn't want to compete with the vice president. The Clinton's found a replacement in New York State Supreme Court Justice Morgan Lewis. Hamilton wasn't happy with this new state of affairs. At a Federalist meeting, he had already declared his support for Lansing. At the same time, he had roundly condemned Burr, and he hinted that Burr's election would encourage the New England states to endorse the idea of leaving the union. Hamilton, faced with what he saw as little choice, threw his support to the Jeffersonian Lewis. As it turned out, Hamilton had little about which to worry. Although Burr carried New York City by a narrow margin, he was soundly trounced in the rest of the state. Lewis won the election capturing 58.2 percent of the vote.

Soon after the election, the *Albany Register* published letters in which Charles Cooper cited Hamilton's opposition to Burr and stated that Hamilton had expressed "a still more despicable opinion" of Burr at a dinner party. Burr saw this as an attack on his honor and demanded an apology. Hamilton refused, saying that he could not recall the incident. There followed an exchange of testy letters between the two, which failed to satisfy Burr. A duel was scheduled for July 11, 1804, at a site in Weehawken, New Jersey. Ironically, Hamilton's son, Philip, had been killed in a duel three years earlier that was fought on this very site.

Early on the morning of July 11th, Hamilton and Burr took separate boats from Manhattan to Weehawken's Heights in New Jersey. Burr reached the spot first, and about a half-hour later, Hamilton arrived. By some accounts, lots were cast for the choice of position. However, according to the historian Joseph Ellis, since Hamilton had been challenged, he

Hamilton vs. Burr

had the choice of both weapon and position. Regardless of which is correct, either Hamilton or his second chose the north side position.

Hamilton's likeness graces the country's ten dollar bill.

All firsthand accounts of the duel agree that two shots were fired. At the time, it was common for duelists to fire an initial shot at the ground, to throw their fire away, to signify courage. Hamilton had pledged to withhold his shot, which he did not do. He fired first and hit a tree limb above Burr. It is possible that Hamilton did this on purpose, thus wasting his shot. Burr, having no way of knowing this, returned the fire and hit Hamilton in the lower abdomen above the right hip. The bullet caused significant damage to Hamilton's internal organs, particularly his liver, and Hamilton collapsed immediately. Burr began to move toward Hamilton but was stopped by his seconds, who rushed him back to his boat.

The paralyzed Hamilton, who declared that his wound was mortal, was taken back to a friend's home in Greenwich Village. There followed visits from family and friends. After considerable suffering, Hamilton died the next day. Gouverneur Morris (See Chapter 14) gave the eulogy at his funeral, and Hamilton was laid to rest in the Trinity Churchyard Cemetery in Manhattan.

Burr was indicted for murder in both New York and New Jersey. These charges were either later dismissed or resulted in acquittal. However, the animosity directed toward the vice president from that day forward effectively ended his political career.

Opinions of Hamilton have changed over the years. Both John Adams and Thomas Jefferson said he was unprincipled and aristocratic. During the eras of Jeffersonian and Jacksonian democracy, he was viewed in a negative light. However, both Theodore Roosevelt and Henry Cabot Lodge praised Hamilton and his views on a strong government by the Progressive Era.

Bust of Hamilton atop the New Jersey dueling site where he lost his life.

If You Go:

There are many other luminaries buried in the Trinity Churchyard Cemetery. **John Jacob Astor,** the businessman, merchant, and investor who became America's first multi-millionaire, can be found at Trinity.

Also buried here is **Robert Fulton,** who is often given credit for inventing the steamboat, which is not the case. He did construct

This monument marks the final resting place of Alexander Hamilton. Based on it's location one would guess that Aaron Burr often passed it during his latter years in New York City.

a steamboat called the *Clermont* and made it a commercial success by establishing the first permanent commercial route on the Hudson River.

Revolutionary War General **Horatio Gates** was laid to rest here. Gates claimed credit for the American victory in the Battle of Saratoga. He was blamed for the defeat at the Battle of Camden in 1780. He remains a controversial figure due to his participation in the Conway Cabal, which sought to replace George Washington as commander of the American forces.

James Lawrence, a United States Naval Officer, whose dying words "Don't give up the ship" made him famous, is buried here.

There are also three Continental Congress members, **Francis Lewis**, **Walter Livingston,** and **Martin Luther**, whose final resting place is at Trinity. Lewis signed the Declaration of Independence.

9

"Lady Day"

Billie Holiday

County: Bronx • Town: New York
Buried at Saint Raymond's Cemetery
2600 Lafayette Avenue

She was born in Philadelphia but spent her formative years in Baltimore and New York. It was in New York that she began her show business career. While still in her teens, she started performing in Harlem clubs, going from table to table, singing for tips. Here she came to the attention of a young record producer named John Hammond (who would later sign Bob Dylan and Bruce Springsteen to their first recording contracts). With Hammond's backing, she recorded her first record at the age of 18. Her distinctive vocal style earned her a reputation as a seminal influence on both jazz and pop singing. Barbara Streisand has stated, "If I hear a record once, I usually never listen to it again. I rarely listen to music—unless it's Billie Holiday."

According to her birth certificate, Holiday was born on April 7, 1915, in Philadelphia and named Elinore Fagan. However, the hospital records show Eleanor, and she said her birth name was Eleanora. Her teenaged parents, Sarah Fagan and Clarence Holiday, were not married, nor did they live together. Her father left mother and daughter behind to become a jazz guitarist. Though Holiday is commonly acknowledged to be the father, the aforementioned birth certificate identifies the father as Frank DeViese. It is a fact that the elder Holiday never publicly stated that he was Billie Holiday's father until she became well known and successful.

Details of Holiday's childhood are sketchy at best. In Baltimore, it appears that she was living with and raised by her mother's half-sister. While being shuttled between relatives, Holiday was at worst abused and

Billie Holiday

at best neglected. The possibility exists that she may have been raped during this period. The youngster frequently skipped school, and in 1925, she found herself in juvenile court at the age of nine as a result of truancy. The court sent her to a Catholic reform school where she spent nine months before being released to her mother's care. By the time she was eleven, Holiday had dropped out of school.

Holiday's mother had started a relationship with Wee Wee Hill, a porter she had met while working in the transportation industry. Leaving the girl behind with her half-sister, the couple moved to Harlem, New York. Once the two separated in1929, Holiday joined her mother, living and working in a Harlem brothel. Holiday, who had yet to reach the age of 14, also became a prostitute. Mother and daughter were both arrested during a police raid in May of 1929. After serving some time in a workhouse, Holiday was released the following October.

Back in Harlem, Holiday began singing in multiple nightclubs. She took the name Billie from an actress and Holiday from her father. Her reputation around Harlem began to grow, and by 1932, she was the leading singer at a club called Covan's. It was during a performance here that John Hammond first heard her perform. Years later, Hammond was asked what it was about Billie Holiday that got his attention. Hammond responded by saying he heard a singer who sounded like an improvising horn player and never sang a song the same way twice. Hammond recalled that he had to be sold on Holiday because he turned down the chance to work with Ella Fitzgerald to concentrate on Holiday.

Through Hammond, Holiday began working with some of the really big names in the music business. Her first recordings were made with Benny Goodman. When she was 18, she appeared in a short film *Symphony in Black* with Duke Ellington. She then began working with the noted jazz pianist Teddy Wilson. The two would take standard pop tunes like "Yankee Doodle" and work their jazz magic on them. Today the recordings made by Holiday and Wilson back in the 1930s are considered classics. Together they recorded more than ninety songs.

In 1937, Holiday took to the road as a big band vocalist with Count Basie. They were booked to play at the Fox Theater in Detroit. The management felt that her skin tone wasn't dark enough to sing with Basie's black band, so they applied makeup to blacken her face. Holiday went on but later recalled, "I had to be darkened so the show could go on in dynamic-asset Detroit. There's no damn business like show business. You have to smile to keep from throwing up."

Basie's saxophonist was the talented Lester Young, and he and Holiday hit it off perfectly. The two would eventually make 49 recordings. Though they teamed on fantastic songs like "Foolin' Myself" and "Easy Living," Young would pick "A Sailboat in the Moonlight" as his favorite piece. Some describe the song by saying that within it, the vocal and the saxophone become one. The two were so close that they gave each other nicknames that stuck; she called him "Pres," and he christened her "Lady Day."

By all accounts, Holiday's short stint with Basie's band was a rocky experience, and she was eventually fired. From her account, she was upset over her wages and the working conditions. Basie's male vocalist said she was unprofessional. The official word was that she was let go for being temperamental and unreliable. It appears that these reports didn't scare off Artie Shaw, who hired her to sing with his band within a month.

Working with Shaw certainly widened her audience. She was among the first black women hired to perform with a white orchestra. This caused some problems when Shaw decided to take his band on a Southern tour. In her autobiography, Holiday tells of not being allowed to perform on the same stage as the other vocalists because of her race. She recalled that Shaw, ignoring the rule, told her to get up here with the band. However, it was a racial incident in New York City that may have caused Holiday to leave Shaw. The band played the Lincoln Hotel, and Holiday was told to use the service elevator after the hotel manager received complaints from white patrons. She was also not permitted to enter the bar or the dining areas though the other band members faced no such prohibition. In addition to the racial slights, she was also upset with the number of songs Shaw was permitting her to perform, so she left the band.

By this time, her recordings for Columbia records had made her an established star. Yet Columbia refused to record the song with which she is most closely associated. She is said to have first performed the song in 1939, at the Cafe Society in New York's Greenwich Village. This was a progressively integrated nightclub that catered to the liberal mindset. Yet even in this setting, Holiday was reluctant to sing the song and did so only after being prodded by Barney Jacobson, the club owner.

Lady sings the blues.

Holiday would recall after the initial performance, the song was met with a stunned silence that was only broken when one person in the audience began to applaud. The rest of the crowd joined in, and the song became her signature piece. It was written by a white Jewish schoolteacher, Abel Meeropol, titled "Strange Fruit."

The song was a protest song written before such a label existed. It focused on American racism, specifically the lynching of black Americans. In the first verse, Holiday sings:

> Southern trees bear strange fruit,
> Blood on the leaves and blood on the root,
> Black body swinging in the southern breeze,
> Strange fruit hanging from the poplar trees.

Columbia, feeling that the song was too controversial and fearing a backlash from Southern record retailers, refused to record it. Holiday was granted a one-session release from her Columbia contract to record the song for Commodore records. That recording became her best-selling record. Ahmet Ertegun, the founder of Atlantic Records, called "Strange Fruit" the beginning of the civil rights movement. In 1978, Holiday's version was inducted into the Grammy Hall of Fame. In 1999, *Time* magazine declared that "Strange Fruit" was the song of the century, and in 2002 the Library of Congress added the tune to the National Recording Registry.

In 1941, Holiday and pianist Arthur Herzog wrote and recorded "God Bless the Child." The record sold over a million copies and was named number three by Billboard when they ranked the year's songs. Holiday said that the song's title came from an argument that she had with her mother that ended with her yelling, "God bless the child that's got his own."

Holiday was quoted as saying, "Somebody once said we never know what is enough until we know what's more than enough." Certainly, that was the way she lived her life. She started smoking tobacco when she was fifteen, and in time she'd be smoking 50 cigarettes a day, not including the marijuana she freely ingested. She also drank heavily and seemed to be attracted to men who abused her. In 1941, she married James Monroe, and though the union didn't last, he introduced Holiday to opium. Her next marriage to trumpeter Joe Guy was short-lived, but he did introduce her to heroin. She became addicted to the latter drug, and on May 16, 1947, she was arrested in New York for possession of narcotics.

One year earlier, Holiday had made her only featured film, *New Orleans,* which also starred Louis Armstrong (See Chapter 1). Holiday was upset that many of her musical numbers ended up on the cutting room floor, but truth be told, her drug addictions were a significant problem during the filming. Joe Guy, who was supplying her with drugs, had to be banned from the set.

As a result of her arrest, Holiday was sentenced to a year and a day in prison. She served eight months before being released because of good behavior. Though she had served her time, her conviction continued to haunt her. As a felon, she could no longer obtain a cabaret card, which meant that she could no longer work in New York nightclubs. Finding work outside of Gotham grew difficult as well since club owners were reluctant to hire her because of her reputation as an addict as well as her unreliability. Her recording sales plummeted, as did the radio play of her recordings. One reviewer writing in *Downbeat* said that she was becoming "Lady Yesterday."

In 1948, John Levy, owner of the Ebony Club, booked her to perform at his New York club even though it was illegal. Levy would become her boyfriend and her manager. Like the previous men in her life, he was physically abusive. Her performance at the club went on uninterrupted and was judged to be a success. However, as Levy hoped it would, it did not result in Holiday regaining her cabaret card.

At this point, her life might be best summed up in the lyrics of a song she recorded and often performed live. The 1920s blues standard titled "Ain't Nobody's Business if I Do" concludes with this final verse:

> Well, I'd rather my man would hit me
> Then follow him to jump up and quit me
> Ain't nobody's business if I do.
> I swear I won't call no copper, if I'm beat up by my papa
> Ain't nobody's business if I do.

Holiday had made a good deal of money but had lost most of it to drugs. By the 1950s, the drinking, drugs, and abusive relationships caught up to her and took their toll on her health. Her voice had changed some say for the worst. The quality of the recordings she made during this period continues to be debated by jazz fans. Miles Davis was not among those who felt that Holiday had lost it. In 1958 he said, "You know she's not thinking now what she was in 1937, and she's probably learned more about different things. And she still has control, probably more control than then. No, I don't think she's in decline."

During the '50s, Holiday kept busy as she toured Europe and began recording for Verve records. In 1956, her autobiography, *Lady Sings the Blues,* was published. William Duffy ghostwrote the book, and it was based on conversations the writer had with the singer. Later, when asked about some of the information in the account of her life story, Holiday claimed, "I ain't never read that book."

In that same year, Holiday performed two concerts to sold-out audiences at Carnegie Hall. The following year she appeared on the television show, *The Sound of Jazz,* where she sang a song she had written called "Fine and Mellow." She was reunited with Lester Young on the show, and their performance has been called the most moving jazz moment ever captured on film. The clip is available on YouTube, and it is indeed brilliant.

Holiday married again in 1957. The groom was Louis McKay, a mafia enforcer, who like the previous men in her life, was abusive, but unlike those who had gone before him, he tried to get her off drugs. He was unsuccessful.

Maya Angelou had a memorable meeting with Holiday around this time that she described in her book *The Heart of a Woman.* Angelou was a calypso singer, and her voice coach brought Holiday to her home in Los Angeles. For five straight days, Holiday visited Angelou. On the fifth day, Holiday accompanied Angelou to watch her perform. With Holiday seated in the front row, Angelou began singing her first song only to be interrupted by Holiday yelling, "Stop that bitch. Stop her goddamit. Stop that bitch. She sounds just like my goddam mamma." Holiday then rose and headed for the women's bathroom with Angelou in pursuit. Once in the bathroom, Angelou said, "Billie, let me tell you something . . ." But that was as far as she got before Holiday interrupted her telling her not to worry about the song since she couldn't help how she sounded. After a very short conversation, Holiday said, "You want to be famous, don't you?" Angelou admitted that she did. Holiday responded, "You're going to be famous. But it won't be for singing."

Early in 1959, Holiday was informed that she had cirrhosis of the liver. Her doctors told her she had to stop drinking, and for a short time,

Tombstone that marks the burial site of the great blues singer.

Grave goods left to honor Holiday show that she hasn't been forgotten.

she did. When she went back to the bottle, she hit it as hard as she ever had. On May 31, 1959, she was admitted to the Metropolitan Hospital in New York. While she was in her hospital bed, the police raided her room where she was arrested for possession of heroin, which was found in her purse. While she lay dying, a police guard was placed at her door.

She died from heart failure caused by cirrhosis on July 17, 1959. She was 44.

A few days later, her funeral was held at Saint Paul the Apostle Roman Catholic Church. More than 3,000 people attended it. She was laid to rest in Saint Raymond's Cemetery in the Bronx.

In 1972, Diana Ross starred as Holiday in the film *Lady Sings the Blues,* which was loosely based on the 1956 autobiography. The movie was a box office smash and was nominated for five Academy Awards. The city of Baltimore erected a statue in Holiday's honor that was dedicated in 1985. In 1988, U2 released the song "Angel of Harlem" as a tribute to Holiday.

One year before Holiday died, Frank Sinatra said, "It is Billie Holiday, whom I first heard on 52nd Street . . . who was and still remains the greatest single musical influence on me. It has been a warm and wonderful influence, and I am very proud to acknowledge it. Lady Day is unquestionably the most important influence on American popular singing in the last 20 years. With few exceptions, every major pop singer in the U.S. during her generation has been touched in some way by her genius."

If You Go:

The great boxing champion **Hector (Macho) Camacho,** who is regarded as one of the top fighters of his era, is buried here.

Singer **Frankie Lymon** of Frankie Lymon and the Teenagers was laid to rest here in 1968. When Lymon was only 13 years old, the group hit it big with the song "Why Do Fools Fall in Love."

Two-time typhoid epidemic source **Mary "Typhoid Mary" Mallon** can be found at Saint Raymond's, as can the actress **Lois Nettleton** who passed away in 2008.

10

"Master of Illusion"

Harry Houdini

County: Queens • Town: New York
Buried at Machpelah Cemetery
8230 Cypress Hills Street

Few performers have ever captured the public imagination like Harry Houdini. His grand illusions and daring, spectacular escape acts made him one of the most famous magicians of all time. He was one of the world's most popular entertainers, a real star of stage and screen. Time and again, his escapes from seemingly impossible predicaments thrilled audiences.

Houdini was born Erik Weisz in Budapest, Austria-Hungary, on March 24, 1874. He was one of seven children born to a Jewish rabbi, Mayer Samuel, and his wife, Cecilia. His family moved to the United States in 1878. The family name was changed to Weiss, courtesy of immigration officials, and Erik's name was changed to Ehrich. They first lived in Appleton, Wisconsin, where his father served as Rabbi of the Zion Reform Jewish Congregation. Rabbi Weiss lost his position there in 1887, and he and Ehrich moved to New York City. The rest of the family joined them when Rabbi Weiss found permanent housing.

The senior Weiss would struggle to provide for his family, taking work anywhere he could find it. Young Ehrich was forced to work from an early age to help out the family. His jobs included selling newspapers and working as a bootblack. He showed an early interest in performing, making his debut in a neighborhood circus as a trapeze artist when he was nine. When his father took him to see a traveling magician, his interest in magic took off, and he began to study magic.

Harry Houdini

He did not, as legend has it, run away with a circus, nor was he an apprentice to a locksmith. He merely turned to magic at age 17 as an alternative to factory work. In 1891, he teamed up with a friend named Jacob Hyman in an act they called "The Brothers Houdini." The name "Houdini" was used in tribute to Jean Eugene Robert-Houdin, the most famous magician of the era. Later in life, Houdini claimed that the first part of his new name, Harry, was an homage to Harry Kellar, another famous magician.

Let's see you get out of this!

After his father died in 1892, Harry left the family and went on the road. The Brothers Houdini performed their act (initially traditional card tricks and other unremarkable tricks) in dime museums and small theaters throughout upstate New York and the Midwest, including the Midway of the 1893 World's Columbian Exposition in Chicago (the Chicago World's Fair). In 1894, Harry's younger brother, Dash, replaced Hyman. While they were performing at Coney Island, Harry met a fellow performer, Wilhelmina "Bess" Rahner, a struggling singer and dancer who was initially courted by Dash but became the love of Harry's life. She and Harry wed that summer. Soon after, Bess replaced Dash, and the act became "The Houdinis."

Life on the dime museum circuit was grueling for the young couple. Harry tried every type of magic, from card manipulations (billed as the "King of Cards") to illusions and run-of-the-mill box escapes. In 1898, though barely 25, Houdini thought about quitting. In the spring of 1899, though, he and Bess went back on the road, and they finally caught a big break. They were performing in a beer garden in St. Paul, Minnesota when they caught the eye of a rising tycoon in the vaudeville world, Martin Beck. Beck was impressed with Houdini's handcuff escapes and challenged him the next day with his cuffs. Houdini escaped easily. Beck advised him to concentrate on escape acts and booked him on the Orpheum vaudeville circuit. Within months he was performing at the top vaudeville houses in the country.

Houdini began performing jail escapes and other public stunts to lure people to the shows. He had a talent for generating publicity and became known as "The Celebrated Police Baffler" and "The King of Handcuffs." His shows often involved local police, who would search him, place him in shackles and lock him in their jails from which he would escape. The shows were a huge sensation, and he soon became the highest-paid performer in vaudeville.

He set out for Europe to spend the next five years (1900-1905) touring England, Scotland, the Netherlands, Germany, France, and Russia. He delighted crowds just as he did in America, challenging local police to shackle him and lock him in jails, water-filled tanks, and nailed packing crates. He was able to escape because of his uncanny strength and his equally uncanny ability to pick locks.

One memorable challenge came from the *London Mirror* newspaper in 1904. They had special handcuffs made by a locksmith from Birmingham, England. The handcuffs were said to have been constructed with a Brahma lock, a complicated mechanism containing many circular tumblers. Houdini accepted the challenge. On March 17, over 4,000 people and 100 journalists turned out for the much-hyped event. During the attempt, Houdini asked if the cuffs could be removed to take off his coat. The request was denied. He promptly took out a penknife and, holding the knife in his teeth, used it to cut his coat from his body. At the 56-minute mark, Houdini's wife appeared on stage and kissed him. After an hour and ten minutes, he emerged free, and pandemonium broke out at the Hippodrome Theater. As he was paraded on the shoulders of a cheering crowd, he broke down and wept. He later said it was the most difficult escape of his career.

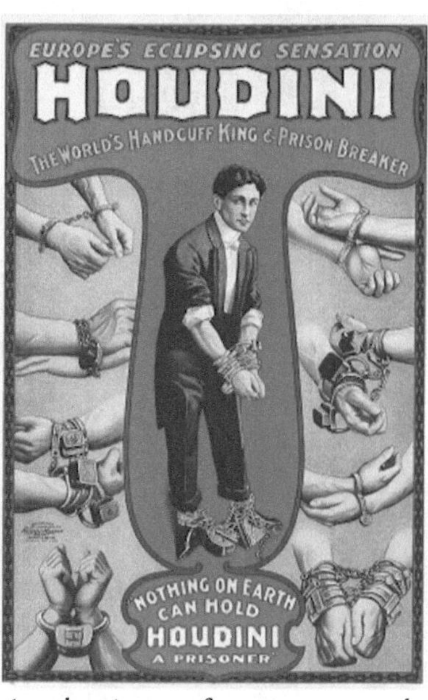

An advertisement for an appearance by the unparalleled escape artist.

In Germany, he caused an even bigger stir when he ran up against Kaiser Wilhelm II, emperor of Germany, and his formidable police force. A Cologne policeman, Werner Graff, accused him of fraud, claiming Houdini attempted to bribe him to allow an escape from the city jail and paid a civilian police employee to help with a public escape act. Rather than letting it slide and blow over, Houdini hired a lawyer and sued both the newspaper, which printed the story, and the policeman for slander. The trial began in February 1902 and received wide coverage in the press. After a parade of witnesses for both sides, the chairman of the jury asked Houdini to vindicate himself by opening the lock without the aid of the tools which Graff claimed he had used. Houdini opened the lock. Then, performing where only the judge could watch him, he slipped out of a set of locked chains.

Houdini won the case.

He was victorious again several months later when he defeated Graff's appeal by again opening one of Graff's prepared locks. Graff had to pay a fine as well as Houdini's expenses and money for lost bookings. Even though he had to reveal some of his tricks to the court, the resulting publicity only enhanced Harry's status.

Houdini at work.

He returned to the United States in 1905, an international celebrity. He bought a farm in Connecticut and a house in Harlem. He went on performing in the U.S. for years with great success. Because of imitators, Houdini put his "handcuff act" behind him and in 1908 introduced the famous milk can escape, reminding audiences that "failure means a drowning death." He staged a series of manacled bridge jumps around the same time, which drew large crowds and great publicity. The possibility of failure and death thrilled his audiences.

He kept expanding his act with his escape challenge in which he invited the public to devise contraptions to hold him. One such challenge had him escape from a cask of beer in Scranton, Pennsylvania. In 1913, he introduced perhaps his most famous act, the Chinese water torture cell, in which he was suspended upside down in a locked glass and steel cabinet filled with water. Many consider it Houdini's greatest trick. It required him to hold his breath for more than three minutes and had all the elements of a Houdini performance: brilliant technical conception, great physical strength, and highly dramatic presentation. This trick was so daring and such a crowd-pleaser that it remained in his act until his death.

In 1913, Houdini's mother died. He was very close to her and would grieve for her the rest of his life. Her death focused his attention on spirit mediumship or the contacting of the dead. Houdini seemed outraged at the victimization of the bereaved and spent the last 13 years of his life in a highly publicized battle with the spiritualists. Spiritualism was gaining popularity in the 1910s and particularly after World War I. Houdini's training in magic allowed him to expose frauds who had successfully fooled many scientists and academics. He was a member of a "Scientific American" committee that offered a cash prize to any medium who could successfully demonstrate supernatural abilities. None was able to do so, and the prize was never collected.

Houdini attended hundreds of séances and never experienced one he considered genuine. In 1924, he published a book, *A Magician Among the Spirits.* He described the mediums and psychics as fraudulent and exposed the tricks they used, including spirit writing, table rapping, and levitation. He often entered a séance disguised as an old man with a fake beard and glasses. When the séance reached its peak, he would jump to his feet and confront the stunned medium with the fraud. Afterward, news reporters hungry for a scoop waited outside, ready to record the skirmish between Houdini and the spiritualist.

One of his most controversial exposures involved Boston medium Mina Crandon, or "Margery," as she liked to be called. In 1922, her husband requested that Scientific American investigate her for the cash prize. Houdini helped to expose her as a fraud after a series of combative séances. At his own expense, he published a 40-page illustrated pamphlet entitled *Houdini Exposes the Tricks Used by the Boston Medium Margery.* These activities cost Houdini the friendship of Sir Arthur Conan Doyle, the author and creator, a firm believer in spiritualism. They became public antagonists.

When the United States entered World War I in 1917, Houdini tried to enlist in the army, but at age 43, he was rejected as too old. Wishing to show his patriotism, he performed many free shows for servicemen. He would perform his "Money for Nothing" routine, producing five-dollar gold pieces from the air and tossing them to the audience. He claimed he gave away $7,000 in that manner.

After almost three decades of public performances, Houdini found a new and powerful way to reach people: the motion picture. He made his first film, a serial called *The Master Mystery*, in 1918, just as the movie business was about to flourish. He became one of Hollywood's first action heroes, and his movies delighted audiences around the world. In 1919, he became a film producer/actor/stuntman, starting his own company called the "Houdini Picture Corporation." He made several movies such as *The Grim Game*, *The Man from Beyond*, and *Haldane of the Secret Service* but gave up on the business in 1923, complaining that the profits were too meager. The famous film comedian Buster Keaton befriended Houdini when the young Keaton and his parents worked in vaudeville with Houdini. The young boy, then known by his given name, "Joseph," was intrigued by Houdini's magic, and Houdini was quite taken with the boy. He nicknamed him "Buster," and the name stuck.

Houdini was protective of his status as the world's most famous magician, and he often distanced himself from the other magicians of his day. Paradoxically, he went out of his way to support the magic community in general. In 1917, he became the tenth president of the Society of American Magicians. While on tour, Houdini, at his own expense, had been recruiting local magic clubs to join the Society. He persuaded clubs in Buffalo, Detroit, Pittsburgh, Kansas City, Chicago, and San Francisco to join. He created the richest and longest-surviving organization of magicians in the world, with almost 6,000 dues-paying members. It's still going strong. He held the position as president for nine terms until his death. He is the only president to serve for more than one year.

Houdini began 1926 with his one-man show on Broadway. The show featured a bit of everything that made him a legend: small scale illusions, blockbuster escapes, and a spiritualism exposé. The show was such a success he took it on the road. While on tour with Bess in October of that year, Harry began to experience stomach discomfort. He refused medical treatment and refused to cancel any shows. Quite possibly, he was suffering from the onset of appendicitis, and his stubbornness may have led to his doom.

While performing in Montreal on October 22, 1926, Harry was punched in the stomach by a McGill University student named Gordon Whitehead, who tested Houdini's well-known ability to withstand such blows. The punch may or may not have been the cause of Houdini's ruptured appendix, but two days later, he collapsed on stage in Detroit and was admitted to Grace Hospital suffering from peritonitis. On October 31, Halloween, with his brother Hardeen at his side, Houdini passed away at 52. His last words were, "I'm tired of fighting." Houdini's insurance company concluded the death was due to the punching incident and paid double indemnity.

In the summer of 1926, a few months before he died, Houdini heard about a magician who had sealed himself inside a box and been lowered into the water, where he allegedly stayed for over an hour, submerged, before coming up and out of the box. Houdini purchased a bronze coffin and had himself locked into it and submerged in a hotel swimming pool (New York's Hotel Shelton, now the New York Marriott East Side) for an hour and a half before the coffin was pulled out and opened to reveal a smiling, healthy Houdini. He claimed he used no trickery or supernatural powers, just controlled breathing. Houdini took the coffin on tour with him in the fall, displaying it in the lobbies of the theaters he played, and he planned to perform the stunt on his tour. He jokingly instructed his wife to use the coffin should anything happen to him while on tour. Sadly, it was in that very coffin his body was returned. Houdini's funeral was held on November 4, 1926, in New York City, with more than 2,000 mourners in attendance. The Society of American Magicians honored him with a broken wand ceremony. At the ceremony, his

Preparing for another escape.

Magnificent grave of the Great Houdini.

fellow magicians broke a wand to symbolize the loss of the magic that came with the death of Houdini. This ritual was so emotionally powerful that the Society members adopted it and still perform it at magicians' funerals. Each year the magic fraternity gathers at Houdini's grave to repeat the ceremony on the anniversary of his death.

He was interred in the Machpelah Cemetery in Ridgewood, Queens, New York, with the Society of American Magicians' crest inscribed on his grave. A bust was added in 1927, a rarity because graven images are forbidden in Jewish cemeteries. In 1975, the bust was destroyed by vandals. Over the years, the site has been vandalized, thieved, and forsaken, and replacement busts have been smashed or stolen four times. The Society of American Magicians once paid for the maintenance and repair of the grave but stopped after a dispute with the cemetery managers. At one point, magician David Copperfield donated $15,000 to help restore the grave. Recently, a committee of the Society claimed they had worked out a deal to restore and care of the site.

Houdini's parents and siblings are all buried there, but not his wife, Bess. She died of a heart attack on February 11, 1943, at the age of 67. Houdini had expressed a desire to have Bess buried with him, and on his gravestone is inscribed her full name, birth year, and "19_ _" for the year of her death. However, Bess is buried at the Gate of Heaven Cemetery in

Bust of Houdini that adorns his final resting place.

Westchester County, New York, about 35 miles away. The reason for this is not completely clear, but it may be her family refused to allow her to be buried in a Jewish cemetery.

For ten years, Bess presided over annual well-publicized séances held on October 31, the anniversary of Houdini's death. Though she eventually stopped participating, the séances continue to this day. Harry and Bess had made a pact about making contact after death. They devised a coded message that only they knew. After ten years, Bess gave up hope.

Houdini's New York house still stands at 278 W. 113th Street in Harlem, and there is a small plaque at the site. After his death, Houdini's props and effects were used by his brother, who eventually sold them to magician Sidney Radner. In 2004, the collection, including the Chinese Water Torture Cell, was auctioned off, with most of it going to David Copperfield. These items are now archived and preserved at Copperfield's warehouse in Las Vegas.

In 1960, Houdini was given a star on Hollywood Boulevard's famous Walk of Fame, and in 2002 an official commemorative postage stamp was issued by the U.S. Postal Service. The stamp does a trick: in normal light, there is an image of Houdini, but under UV light, the image is shackled in chains.

There are Houdini museums in New York and Scranton, PA. The New York museum is located in a magic store, Fantasma Magic, at 421 7th Avenue. The museum in Scranton is at 1433 N. Main Avenue and is billed as the only building in the world entirely dedicated to Houdini. Houdini performed in Scranton and did several special challenges there.

If You Go:

Machpelah Cemetery is located amidst a cluster of cemeteries containing famous graves:

At Cypress Hills Cemetery, you'll find Hall of Famer **Jackie Robinson** (1919–1972), legendary actress **Mae West** (1893–1980), and heavyweight champion **Gentleman Jim Corbett** (1866–1933), 833 Jamaica Ave, Brooklyn, New York.

Comedian **Henny Youngman** (1906–1998) is buried in nearby New Mount Carmel Cemetery, 82–99 Cypress Avenue & Cypress Hills Street, Glendale, New York.

Actor **Bert Lahr** (1895-1967) and renowned attorney **Roy Cohn** (1927–1986) are buried in adjacent Union Field Cemetery, 8211 Cypress Avenue, Flushing, New York.

11

"King of Comedy"

Alan King

County: Queens • Town: New York
Buried at Mount Hebron Cemetery
130-04 Horace Harding Expressway

Alan King was a high school dropout who became an actor and one of the most famous and respected stand-up comedians of all time. His show business career lasted more than half a century.

He was born Irwin Alan Kniberg on December 26, 1927, in New York City. He was the eighth and last child of Russian Jewish immigrants Minnie and Bernard Kniberg. His father worked as a handbag cutter. At first, he lived on Manhattan's Lower East Side, and later the family moved to the Williamsburg section of Brooklyn. It was a tough neighborhood, and King used humor to get by.

When he was 14, he appeared on *Major Bowes Amateur Hour* as a contestant. This was radio's best-known talent show and one of the most popular programs in the 1930s and '40s. King didn't win but was invited to join a nationwide tour. When he returned, he began telling jokes in clubs around the Bronx for a dollar a night. He sensed he might have a future in making people laugh, and at age 15, he dropped out of high school to accept an offer to perform comedy at the Hotel Gradus in the Catskill Mountains. He was told that if he did well, he could stay and perform all summer. King walked to the stage and opened with: "When you work for Gradus, you work for gratis!" He was fired the next day.

However, he did land on his feet and spent that summer and the next as Master of Ceremonies at Forman's New Prospect Hotel in Mountaindale, New York. He later worked in Canada in a burlesque

Alan King

house and began to box professionally. He was quite successful as a boxer, winning his first 20 fights. He quit boxing after his first loss and decided to focus on comedy. He took the name of the fighter who beat him, "King," and from then on was known as Alan King.

He began working at a popular nightclub as a doorman and comedian. The club was called Leon and Eddie's. It started as a speakeasy and became one of New York's leading nightclubs in the '30s and '40s. It was there he met the legendary comedian Milton Berle. Berle recognized King's talent and became his mentor. King was often referred to as "Milton Berle's protégé."

King began his comedy career with one-liners and other material concerning mothers-in-law and Jews. He changed his style when he saw Danny Thomas performing in the early 1950s. He noticed Thomas was talking *to* his audience, not *at* them. He quit being a traditional joke-telling comedian and became a more conversational-style performer using everyday life for humor. In short, he'd evolved into an astute addresser of audiences.

In the early '60s, after a series of civil rights protests involving lunch counter sit-ins at Woolworth's, he asked a mostly black audience, "Why is everybody carrying on about Woolworth's? Have you ever eaten at the counter at Woolworth's? If you wanted to sit in the Colony Club, I could understand."

In 1947, King married Jeanette Sprung. The couple adopted three children, and at the urging of his wife, the family moved out of Manhattan to the suburbs. He used suburban life as the basis for much of his comedy, and as America was moving to suburbs, his humor resonated. He moved up in the show business ranks, performing at clubs around New York. His first big break came in 1949 when he headlined at New York's Paramount Theatre. He began opening for many celebrities, including Patti Page, Nat King Cole, Lena Horne, Frank Sinatra, and Tony Martin.

It was Martin who suggested King for his first movie role; the 1955 film *Hit the Deck*. The following year, he appeared in Judy Garland's one-woman show at the Paramount and accompanied her when she performed it in London, propelling him to stardom. When asked why the brilliant but chronically unreliable Garland had employed him for so long, he replied, "Because no one could make the announcement 'Miss Garland will not appear tonight' better than I could." King became a regular on *The Ed Sullivan Show* and made many appearances on *The Perry Como Show* and *The Gary Moore Show*.

Ed Sullivan's go-to guy was laid to rest here.

Living near New York City, King was frequently available when Sullivan needed an act to fill in for a last-minute cancellation. He made his first appearance on *Sullivan* in December 1956. It was scheduled at the last minute after Victor Borge canceled. The audience loved him, and he would appear 55 more times on the show, becoming one of Sullivan's favorites and gaining enormous national exposure. He also became a regular guest host for *The Tonight Show Starring Johnny Carson,* and frequently worked the club circuit from New York to Las Vegas—hobnobbing with superstars like Sinatra, Dean Martin, and Sammy Davis, Jr. "I worked with Frank Sinatra," King said years later. "He was the best. Even if he wasn't, who would dare say he wasn't?"

King became active in politics and was the emcee for John F. Kennedy's presidential inauguration party in 1961. He was also a strong supporter of Robert Kennedy and accompanied Senator Kennedy's body to Washington, D.C., after being assassinated in 1968.

He hosted the Oscars in 1972 and was the long-standing host for the New York Friar's Club celebrity roasts. After performing for the British royal family, he was introduced to Queen Elizabeth. "How do you do,

This stone pays tribute to the man who had the ability to make us laugh.

Mr. King?" she is reported to have said. "How do you do, Mrs. Queen?" he replied.

His success as a comic allowed him to venture into Broadway productions and Hollywood films. On Broadway, he starred as Nathan Detroit in *Guys and Dolls*. He made a name for himself in a wide variety of films. He frequently worked for director Sidney Lumet, beginning with *Bye Braveman* (1968) and later *The Anderson Tapes* (1971), as well as a starring role in *Just Tell Me What You Want* (1980). He often portrayed a gangster, as in *Casino* (1995) and *Night and the City* (1992), both starring Robert DeNiro. He also had a significant role in *Memories of Me* (1988), portraying Billy Crystal's terminally ill father.

King is also the author of five books, including his autobiography, *Name Dropping: The Life and Lies of Alan King*, published in 1996. He was the first recipient of the award for American Jewish humor from the National Foundation for Jewish Culture in 1988. The award was ultimately renamed in his honor.

Less well known was his charity work. He is the founder of the Alan King Diagnostic Medical Center in Jerusalem, raised funds for the Nassau Center for Emotionally Disturbed Children on Long Island, and established a chair in dramatic arts at Brandeis University. He also created the Laugh Well program, which sends comedians to hospitals to perform for patients. This idea came from his own experiences with oral cancer.

An avid cigar smoker, King struggled with cancer in his later years and died at the Memorial Sloan Kettering Cancer Center in Manhattan on May 9, 2004, from lung cancer. He is buried in Mount Hebron Cemetery in Flushing, Queens. His tombstone reads: "His passion for life brought life to us."

If You Go:

Mt. Hebron Cemetery contains a few interesting surprises. There are Olympic medal and Nobel Prize winners buried at Mt. Hebron, including:

- **Dr. Rosalyn Yalow** (1921–2011) won the Nobel Prize for Medicine in 1977.
- **Dr. Marshall Nirenberg** (1927–2010) won for Biology in 1968.
- **Henry Wittenberg** (1918–2010) won the Gold Medal in Freestyle Wrestling for the United States in the 1948 London Summer Olympics.

In contrast, there are at least seven notorious organized crime figures buried at Mt. Hebron, including three members of the murder-for-hire gang known as "Murder, Inc.":

- **Martin "Buggsy" Goldstein** (1905–1941).
- **Emanuel "Mendy" Weiss** (1906–1944).
- **Louis "Lepke" Buchalter** (1897–1944).

All three of these men were executed by electric chair at Sing Sing Prison (Weiss and Buchalter on the same day, just minutes apart). The other four:

- **"Kid Dropper" Nathan Caplin** (1891–1923).
- **Abraham Landau** (1895–1935).

- **Morris L. Kessler** (1912–1935).
- **Louis Kerzner** (1904–1939).

. . . were all shot to death in separate killings between 1923 and 1939. Caplin was shot and killed by Kerzner, and Kerzner was shot and killed on orders of Louis Buchalter.

Another item of interest at Mt. Hebron is the mausoleum and apparent future burial site of **Barbra Streisand**.

12

"Give Peace a Chance"

John Lennon

County: Manhattan • Town: New York
Buried at Strawberry Fields Section of Central Park
Between 71st and 74th Streets

He was born while Hitler's Luftwaffe was pounding England during the Battle of Britain. His father left him when he was still a young child, and his mother's family sent him to her older sister to care for and raise him. At school, he developed a reputation as a troublemaker whose chances for future success were slim. He would go on to publish two critically acclaimed books, lead a band that would revolutionize music worldwide, come to be recognized as one of the greatest composers of his time, and earn the well-deserved title of a peace activist. If Bob Dylan was the "Voice of a Generation," then he was its conscience. A musician, a poet, a philosopher, and a humanitarian is how the world came to know John Lennon.

On October 9, 1940, John Lennon took center stage for the first time. As soon as she had been informed of his arrival, Lennon's Aunt Mimi ran to the hospital, ducking into doorways to dodge the bombs being dropped by the Germans. At the time of his birth, Lennon's father, Alfred, was fittingly at sea working as a ship steward. It proved fitting because his father's absence would be the norm in Lennon's life. His mother, Julia, was beautiful and free-spirited. She had married Alfred against her family's wishes.

Alfred Lennon returned to port after one of his sea trips to find Julia pregnant by another man. To the surprise of few, the marriage failed, but not before scarring the young Lennon. Alfred received permission from

John Lennon

Julia to take his son on a day trip. Lennon's father's real plan was to have his brother adopt the boy. When the day trip turned into a multiple day trip, Julia did some detective work and tracked down Alfred and Lennon. It was Alfred who presented the four-year-old with a Hobson's choice saying, "You have to decide whether you want to stay with me or with mummy." In tears, Lennon initially chose his father but watching his mother turn and go was too much for him, and he ran after her, pleading that she not leave him. Julia took her son back to Liverpool, where her family decided he should be raised by her older sister Mimi.

So, it came to be that Lennon grew up in the home of Mary Elizabeth Smith (his Aunt Mimi and her husband, Uncle George). While Julia remained in his life, his aunt and uncle provided him with structure and care. The couple had no children of their own. It is not an understatement to say that both treasured the young Lennon. At the same time, it is equally accurate to state that the absence of parental love tugged and pulled at Lennon throughout his life.

From the time he entered school, Lennon excelled at art, and he was a ferocious reader. Even today, his classmates from his early days in primary school recall that he stuck out as somebody unusual or different. Some thought him odd and remembered that Lennon was usually involved if there were fights on the playground. Looking back on his early school days years later, Lennon said he thought he was either a genius or a madman. Of course, he added, that he knew he wasn't a madman.

When Lennon was 14, his uncle George died suddenly. Three years later, his mother was killed when a car went out of control and struck her as she was waiting at a bus stop. He got over his uncle's death in time, but his mother's loss would stay with him. Later he would write two very different songs about his mother. The hauntingly beautiful "Julia" that he recorded on the Beatles *White Album*, and the searing song titled "Mother" appearing on his first solo effort.

Through movies like Rock Around the Clock and recordings by American artists like Elvis and Buddy Holly, Lennon's interest in Rock and Roll was first ignited. When he was unable to convince his aunt or his mother to buy him a guitar, he went the mail-order route and ordered one himself (Aunt Mimi would later buy him a better guitar, though she was quick to tell him that while playing it was all well and good, he'd never make a living that way). It didn't take Lennon long to form his first band, which he named the Quarrymen, taking the name from the Quarry Bank High School where he was a student. One of the band's early performances took place on July 6, 1957, and it is noteworthy as it was the day Lennon met Paul McCartney. A friend recalling that fateful day said the two "circled each other like cats."

As Lennon learned more about McCartney, one thing was evident to him. McCartney was a better musician. As the Quarrymen's leader, Lennon alone had the authority to choose who was in the group. Though he recognized that he was risking his authority, Lennon invited the 15-year-old McCartney to become a part of the band. In his excellent book *Lennon Revealed,* Larry Kane quotes Lennon, who stated, "I made a decision to have a better person in the group."

McCartney accepted the invitation and later spoke of his feelings at the time to Beatles biographer Hunter Davies. "I idolized John. He was the big kid in the chip shop. I was the little guy."

Meanwhile, back at Quarry Bank High School, the individualism that Lennon had exhibited in the primary grades had continued, except now he was viewed as a behavior problem. The teaching staff's general view was that he rebelled against any restraint or discipline. It was against this background that the school's headmaster sat down with Aunt Mimi to discuss Lennon's future after graduation. The headmaster suggested art college, and Mimi agreed, saying, "Any port in a storm." With the aid of the headmaster's recommendation, Lennon was accepted at the Liverpool College of Art.

It was in an art class that Lennon would meet Stuart Sutcliffe. Sutcliffe was a talented young artist who was a year ahead of Lennon at the school. By the time Lennon arrived at the art school, Sutcliffe's artistic talent had made him well known to the other students and teachers. Lennon sought him out, and the two became fast friends. If there was a peer that Lennon looked up to, it was Sutcliffe who, unlike the majority of his friends, was not afraid to hold Lennon responsible for his behavior. In speaking of Sutcliffe, Aunt Mimi said, "That was his only friend, he was the only other boy he really enjoyed being with for long periods of time." Yoko Ono, who never met Sutcliffe, said that Lennon had told her that he really cared for Sutcliffe and respected him as an artist.

In 1958, a friend of McCartney's named George Harrison joined the band, and in1960, Lennon brought Sutcliffe on board as the band's bass player. It was around this time that the Quarrymen changed their name to the Silver Beetles. By now, the group had five members with Pete Best working the drums. That August, the group played 48 straight nights at a club in Hamburg, Germany, as The Beatles.

By the time The Beatles arrived in Hamburg, Lennon had already flunked out of art college. Both Lennon and McCartney had begun writing songs. Some were written as a team and some individually, but the two agreed that whatever they wrote would be credited as a Lennon-McCartney composition. Also, the tension between McCartney and Sutcliffe was on the rise. For one thing, McCartney was jealous of the attention that Lennon gave Sutcliffe. Added to that was the fact that Sutcliffe was a gifted artist but not much of a musician. During the band's performances, he would turn his back to the audience to hide his ineptitude at playing the bass, which happened to be the instrument that McCartney wanted for himself. It was against this background that the group entered into what they would call the Hamburg Experience.

All told, The Beatles would make three trips to Hamburg as they honed their skills as a group with long non-stop performances and the beginning of their use of drugs, particularly uppers, to help them get through their shows. Among the German fans, they attracted was a beautiful photographer named Astrid Kirchherr. She is credited with creating The Beatle hairdo, and the first member of the band to wear it was Sutcliffe.

Kirchherr and Sutcliffe fell in love, and he decided to leave the group and stay in Germany to pursue his art. This decision depressed Lennon, though both McCartney and Harrison viewed the event favorably as it related to the group. Lennon's depression grew worse when Sutcliffe died on April 10, 1962, due to a cerebral hemorrhage. Kirchherr broke the news to Lennon as The Beatles arrived in Hamburg. She recalled that he reacted by bursting into hysterical laughter. In her view, it was his way of not having to face the truth. Lennon never forgot Sutcliffe, as evidenced by his dead friend's appearance on The Beatles' *Sergeant Pepper's* album cover.

Back in England, the band began making frequent appearances at Liverpool's Cavern Club. In all, they would make 292 appearances at the club. While they were working at the Cavern, The Beatles came to the attention of a local businessman named Brian Epstein. One day a customer walked into his shop and asked for a record *My Bonnie* by the Beatles. Epstein had never heard of it but promised to try and locate the recording. He made some inquiries and found that the group had recorded the song in Hamburg. He also found out that the same group on that record played in the Cavern Club, located a couple of football fields away from his shop.

Epstein took a trip to the club to see the group. He was captivated by their raw talent. He then arranged a few meetings with the boys, as he called them, where they discussed the future. Finally, Epstein told them they needed a manager, and he offered to do it. It was Lennon who accepted, saying, "Where's the contract? I'll sign it." On January 24, 1962, the others took pen in hand as well and signed on with Epstein for five years. That same year Lennon married his longtime girlfriend Cynthia Powell, who was pregnant with their first son, Julian.

Epstein never tried to influence The Beatles musically in any way. However, he did take charge in other ways. He set down rules that they take the stage on time, that eating and drinking during performances stop, and that there would be no yelling at the audience. The latter regulation was aimed directly at Lennon, who had taken to yelling insults at audiences during the Hamburg days. The Epstein decision that provoked the group's most significant debate occurred when he decided the band would wear suits and ties. It was an idea McCartney supported, and Lennon and Harrison fought. Even after the two gave in to Epstein's packaging plan, Lennon would appear onstage with his tie loosened and his top shirt button undone. It was his little rebellion.

With the packaging of his product complete, Epstein set about getting The Beatles a recording contract. In making the rounds, Epstein told people that The Beatles would be bigger than Elvis, but nobody was buying. Finally, he convinced E.M.I. to take a chance on the group. Before making their first record, The Beatles replaced their drummer. Pete Best was out, and Ringo Starr was in.

E.M.I. teamed The Beatles with producer George Martin. Martin's forte to that point had been classical music, a little pop but mainly comedy albums. When The Beatles arrived to make their first record with Martin, they only had a few original compositions. The band wanted to record the Lennon McCartney tune "Love Me Do," with which Martin wasn't impressed. He offered them other songs, but they wanted to do one of their own. So, "Love Me Do" it was. The record reached number

17 on the British charts. When Lennon played the record for his Aunt Mimi, she was unimpressed.

The Beatles then recorded a tune Lennon had written, which he said was inspired by Roy Orbison. Upon hearing the song, George Martin insisted that the band increase the tempo. When the recording was finished, Martin said, "Congratulations, gentlemen, you've just made your first number one record." When Lennon played it for Aunt Mimi, she told him, "That's more like it." "Please Please Me" did indeed rise to the top of the charts.

By 1963 Beatlemania had already engulfed England, and word of the band reached the United States. Contrary to popular belief, The Beatles' first American television appearance was not on the *Ed Sullivan Show* (see Chapter 23). A month before the Sullivan appearance, Jack Parr showed a film of The Beatles performing "She Loves You." After playing the film, Parr joked that it appeared that England had caught up to us culturally.

While it wasn't their first, The Beatles' February 1964 appearance on Sullivan's show was nothing short of historic. The four became international stars, led by the songwriting duo of Lennon and McCartney. The band ruled the pop charts for the remainder of the decade. Between 1964 and 1966, they made two successful movies. Lennon wrote two critically acclaimed books, and the band toured worldwide.

In 1966, just as The Beatles' last American tour was to begin, the United States magazine *Datebook* published a quote from an interview Lennon had given four months earlier. Lennon said, "Christianity will go, it will vanish and shrink. I needn't argue with that, I'm right, and I will be proved right. We're more popular than Jesus now; I don't know which will go first, rock and roll or Christianity. Jesus was alright, but his disciples were thick and ordinary. It's them twisting it that ruins it for me." Wire services picked it up, and in no time, there were headlines worldwide reporting that Lennon had said that The Beatles were more popular than Christ.

The reaction to the quote may have been most intense in the United States. Nearly 50 radio stations refused to play Beatle records. Rallies were held where teenagers were encouraged to toss Beatle records and memorabilia into bonfires. One can only imagine that had Christ been around, he might have said let he who has not sinned burn the first LP.

Epstein hurried to America to do damage control. Before leaving, he begged Lennon to issue a public apology, but Lennon refused, saying he had done nothing wrong. Only after being told that he was letting the band down did Lennon agree to go before the press in Chicago, where he said, "I apologize if it will make you happy. I still don't know what I've done." No doubt Epstein had hoped for more, but that was the best he was going to get.

Up to this point, there is little doubt that Lennon was the leader of the best-known band in the world. McCartney compared him to Elvis and said, "We all looked up to him." In his book, Larry Kane quotes The Beatles press officer, Tony Barrow, who said, "but the fact remains during the height of Beatlemania, John did the heavy lifting. When one of the boys was upset over something, Paul would go to John and complain. John would confront Brian. Brian would fix it or try to. And Paul would sometimes look like the good guy because he didn't want to engage in uncomfortable situations. Both were born leaders, but John was the risk-taker in dealing with heavy issues."

The Beatles gave their last full concert in San Francisco on August 29, 1966. Some believe the decision to stop touring was influenced by the band's death threats after Lennon's Christ comments. While that may have been a factor, the band's music's evolution certainly played a part. The Beatles abandoned the pop sound that had catapulted them to the top of the music world. Their recordings became more complicated, both musically and lyrically. While most of the songs were still credited to Lennon and McCartney (Harrison had begun writing), the two worked separately. Generally, whoever wrote the song was the lead vocalist. For example, McCartney was tugging at the heartstrings with songs like "Yesterday" and "Here, There and Everywhere." Lennon, heavily influenced by Bob Dylan, was penning "In My Life" and "Tomorrow Never Knows."

That November, Lennon went to London's Indica art gallery to view an exhibit by an avant-garde artist named Yoko Ono. The artist told Lennon that he could climb a stepladder and hammer an imaginary nail into the wall for five shillings. Lennon responded that he would give her an imaginary five shillings to hammer the imaginary nail. Though they were both married, the two felt an immediate connection, and Lennon made it a point to stay in touch with Ono.

On June 1, 1967, The Beatles released the album *Sgt. Pepper's Lonely Hearts Club Band.* The recording met with immediate commercial and critical success. It would top the charts in both England and the United States for months. It was The Beatles' psychedelic masterpiece. Lennon, who, along with the other Beatles, was experimenting with LSD, wrote many memorable songs on the LP. These include "Lucy in the Sky with Diamonds" and, aside from McCartney's middle eight, "A Day in the Life." Decades later, *Rolling Stone* magazine would name *Sgt. Pepper's* the greatest album ever made.

Later Lennon would say that by this time, he was already growing tired of The Beatles. He was actively pursuing Yoko Ono though she initially showed little interest in a romantic relationship. A big blow came to the group on August 27, 1967, when Brian Epstein died from a drug overdose. According to his biographer, Ray Coleman, the death hit Lennon hard. Lennon said, "The Beatles were finished when Eppy died. I knew, deep inside me, that that was it. Without him, we'd had it."

McCartney moved in to fill the void left by Epstein's death. He came up with the idea to do a TV movie titled *The Magical Mystery Tour.* The film was shown on British TV on the day after Christmas in 1967. It was a critical disaster and constituted The Beatles' first failure. Lennon, whose attention had been diverted by Ono, participated half-heartedly in the project. He would later complain about the production cost, calling it the most expensive home movie ever made.

While The Beatles being finished may have been Lennon's view in retrospect, 1968 would prove to be a hectic year for both him and the band. In February, the group traveled to India to study transcendental meditation with Maharishi Mahesh Yogi. Lennon took his wife, Cynthia, on the trip, but he remained in contact with Ono through letters. In India, both Lennon and McCartney composed many of the songs on the album titled *The Beatles,* which came to be known as *The White Album.*

Paul and Ringo were the first to tire of Maharishi and leave India. Lennon grew to find the man annoying, and he decided to leave as well. When Maharishi asked him why he was departing early, he said, "If you're so bloody cosmic, you'll know why."

Lennon had decided to end his marriage, and he and Cynthia were divorced that November. By this time, Lennon and Ono had already announced that she was pregnant with his baby. She would suffer a miscarriage that same month. While this was going on, The Beatles had formed the Apple Corporation, and the animated movie *Yellow Submarine* had been released. In August, the McCartney-composed "Hey Jude" climbed to the top of the record charts, where it stayed for nine weeks.

Lennon quickly grew disenchanted with Apple. One of its employees, Richard Dilello, would later write a book about the company describing it as an extended cocktail party. Lennon's concern was that through Apple, The Beatles were losing substantial amounts of money every month. The group held a meeting to discuss matters, and McCartney began suggesting that The Beatles perform live, perhaps at a Roman amphitheater or on a cruise ship. Lennon was having none of it and told the others that he was breaking up the group. While the albums *Abbey Road* and *Let It Be* were released later, for all intents and purposes, The Beatles broke up long before McCartney's official announcement on April 10, 1970. That announcement angered Lennon, who said, "I started the band. I disbanded it. It's as simple as that." He told *Rolling Stone*, "I was a fool not to do what Paul did, which was use it to sell a record." The comments started a public feud between the two that would explode in their music in the early '70s.

By the time McCartney made the split official, Lennon had already married Ono. The newlyweds made their honeymoon a peace event when they checked into an Amsterdam hotel and held a bed-in for peace. The couple knew that they would be covered by the press regardless of what they did, so they used the moment to promote a cause they both believed.

Lennon and Ono staged yet another bed-in in Montreal, Canada. A reporter asked Lennon what he was trying to accomplish through these antics. His response was, "Just give peace a chance." On June 1, 1969,

Lennon recorded the song with that title in the Queen Elizabeth Hotel room where he and Ono were staying. Though he was still technically a Beatle, he released it as a solo work. The song became an anthem of the American anti-war movement.

In December of 1969, Lennon organized a supergroup to perform at London's Lyceum Ballroom. The purpose of the show was to support the United Nations Children's Emergency Fund. He called the group the Plastic Ono Band, and it included George Harrison, Eric Clapton, Keith Moon, Billy Preston, and Klaus Voormann. During most of the performance, Ono sat at Lennon's feet, covered by a white bag.

In 1970, Lennon released his first solo album titled *John Lennon/ Plastic Ono Band.* The work received critical acclaim. Rock critic Greil Marcus said that Lennon's singing on the final verse of the song "God" "may be the finest in all of rock." The *Village Voice* named it the album of the year. Today it is considered by many to represent Lennon's finest solo work. In 2003 *Rolling Stone* placed it at number 22 in the magazine's listing of the 500 greatest albums ever made.

Lennon's next solo effort *Imagine* didn't receive his first album's critical praise, but it was a commercial success. Lennon left out what, to some, was offensive language so that the fans would listen to it. He said

Tribute to Lennon located in New York's Central Park.

the song "Imagine" was "Working Class Hero" with chocolate on it. The record did include a song directly aimed at McCartney titled "How Do You Sleep." A few months earlier, McCartney had written and recorded a song called "Too Many People." Lyrically McCartney's song took a shot at Lennon and his new lifestyle with the words:

Too many people going underground
Too many reaching for a piece of cake
Too many people pulled and pushed around
Too many waiting for that lucky break.
That was your first mistake
You took your lucky break and broke it in two
Now what can be done for you
You broke it in two.

Why McCartney chose to attack Lennon lyrically (when he above all people knew that was Lennon's strength) is anybody's guess. Lennon pulled no punches in his response:

You live with straights who tell you you was king
Jump when your momma tell you anything
The only thing you done was yesterday
And since you've gone you're just another day.
How do you sleep?
How do you sleep at Night?

A pretty face may last a year or two
But pretty soon they'll see what you can do
The sound you make is musak to my ears
You must have learned something in all those years.
How do you sleep?
How do you sleep at night?

Many thought the song "Crippled Inside" was also aimed at McCartney. Music fans followed the feud between the greatest songwriting team of their time with interest. As they say, time heals all wounds, and by the middle of the decade, the two had buried the hatchet and put their bad feelings behind them.

By 1971, Lennon and Ono had taken up residency in New York City. That December, the couple released their Christmas tune "Happy Xmas (War is Over)." The following year the Nixon administration, fueled by Lennon's anti-war and anti-administration political stances, took steps to deport the former Beatle. By March of1972, Lennon had been ordered to get out of the country within two months. Lennon hired the attorney Leon Wildes to represent him in what would become a four-year battle. Throughout the conflict, Wildes successfully obtained extensions that allowed Lennon to stay in the United States. He was a prisoner of sorts since he knew that he wouldn't be permitted to return if he left the country.

Given the circumstances, one would think that Lennon would tread lightly when it came to political topics. That was hardly the case, as evidenced by the release of his next album, *Some Time in New York City.* The album was loaded with political statements from women's rights to England's presence and role in Northern Ireland's troubles. A single from the record "Woman is the Nigger of the World" was released but received very little radio airplay because of Lennon's use of the word "nigger." The album itself was a critical disaster. It was widely viewed as poorly written, and the backing band was viewed as mediocre at best.

At this point, Lennon and Ono were having relationship problems. In her view, she was pursuing her art while Lennon was partying into the wee hours. He had never been able to handle alcohol, and now he was doing a lot of drinking. Ono didn't want any part of the situation. While Lennon was working on his next record, Ono was deciding how to proceed. She decided that the two needed to be separated. Ono told John he had to leave and set him up with a female companion named May Pang. According to Larry Kane, Ono called Pang, who was working for the couple at the time, into her office and suggested that she'd be good for her husband. Though Pang was reluctant, Ono got her way, and Lennon and Pang began an affair. While the two were together, he released the album *Mind Games* near the end of 1973. While more successful than his previous LP, it was an inconsistent offering at best.

The year 1974 found Lennon and Pang heading to California for what became known as the "Lost Weekend." He continued his drinking, and his exploits with the singer Harry Nilsson were finding their way into the press. Two of the more publicized events took place at the Troubadour Club in Los Angeles. The one became known as the "Kotex Incident" when an intoxicated Lennon returned from the bathroom with a Kotex on his forehead. Seeing a waitress, he asked, "Don't you know who I am?"

She responded, ". . . some asshole with a Kotex on his head."

A few days later, Lennon and Nilsson were back at the same club to see the Smothers Brothers. Both men began drinking heavily, and Lennon began loudly heckling the performers. Peter Lawford, seated a few tables away, began yelling at Lennon to shut up. Ignoring Lawford, Lennon continued his harangue until bouncers removed both Lennon and Nilsson from the club.

Lennon and Pang headed back to New York, where they set up house together. That October, he released the album *Walls and Bridges.* Lennon produced the record himself, and it was a strong effort featuring quality songs like "Old Dirt Road" and "Nobody Loves You (When You're Down and Out)." The album's biggest hit was a sax-driven tune Lennon sang with Elton John titled "Whatever Gets You Through the Night." It became Lennon's only number one record as a solo artist. Elton John had bet Lennon that the song would reach number one and as payment Lennon agreed to appear with John at one of his live performances.

The two performed together on Thanksgiving Day, November 28, 1974. John tried to persuade Lennon to sing "Imagine," but Lennon refused, saying he didn't want to look like an old crooner doing his old hits. Instead, the two sang "I Saw Her Standing There," which Lennon introduced by saying it was written by an old fiancé of his, "Lucy in the Sky with Diamonds" and "Whatever Gets You Through the Night." The show was also noteworthy because it reunited Lennon and Yoko Ono, who met him backstage before the performance. Shortly after that, the two began living together again as man and wife.

In 1975 Lennon released the album *Rock and Roll.* While critics were unimpressed by the work, it does highlight Lennon's vocal talent.

New York's Strawberry Fields where fans gather to remember the man who brought The Beatles together.

Covering the hits when he was a boy, he does a great job on tunes like "Stand by Me" and "Rip It Up."

The rest of 1975 proved to be a banner year for Lennon. By October, he had won his immigration case and now had a green card. On the 9th of that month (Lennon's birthday), his second son, Sean, was born. A father again, Lennon devoted himself to raising Sean, saying, " we have basically decided, without any great decision, to be with our baby as much as we can until we feel we can take time off to indulge ourselves in creating things outside the family." True to his word Lennon became a house husband, and little was heard from or about him for the rest of the decade.

The retirement lasted until October 1980, when the single "(Just Like) Starting Over" was released. One month later, Lennon and Ono were back in the news with their new album *Double Fantasy.* Both the single and the album were big hits, and the two artists began planning a tour to place the following year.

On the night of December 8, 1980, Lennon and Ono returned to their apartment in New York's Dakota building just across the street from Central Park. As they were making their way into the building, a deranged

Lennon fan stepped from the shadows and began firing his gun. Four of the bullets struck Lennon, who fell at the entrance to the building. Lennon was rushed to a nearby hospital, but efforts to save him proved futile. He was pronounced dead at 11:07 P.M.

Not far from this quiet zone one can find street musicians remembering Lennon through his music.

Lennon was cremated, and some believe that his ashes were scattered in New York's Central Park in the area now known as Strawberry Fields. There fans still gather to pay tribute to the memory of a man who became known for his honesty and humanity as much as for his talent. When we visited, we were surprised at the number of young people present, many of whom had to have been born after Lennon's untimely passing.

Lennon has been honored numerous times since his death. For example, he has been inducted into the Rock and Roll Hall of Fame twice, once as a Beatle and once as a solo artist. Numerous artists have paid tribute to Lennon through their work, including George Harrison, Paul Simon, Joan Baez, Elton John, Queen, Bob Dylan, and yes, Paul McCartney. We like to believe that Lennon would have especially cherished his co-composer's effort.

If You Go:

The Imagine Memorial is in the Strawberry Fields section of Central Park across from Lennon's last home in the Dakota. You will undoubtedly run into many fans and a few musicians who gather daily to sing Lennon's compositions. You will also find street vendors selling Lennon related items like buttons and posters.

13

"The Batman"
William Barclay "Bat" Masterson

County: Bronx • Town: New York
Buried at Woodlawn Cemetery
517 East 233rd Street

He is still best remembered as one of the Wild West's most famous lawmen. Before donning a badge, he was a buffalo hunter and an Army scout. He counted Wyatt Earp among his friends and had more than a passing acquaintance with Doc Holiday. He was very fond of sports and gambling and later in life became a boxing referee. This man, who made a name for himself in places like Dodge City and Tombstone, ended up as a sports columnist in New York City, where he also served for a time as a United States marshal. Though baptized as Bartholomew, he would come to use the name William Barclay Masterson. However, he is best known by the nickname given to him by his parents, "Bat."

Bat was born on November 26, 1853, in Quebec, Canada. He was the second of eight children parented by Thomas and Catherine Masterson. All the children but one, the youngest girl named Emma, were born in Canada. By the time Emma arrived on the scene, the family had moved to a farm in upstate New York. The family next headed to Illinois and then to Missouri before finally settling near Wichita, Kansas, in 1871. Bat's father, Thomas, would remain on the family's farm in Kansas until he died in 1921.

Very little is known about Bat's childhood. It is believed he received the typical frontier education by attending school in a one-room schoolhouse. Based on the path he took as he grew older, it is safe to assume the goings-on in the nearby cattle town of Wichita heavily influenced young

Bat Masterson

Bat. Buffalo herds numbering in the millions still roamed the Kansas plains attracting hunters looking to make their fortunes. By the time he turned 21, Bat and his older brother Ed had joined their ranks.

While hunting down buffalo, the hunters set up camps. It was in these camps that Bat learned about both gambling and drinking. Salesmen would seek out these camps to peddle their liquid wares, generally grain alcohol or some other concoction to which they added red pepper. It is safe to say that the liquor Bat grew fond of and enjoyed throughout his life was relatively tame compared to what he digested in those hunting camps.

Bat's buffalo hunting adventures took him to Texas, where he joined a group of men who left Dodge City to head for a trading post called Adobe Walls. It was here where Bat and 27 other men, including the famous rifleman, Billy Dixon (who is still one of just eight civilians ever awarded the Congressional Medal of Honor), were attacked by an Indian force estimated to number more than 700. On day one of what became known as the "Second Battle of Adobe Walls" (in 1864, Kit Carson was involved in the first battle at this location), the initial Indian attack came close to success, but the hunters held on to repulse the advance. After the first attack, the Indians were forced to keep a distance because of the hunters' accuracy using their long-range rifles. On the third day of the attack, a number of the Indians retreated to a bluff about a mile away from the hunters to survey the site and decide on their next move. At this point, Billy Dixon took what he later termed "a scratch shot" that dropped one of the Indian warriors. Dixon's accuracy so discouraged the Indians that they gave up the fight. Bat had survived his initial Indian fight and, in all probability, killed a Comanche or two himself.

Bat's reputation as a hunter and his ability to handle firearms resulted in a growing reputation. In his later years, Bat would claim that General Nelson Miles, who became famous as an Indian fighter and whom Teddy Roosevelt called the "Brave Peacock," recruited him to be an Army scout. It was a job he took for a few years in the 1870s; a time Bat described as "when the Indians got obstreperous."

In 1876, Bat was back to hunting buffalo in the area around Sweetwater, Texas. On January 24th, he was playing poker in one of the local establishments called the Lady Gay. The owner of the saloon, a man by the name of Melvin King, was one of the participants in the game. Things did not go well for King that night, and when the game ended, he had lost a considerable amount of money. With the gambling over, Bat began talking to a woman named Mollie Brennan, one of the popular prostitutes in town and known to have spent time with King. It was about midnight when Brennan, accompanied by Bat, and a man named Charlie Norton headed to Norton's tavern and dance hall. Soon after Bat and Brennan found a couple of seats, King burst in, pulled out a Colt 45, and fired a shot that hit Bat in the abdomen and ended up in his hip. King fired again, and this shot struck Brennan, killing her. Bat pulled his gun from the floor and fired, striking King in the chest; he would die the following day. The incident became known as the Sweetwater Shootout, and it contributed to Bat's reputation as a cold-blooded killer. Bat himself always downplayed the shooting claiming that he only fired in self-defense. For a short time, while he was recuperating from his wound, Bat used a cane. Contrary to popular belief, primarily based on the *Bat Masterson* television series starring Gene Barry, Bat did not use a cane for the rest of his life. Nor was it his weapon of choice when he ran into trouble.

Having recovered from his wounds, Bat considered what to do next. He later claimed to have thought about heading for the Black Hills after General George Armstrong Custer announced that gold had been discovered. What is known that he made his way to Cheyenne, Wyoming, where he decided to "buck the tiger," which meant he decided to challenge the dealer at one of the local gambling tables. Bat got hot with the cards and ran his winning streak, which lasted five weeks, out to the very end. He thought about heading for Deadwood, where he would have joined the likes of Wild Bill Hickok and Calamity Jane. Instead, according to Bat, Wyatt Earp, who he had met a few years earlier, convinced him to join the Earp brothers as a law enforcement officer in Dodge City. Later in life, Bat would write about Wyatt Earp, saying, "Wyatt Earp is one of the few men I personally knew in the West in the early days, whom I regarded as absolutely destitute of physical fear."

After arriving in Dodge, Bat served as a sheriff's deputy alongside Earp and then was elected county sheriff of Ford County, Kansas. Upon being elected, he quickly named three under-sheriffs, including his brothers Jim and Ed. Bat was only in office for three days when outlaws made two unsuccessful attempts to rob trains that were part of the Atchison, Topeka & Santa Fe railroad system. Although these attempts failed, the

Wyatt Earp and Bat Masterson

railroad company offered a high monetary reward for the capture, dead or alive, of the unsuccessful train robbers. When this failed, the company approached Bat and asked him to organize a posse and search for the outlaws. He agreed to do so.

The search began but was slowed by a snowstorm. Bat and his men were about 35 miles outside of Dodge City when they sought shelter from the storm at a ranch in the area. The ranch owner said he had no other visitors, but Bat had a hunch that the bandits would also show up

seeking a place to ride out the storm. The young lawman's intuition served him well as Dave Rudabaugh and Ed West, two well-known outlaws, arrived at the ranch only to be arrested by Bat and his men. This episode further enhanced Bat's growing reputation as a western lawman.

During the summer of 1878, a woman by the name of Dora Hand arrived in Dodge. She was a dancehall girl who was called the "Queen of the Fairy Belles." She caught the attention of a cowboy by the name of James Kenedy. Kenedy's father was a wealthy cattleman who had raised a son who believed he was above the law. Indeed, the elder Kenedy had already used his influence to get his boy out of trouble. Hand soon became a performing fixture at the Alhambra Saloon and Gambling House, co-owned by the town's mayor, James Kelly. Kelly, much to the annoyance of Kenedy, began spending considerable time with Hand. On one night in the saloon, Kenedy and Kelly got into a fight, and Kelly roughed the young man up before throwing him out into the street. Kenedy left town but, as it turned out, not for good.

A couple of months went by before Kenedy returned under cover of night with a plan to get his revenge. The young cowboy didn't know that Kelly was away at the time, and he was letting Hand and another woman named Fannie Garretson stay at his house. The two women were asleep when Kenedy fired two shots through the door of the residence. One bullet caused no harm, but the other went through a wall and struck and killed Hand.

While there were no witnesses, Wyatt Earp and Bat both suspected that Kenedy was the culprit. They organized a posse and headed out of town, eventually catching up with Kenedy, who attempted to flee. Bat shot and struck the cowboy in the shoulder. From the ground, Kenedy asked if he had killed Kelly. When he was informed that he had killed Hand, he said, "You ought to have made a better shot than you did." Bat responded, "I did the best I could." Although Kenedy was acquitted (probably thanks to Dad), the story of Bat's actions in the case spread throughout the region, adding to his growing legend.

Meanwhile, the good citizens of Dodge City were taking action to try to calm down the violence that often erupted in the town's gambling establishments. They had concluded that losing gamblers and guns were a combination that didn't mix well. As a result, the town enacted a series of local ordinances. Concealed weapons (unless you were a lawman) were prohibited, and upon entering Dodge, you were required to give up any weapons you had in exchange for a receipt you could use to reclaim them as you left town.

In April of 1878, Ed Masterson, who was then the marshall, and a deputy, paid a visit to the Lady Gay Saloon. Once inside, they confronted an armed cowboy named Jack Wagner. Masterson told him he would need to give up his gun. Wagner surrendered his weapon, and Masterson gave it to Wagner's trail boss, Alf Walker, telling him to check it in with the bartender. Thinking the job completed, both Masterson and his deputy exited the saloon. They were both still outside the establishment when Wagner appeared with his gun. At this point, Masterson and Wagner got into it as Masterson attempted to grab the firearm forcibly. Alf Walker appeared, pointed his gun at the deputy, and pulled the trigger, but the pistol failed to fire. By this time, Wagner had gotten control of his gun and shot Masterson in the abdomen.

What followed is open for debate. Some say that the mortally wounded Ed Masterson managed to fire three shots and hit Wagner, who made it to another saloon before collapsing. He would die the next day. However, in 1913, Bat, who was testifying at a libel trial, told a different story. According to Bat, he was in the vicinity when he heard the shots, and he chased both Wagner and Walker as they fled. Bat said he opened fire on the two, killing Wagner and wounding Walker. Walker would die later due to complications from his wounds. Bat then returned to care for his brother, who was past helping. Some believe that Bat's role in the episode wasn't reported in the local papers to protect him from friends of the cowboys who might come to Dodge seeking revenge. At any rate, by 1913, Bat must have felt safe enough to tell the story.

Bat faced reelection in 1879, and the town of Dodge was divided between a group known as "the gang" and another that went by the name "the reformers." Members of the gang were those who were making a living off gambling, prostitution, and drinking. The reformers put up a candidate who defeated Bat in a close election. Bat decided to leave Dodge, and for the next couple of years, he made a living as a gambler.

In February 1881, Bat heard from his old friend Wyatt Earp. Earp invited Bat to join him in Tombstone, Arizona, where Earp was making money managing the gambling operations at the Oriental Saloon as well as acting as the tavern's enforcer. Bat traveled to Tombstone, where he began giving Earp a hand running the saloons faro tables. Fate intervened at this point when Bat received an unsigned telegram from someone in Dodge City that referred to Bat's brother Jim. The telegram was to the point it read, "Come at once. Updegraff and Peacock are planning to kill Jim."

Bat knew the men referenced in the telegram. Jim Masterson had entered into a partnership with A. J. Peacock as co-owners of the Lady Gay Saloon and Dance Hall. Al Updegraff worked at the Lady Gay as a bartender, and he was also Peacock's brother-in-law. Jim held the view that Updegraff was a dishonest drunk, and he wanted him fired. Peacock refused to fire him, and the argument between Jim and his co-owner grew so heated that threats were made prompting the wire to Bat.

Having already lost one of his brothers, Bat left for Dodge. As his train was arriving, Bat saw Peacock and Updegraff walking the streets, so he jumped off the moving train and called out, "Hold up there a minute, you two. I want to talk to you." When the duo saw that Bat had called to them, they began running toward the town jail. Shots rang out, though who began shooting remains unknown. However, once guns were fired, other men in the area joined in, and soon multiple guns were involved in the fight. When the shooting ceased, Bat was arrested, and Updegraff had been struck in the lung: a wound described as serious but not life-threatening. It was impossible to determine who had inflicted the wound, so Bat was released after paying an eight dollar fine. He found his brother Jim unharmed. Jim then sold his share of the saloon to Peacock, and the two brothers decided it was time to get out of Dodge.

Bat decided not to return to Tombstone and, as a result, in all probability, did not participate in the old west's most famous gunfight, "The Shootout at the O. K. Corral." That fight pitted the Earp brothers and Doc Holiday against Ike and Billy Clanton and Tom and Frank McLaury. In thirty seconds, about thirty shots had been fired. Ike Clanton, who was unarmed, was sent on his way by Wyatt Earp, but his brother Billy and the McLaury brothers were lying on the street dead. Doc Holiday, as well as Morgan and Virgil Earp, had been wounded. Bat, who was never fond of Holiday, would later describe him thusly, "Holiday had a mean disposition and an ungovernable temper, and under the influence of liquor was a most dangerous man."

The gunfight did not end the violence. About two months later, Virgil Earp was shot as he left the Oriental Saloon. The shooter was never apprehended, but Ike Clanton and Will McLaury were considered suspects. Virgil was hit in the arm, but he made it down the street, where he collapsed in the arms of his brother Wyatt. Virgil never regained the use of his injured arm.

On March 17, 1882, Wyatt and Morgan Earp were playing pool at a local billiard hall. All of a sudden, they were interrupted by a volley of gunfire. Morgan was hit in the back, and he collapsed while two other bullets hit a wall just over Wyatt's head. Within an hour, Morgan was dead.

These shootings set the stage for Wyatt Earp's noted vendetta posse, a group he had organized to track down his brother's killers. Wyatt had already killed Frank Stilwell, who he believed was one of the men involved in Morgan's death. Earp was wanted for Stilwell's murder. The sheriff of Tombstone was a man named Johnny Behan. Behan had a famous meeting with Earp where Earp told the sheriff, "Johnny, if you're not careful, you'll see me once too often." By the end of the month-long vendetta ride, the posse had killed four men. Earp, who remained wanted for murder, never returned to Tombstone.

Meanwhile, Doc Holiday headed for Denver, where he was arrested for the Stilwell murder. Behan, who said he would hang Holiday, requested that he be extradited to Arizona. When news of Holiday's arrest reached Earp, he contacted Bat, who was now the marshall in Trinidad, Colorado. Earp asked Bat to help Holiday out. Bat did so out of respect for Earp. Holiday was released before he could be extradited.

By this time, Bat had become a huge boxing fan. He was as fond of the "Sweet Science" as he was of gambling. Bat was among the spectators at a bout in February of 1883 in Gulfport, Mississippi. It was a heavyweight contest that pitted the Boston Strong Boy, John L. Sullivan, against Paddy Ryan. Sullivan emerged the winner by knocking out his rival. Some believe that the boxing term knockout was invented because of this fight.

Bat then returned to Dodge City to help an old friend, Luke Short, who was also friends with Wyatt Earp. Short was co-owner of the Long Branch Saloon. The other owner was a cattleman by the name of W. H. Harris. In 1883, Harris ran for mayor but was defeated by Lawrence Deger. That April, prostitutes working at the Long Branch were arrested by the local authorities, who ignored the other working girls in town who plied their trade at similar establishments. Short interpreted the arrests as an attack on his business, which it indeed was. Short armed himself and headed to the jailhouse. Before reaching his destination, he encountered a deputy by the name of Louis Hartman. No one knows who fired first, but a shooting occurred, and Hartman fell to the ground, though he was not hurt. Thinking that he had killed the deputy, Short went back to his saloon and locked the door. Within a couple of days, Short was arrested and taken to the train station, where he was ordered to leave town. Short headed for Kansas City, where he met up with both Bat and Earp.

In May, Bat, Earp, and three associates arrived in Dodge where the town constable, Dave Morrow, met them. Earp had Morrow deputize the five so that they could legally carry guns within the city limits. Morrow did so, and the group became known as the Dodge City Peace Commission. Faced with Bat and Earp, the powers that be reached a compromise with Short, who was allowed to return to town and run his business.

By the late 1880s, Bat was living in Denver, Colorado, working as a faro dealer. It was here he met a singer and dancer named Emma Walters. In 1889, it was believed (there is no legal record) the two were married. Emma would stay with Bat for the rest of his life. In Denver, Bat began to settle down and worked as a boxing referee, promoter, and writer. He composed a weekly sports column for a newspaper called the *George's Weekly*.

During this period, Bat entered into a boxing promotion partnership with a man named Otto Floto. Things didn't work out, and the two parted on less than amicable terms. Floto wrote for the *Denver Post*, and he and Bat continued to feud through their columns. The story goes that Floto eventually hired a gunman to settle things with Bat. Unknown to Floto, the gunman he hired had crossed paths with Bat in the past, and he proceeded to let Bat and Emma take a train out of town. The two eventually made their way to New York City, and within 24 hours of their arrival, Bat was arrested for being part of a gambling ring.

Bat and three other men were accused of running crooked faro games. A man named George Snow, a Mormon from Salt Lake City, claimed that he had lost $16,000 to Bat and his cohorts. Bat vehemently denied the charges, and Snow couldn't identify Bat at the police station. Finally, Bat and the other men were released when they made bail. When Snow failed to appear in court, the charges were dropped. This development failed to satisfy Bat, who promptly sued Snow for $10,000 because the accusations had damaged his reputation. There was no denying that the newspapers played up the story of how the famous western lawman, Bat Masterson, was arrested immediately after setting foot in the city. The case was settled out of court.

While Bat may not have liked his New York reception, he found the city itself to be the perfect place to establish a new home. Boxing was big in New York, and based on his notoriety; Bat was offered a job writing a sports column for the *New York Morning Telegraph*. He would hold that job for the next 18 years.

In 1907, Bat wrote a magazine article titled "My Friend Wyatt Earp." It was a big success and is widely considered the starting point of the Wyatt Earp legend we know today. Many believe that Bat glossed over a

Though Masterson made a name for himself in the Wild West is final resting place is pictured here in New York City.

few parts of Wyatt's life that would have contradicted the Western hero's actions we've come to know.

Bat also became friends with an avid boxing fan, President Teddy Roosevelt. Roosevelt made Bat a U. S. Marshall for the Southern District of New York. Bat served in the position from 1905 until 1909.

On October 25, 1921, Masterson was at his desk working on his next column. It was there that he was found dead of a heart attack at the age of 67. Left behind on his typewriter was the following: "There are those who argue that everything breaks even in this old dump world of ours. I suppose these ginks who argue that way hold that because the rich man gets ice in the summer and the poor man gets it in the winter, things are breaking even. Maybe so, but I'll swear I can't see it that way."

Damon Runyon, who had befriended Bat, stayed with his body the night before the funeral. On the day he was laid to rest, more than 500 mourners paid their final tribute at a small New York funeral parlor. Bat was buried in Woodlawn Cemetery. His tombstone bears the name Masterson, and underneath, one finds the words, "Loved by Everyone."

If You Go:

Fiorello H. La Guardia, considered one of the greatest mayors in American history, is also buried in Woodlawn Cemetery. La Guardia served as New York's mayor from 1934 to 1945. He ran New York during the Depression and World War II and succeeded in cleaning up public corruption and making the city a model for public works programs. He has been credited with restoring the faith of the citizenry in City Hall.

The renowned singer and lyricist **Samuel M. Lewis** was also laid to rest at Woodlawn. Lewis began writing songs in 1912 and is known for penning such standards as "I'm Sitting on Top of the World" and "Rock-a-bye Your Baby with a Dixie Melody." Plus, you can't help but admire the man who wrote the lyrics for "Where Did Robison Crusoe Go with Friday on Saturday Night." Lewis is a member of the Songwriter's Hall of Fame.

Sam Harris, who was partner and brother-in-law of George M. Cohan, is also buried at Woodlawn.

For more information on Woodlawn Cemetery, see the chapters on **Nellie Bly** and **George M. Cohan** (Chapters 3 and 5).

14

"The Penman of the Constitution"

Gouverneur Morris

County: Bronx • City: New York
Buried at Saint Ann's Churchyard
295 Saint Ann's Avenue

He was a founding father who hailed from New York City. He argued with his family over the issue of American independence. He served in the army during the Revolutionary War. He signed both the Articles of Confederation and the United States Constitution. He is credited with writing large sections of the latter document, including the preamble. He was also a United States Senator from 1800 to 1803. His name was Gouverneur Morris.

On January 31, 1752, Morris was born in what is now called the Bronx section of New York City. As a boy, he exhibited a keen intellect—so keen in fact that he enrolled in King's College at the age of twelve, which is now known as Columbia University. He began his studies in 1764 and graduated in four years. Since he was too young at age sixteen to start a career, he stayed at King's and received his master's degree in 1771. Next, Morris studied under the noted New York law scholar William Smith. Through Smith, who opposed British tax policies in the colonies, Morris met patriots such as John Jay and Alexander Hamilton.

In 1775, Morris was elected to the New York Provincial Congress. This Congress was organized by patriots seeking an alternative to the Province of New York Assembly, the official pro-British body. During his service in the Provincial Congress, Morris began supporting turning the colony of New York into an independent state. This put him at odds

Governor Morris

with his family and his mentor, William Smith, who had turned away from the patriot cause when it moved towards pursuing independence.

When the Revolutionary War began, Morris favored reasoning with those Americans who stayed loyal to the king. This is hardly surprising since this group, known as Tories, included his mother and his half-brother. His mother gave the family estate to the British army to be used for military purposes. As the war went on, Morris changed his views on the treatment of Tories and favored tarring and feathering, whippings, and the confiscation of property.

The image above is of the man credited with writing much of the Constitution of the United States.

In 1778, Morris was appointed to be a delegate to the Continental Congress. He was placed on a committee charged with reforming the Continental Army. Upon visiting the army at Valley Forge, he was so affected by the conditions that he became a spokesman for the army in Congress and was instrumental in reforms in training, methods, and financing. That same year, the Conway Cabal took place. Its purpose was to remove George Washington as Commander-in-Chief of the army. Morris cast the deciding vote that kept Washington in his job. In 1779, Morris was defeated in an election that cost him his seat in Congress. The defeat was most likely caused by his support for a strong central government, a view not popular in New York at the time. After his defeat, he left New York and moved to Philadelphia.

In 1780, Morris shattered his left leg, and it had to be amputated. He said he had done it by getting his leg stuck in the spokes of a carriage he was driving. However, Morris had a reputation for having affairs with both married and unmarried women, and there was gossip that the accident occurred while a jealous husband was chasing him.

In Philadelphia, he served as superintendent of finance from 1781 to 1785. He also worked as a merchant, which put him in contact with the financier and Founding Father Robert Morris (no relation). With the support of both George Washington and Robert Morris, he was appointed to be a Pennsylvania delegate to the 1787 Constitutional Convention.

Morris certainly made his presence known at the Convention. According to Catherine Drinker Bowen in her book *Miracle at Philadelphia*, Morris has been described as the most brilliant man at the

Morris as a young man.

convention. She noted that he spoke often, giving 173 speeches, while never saying anything foolish or tedious. She describes his tactics as abrupt, first an eloquent explosive expression of his position and then cynically waiting for the convention to catch up with him. He continued to favor a strong central government. He said, "When the powers of the national government clash with the states, only then must the states yield." Many others at the convention, including Washington, shared his desire for a strong central government. Morris served on the Committee of Five, who drafted the final language of the proposed Constitution. Bowen called Morris the Committee's "amanuensis," meaning that he was responsible for most of the draft, as well as its final form. Also, Morris

The tombstone of an underrated founding father.

was one of the few delegates at the convention who spoke openly against slavery. According to James Madison's notes, Morris attacked slavery calling it a nefarious institution. After the Constitution was adopted, Morris was proud to put his signature on it.

Morris went to France on business in 1789. He would not return for a decade. He served as Minister Plenipotentiary to France from 1792 to 1794. His diaries from this period have become a valuable resource concerning the French Revolution, and they also serve to document his ongoing affairs with women. He was openly critical of the French Revolution, which led to the French government's request to recall him, which the United States eventually did.

Upon his return to the States, he resumed his law practice and entered politics. In 1800 he was elected to the United States Senate as a Federalist. He would serve until 1803. During this time, he championed improving transportation from the eastern part of the country to the interior. After being defeated in his reelection bid, he became chairman of the Erie Canal Commission from 1810 to 1813. The canal was instrumental in transforming New York into a financial capital. That much was clear to Morris when he said, "the proudest empire in Europe is but a bubble compared to what America will be, must be, in the course of two centuries, perhaps of one."

Morris married at the age of 57. His wife was Ann Cary Randolph, the sister of Thomas Mann Randolph, who was the husband of Thomas Jefferson's daughter Martha. Morris and his wife had one son, Gouverneur Morris Jr., who became a railroad executive. On November 16, 1816, Morris passed away after causing himself internal injuries while using a piece of whalebone to clear a blockage in his urinary tract. He was laid to rest in Saint Ann's Episcopal Churchyard Cemetery.

If You Go:

Also buried at Saint Ann's is the brother of Gouverneur Morris, **Lewis Morris,** who signed the Declaration of Independence. He is also considered most responsible for New York adopting the Constitution by the very close vote of 30-27. His grandson **William Walton Morris**, a West Point graduate and a Civil War Brevet Major General, is buried here.

15

"The Master Builder?"

Robert Moses

County: Bronx • Town: New York
Buried at Woodlawn Cemetery
517 East 233rd Street

Robert Moses is probably the most controversial bureaucrat in American history and one of the most polarizing figures in urban planning annals. Although he was never elected to any public office, Moses amassed tremendous power as the leader of numerous public authorities that built 13 bridges, 416 miles of parkways, 658 playgrounds, and 150,000 housing units, spending $150 billion in the process. He was called a visionary who gave all this to New York, along with the Lincoln Center and Jones Beach. He was also called a bulldozing bully who callously displaced thousands of New Yorkers and championed highways as he starved mass transit.

Moses was able to wield such power from the mid-1920s through 1968 and once occupied 12 positions simultaneously, including New York City Parks Commissioner, head of the State Parks Council, head of the State Power Commission, and chairman of the Triborough Bridge and Tunnel Authority. He gained autonomy from the general public and elected officials and once had 80,000 people working under him.

It all began in New Haven, Connecticut, in 1888, when Robert Moses was born to German-Jewish parents who moved to Manhattan in 1897. The family was well off; Robert graduated from Yale and earned a Ph.D. in political science from Columbia University. At that time, he was an idealist and progressive reformer who developed plans for merit hiring of civil servants and became part of the movement to reorganize the New York state government.

Robert Moses

Moses was working within New York's Bureau of Municipal Research, where his intelligence and hard work brought him to Belle Moskowitz's attention. At the time, Moscowitz was a key advisor to Governor Al Smith (See Chapter 21). With Moscowitz's backing, Moses gained both power and influence as he became the man who put the governor's vision of the state's future down on paper. Governor Smith called him "the best bill-drafter I know." Together they would eventually reorganize and consolidate many aspects of state government.

It was Moscowitz who created and advanced the most important initiative of Smith's first administration. She convinced the governor

Jones Beach

to set up a committee that became known as the "Reconstruction Commission." The committee's purpose was to develop a comprehensive plan to guide the state to transition from World War I to peace. The committee would tackle all the day's issues, such as education, immigration, housing, and taxes. Moscowitz convinced noted leaders in business, labor, agriculture, and education to serve on the committee. She served as Executive Secretary, and she selected Moses to be chief of staff. The committee's recommendations related to restructuring state government were mainly implemented during Smith's terms as governor.

At the time, parks were part of the Good Government agenda, and Moses became Smith's parks guy. Here he began his first foray into large-scale public works initiatives. He demonstrated skill as a project manager, a bill drafter, and a public persuader able to divide and defeat any local opposition to his projects. His first major public project was Jones Beach State Park, which was developed while Moses was president of the Long Island State Park Commission (for which he wrote the legislation in 1923). Located in southern Nassau County on Jones Beach Island, the State Park opened in 1929 and was a huge success. Moses was also appointed head of the State Council of Parks.

During this period, Moses began earning a reputation for the arrogance that would stay with him throughout his life. He paid little attention to who he insulted. Even though the state budget was outside his area of expertise, he decided to send a letter to the Director of the Budget, explaining exactly how the state's accounts should be managed. He was so sure of himself that in the missive, he stated that he and the director were "sufficiently good friends so that you would rather have me tell you this point-blank." It appears that Moses was a poor judge when it came to the depth of their friendship since the director responded by saying that the letter from Moses was "illuminating in so far as it reflects your entire ignorance of the details that go into making a budget."

It was in the mid-1920s that Moses first clashed with Franklin D. Roosevelt. Roosevelt was appointed chair of the newly created Taconic State Parks Commission and proposed a parkway and a specific route that differed from Moses's plan. The Taconic Parkway would become the subject of regular clashes between the two men over the next few years. Moses succeeded in diverting funds to his Long Island parkway projects, while the Taconic Parkway was not completed until the 1960s. The antipathy between Moses and Roosevelt was intense and personal. Yet, when the latter became president in 1933, the federal government found itself with millions of New Deal tax dollars to pump into the economy. Moses was one of the few local officials who had projects planned and ready to go. As a result, New York City obtained significant Depression-era funding.

New York City Mayor Fiorella La Guardia discontinued the five independent borough Parks departments in 1934. In their place, he formed a new consolidated, city-wide Parks Department and appointed Robert Moses as its first Commissioner. Meanwhile, Moses retained his state park offices and added "head of the Triborough Bridge Authority" to his ever-growing resumé. He assembled an enormous park design and construction team, which in 1934 had a workforce of 70,000 (all paid by the federal government).

In the first few years of the New Deal, New York built hundreds of playgrounds, three zoos, ten golf courses, and 53 recreational buildings. Orchard Beach opened in the Bronx, and Riis Beach opened in Brooklyn.

Moses inspecting a model of one of his plans for the city.

During the sweltering summer of 1936, 11 gigantic swimming pools opened in neighborhoods all over New York.

It was, however, the chairmanship of the Triborough Bridge Authority which gave Moses the most power. The enabling legislation gave it a great degree of independence and made it mostly impervious to pressure from mayors and governors. It was created in 1933 to complete the construction of the Triborough Bridge, which started in 1929 but stalled due to the Depression. The Triborough Bridge (now the Robert F. Kennedy Memorial Bridge) opened in 1936 and connected the Bronx, Manhattan, and Queens via three separate spans. The bridge's toll revenues amounted to tens of millions of dollars each year and rose quickly as traffic exceeded all projections. Rather than pay off the bonds, Moses sought other toll projects to build—a cycle that would feed on itself. By 1946, under Moses' chairmanship, the Authority grew via a series of mergers with four other agencies and became the Triborough Bridge and Tunnel Authority.

Robert Moses used the public authority's power to sell bonds, build roads, bridges, and tunnels, collect tolls, and put the money back into new projects. The Triborough Bridge and Tunnel Authority operated like a sovereign state. Its leader answered to no one; it had its own source of revenue, its own communications system (complete with networked phones, short wave radios, and walkie-talkies), its own police force (Bridge and Tunnel Officers) who were authorized to make arrests and carry firearms, and its own transportation system (a fleet of cars and trucks).

In 1939, the World's Fair opened in Flushing Meadows. Robert Moses chose the site, and the Parks Department oversaw construction. A year later, the Department completed the Belt Parkway, one of the most ambitious of all the pre-war parkway projects, covering a distance of almost 35 miles in a series of connected highways that formed a belt-like circle around the New York City boroughs of Brooklyn and Queens.

World War II halted public construction, but Moses's power increased after La Guardia retired. Newly elected Mayor William O'Dwyer named Moses the city's "Construction Coordinator" and "de facto" representative in Washington, D.C., in 1946. He was also given powers over public housing that had eluded him under La Guardia. By 1959, Moses had overseen the construction of 28,000 apartment units on hundreds of acres of land. In clearing the land, he sometimes destroyed as many housing units as he built.

From the '30s to the '60s, Moses was responsible for constructing the Throgs Neck, Bronx-Whitestone, Henry Hudson, and Verrazano-Narrows Bridges, and the Brooklyn-Queens, Staten Island, and Cross Bronx Expressways, just to name the major projects. He was the mover behind the Lincoln Center and contributed to the United Nations headquarters being placed in New York rather than Philadelphia.

Moses is viewed as the man directly responsible for the 1958 move of the Brooklyn Dodgers to Los Angeles, which broke this author's heart and may have caused permanent emotional damage. Dodger owner Walter O'Malley wanted to build a new stadium to replace the outdated Ebbets Field. He wanted it in Brooklyn near the end of the Long Island Railroad. On the other hand, Moses wanted to use that site

Henry Hudson Bridge

for a parking garage and proposed that the new stadium instead go in Flushing Meadows. He envisioned the stadium hosting all three of the city's major league baseball teams (the Dodgers, the New York Giants, and the Yankees). O'Malley was vehement in his opposition to Moses's plan, citing the team's Brooklyn identity. Moses refused to budge, and after the 1957 season, the Dodgers and the Giants both left for the West Coast. In 1961, Moses did get to break ground for a stadium on his site. Three years later, Shea Stadium opened as home to baseball's New York Mets and football's New York Jets.

Moses's reputation began to decline in the 1960s, as the view of urban planning began to change. His campaign against the free Shakespeare in the Park festival in Central Park, in which he fought against the legendary director/producer Joe Papp received much negative publicity. This image was enhanced when he tried to destroy a shaded playground in Central Park to construct a parking lot for the expensive Tavern-on-the-Green restaurant.

His popularity suffered another blow in 1963 over Penn Station's demolition, which was one of the most spectacular buildings and architectural landmarks to grace the New York landscape. Madison Square Garden replaced it. This casual destruction of one of New York's jewels led many residents to oppose Moses's plan for a Lower Manhattan

Expressway, which would nearly destroy Greenwich Village and SoHo. This opposition included urban activist Jane Jacobs, whose book *The Death and Life of Great American Cities* was instrumental in defeating Moses' plan in 1964.

Moses's power was further sapped by his involvement with the 1964 World's Fair. His arrogance caused the major European countries and Canada, Australia, and the Soviet Union to decline to participate. His projections for attendance were wildly overestimated, and his generous contracts led to financial disaster.

After the Fair, Mayor John Lindsay and Governor Nelson Rockefeller sought to use toll revenue from the Triborough Bridge and Tunnel Authority to cover New York City's deficits. Moses opposed the idea and fought to prevent it. The mayor then removed Moses as the city's chief advocate for federal highway money. Governor Rockefeller threw his support behind legislation to create a new Metropolitan Transportation Authority that would include the Triborough Bridge and Tunnel Authority. In 1968, the bill passed, and Moses was no longer its chairman. He was promised a key role, but it never materialized, and for all practical purposes, Moses was out of power.

In 1974, Robert Caro published *The Power Broker*, a Pulitzer Prize-winning biography of Robert Moses that severely tarnished his reputation. It won the Francis Parkman Prize awarded by the Society of American Historians, and the Modern Library selected it as one of the hundred most important books of the 20th century.

The power broker himself.

Modest tomb of Robert Moses.

In *The Power Broker*, Caro describes how Moses used his public authorities' wealth to build an empire and live like an emperor. The records of the various authorities he ran were not open to the public, and thus Moses used that to keep the public from finding out what he was doing. Caro describes Moses as the "locus of corruption," the "ward boss of the inner circle," and describes how he enriched those who supported him in public and private life. He doled out contracts for public relations, insurance commissions, and legal fees as he willed and to whom he pleased. He united the banks, labor unions, contractors, bond underwriters, insurance companies, and real estate firms behind him as they stood to gain millions from his projects. Although never elected to any office, Moses was a master politician. His constituency was not the public but rather the most powerful men in the state. Caro claims that Moses was so incredibly wasteful that he paid $40 million more in interest than he had to on one single bridge alone.

To build his highways, Moses threw 250,000 people out of their homes and wrecked scores of neighborhoods. His highways flooded the city with cars and fostered low-density development on Long Island and other suburbs, a pattern that relies primarily on roads instead of mass transit. He systematically starved the subways and commuter railroads and defeated every attempt to create a master transportation plan. He also learned the trick of misleading the state legislature to get his projects underway. Moses called the practice "stake driving": he would grossly underestimate the cost of a project to get it underway, then blackmail politicians into funding the rest, saying that their ignorance about the real cost made them derelict of their duty and unfit for office.

Robert Moses died of heart disease on July 29, 1981, at the age of 92, at Good Samaritan Hospital in West Islip, New York. He is interred in a crypt in an outdoor community mausoleum in Woodlawn Cemetery in the Bronx.

It is likely the debate over Moses's legacy will continue. It is impossible to say that New York would have been a *better* city without Robert Moses, but it almost certainly would have been a *different* city.

If You Go:

As previously mentioned in earlier chapters (Bly, Cohan, Masterson), Woodlawn Cemetery contains many interesting graves of famous people. Three more to note are:

- **Joseph Pulitzer** (1847–1911), best known as the founder of the Pulitzer Prizes, the most prestigious awards in American journalism.
- **Joseph Bulova** (1851–1936), founder of Bulova Watch Co., broadcast American's first national radio commercial in 1926.
- **Thomas Nast** (1840–1902), considered the father of American political cartooning, first featured an elephant as the symbol for the Republican Party.

16

"New York's Finest"

Joseph Petrosino

County: Queens • Town: New York
Buried at Calvary Cemetery
49-02 Laurel Hills Boulevard

Joseph Petrosino was one of New York's finest. He was a pioneer in the fight against organized crime, a protector of his community, and had unique experiences as a New York City police detective.

He was born Giuseppe Petrosino in Padula, a village in southern Italy, on August 30, 1860. In 1873, at the age of 13, he was sent, along with a young cousin (Antonio Puppolo), to New York City to live with his grandfather, who, shortly after Giuseppe's arrival, was killed in a streetcar accident. In 1874, Giuseppe's father, Prospero, a tailor, and his mother, two sisters, and three brothers joined him in New York. At that time, many middle-class Italians came to America, hoping for a better life for their children. Such was the case for the Petrosinos. Prospero opened a shop in Manhattan that became successful enough to support his family.

Giuseppe, or "Joe," being the eldest son, would take any job not to be a burden to the family. He was a newsboy in Little Italy and then a shoe-shine boy in front of Mulberry Street's police headquarters. He developed friendships with many of the policemen who were customers. Being a police officer was his dream. He studied the English language and attended evening classes. In 1878, he obtained American citizenship and applied to the police department. He was rejected. He applied repeatedly, but at five-feet three-inches tall, he did not meet the minimum height requirement of five-feet seven-inches. His friendship with the police, especially with a captain, led to him getting a job as a "white winger"

Joseph Betrosino

or street cleaner. White wingers were named for the white uniforms they wore as they made their way through the streets picking up litter with small brooms and dustpans and depositing the trash in barrels on wheels that they pulled along. At that time, these jobs were controlled by the police department.

In the late 1800s, New York was hit with a great wave of poor southern Italian immigrants. Crime in the Italian ghetto was out of control.

Knowing Italian, Petrosino soon became helpful to the police, who used him as an informant to catch Italian criminals. Finally, the police commissioner bent the height requirement, and on October 19, 1883, he joined the NYPD and was issued badge number 285. He was the first Italian-speaking officer to join the police department. Being fluent in several Italian dialects, he investigated and solved cases that other officers couldn't. His ability to solve crimes in the Italian community was such that his supervisors would call out "send for the Dago" whenever a serious crime took place in that area. By all accounts, he was a tough cop. He befriended future president Theodore Roosevelt, a police commissioner (a council of police commissioners governed the NYPD) and loved Petrosino's toughness and courage during this time.

On July 20, 1895, Roosevelt promoted him to detective sergeant and placed him in charge of the Homicide Division. During one months-long undercover investigation while on loan to the U.S. Secret Service, Petrosino worked as a tunnel digger and lived in a rooming house with suspected anarchists in New Jersey. This group had previously been involved with the assassination of King Umberto I of Italy. During this mission, he discovered evidence that this group would seek to assassinate President McKinley during a visit to Buffalo. He reported this to the Secret Service, and McKinley's reception was initially canceled. But even after Petrosino's competence and reliability were vouched for by Vice-President Roosevelt, McKinley had the event placed back on his schedule. At this public reception on September 6, 1901, McKinley was assassinated by Leon Czolgosz, an anarchist.

Petrosino was tough on Italian criminals who he saw as a shame upon decent Italians and Italian Americans. He was particularly upset by the Black Hand, a criminal organization formed by some Italian immigrants near the turn of the 19th century. Typical Black Hand tactics involved sending a letter threatening bodily harm, kidnapping, arson, and murder. The letters would demand a specific amount of money delivered to a specific place. It usually contained threatening symbols and was signed with a hand drawn in black ink. One of the men considered the Black Hand Gang leader was Ignazio Lupo, also known as "Lupo the Wolf."

Lupo got involved with the Unione Siciliana, a charitable organization that helped Sicilians living in America. The Black Hand infiltrated the Unione for its own purposes, and Lupo was elected chairman.

In 1901, Petrosino obtained a search warrant for the Unione Siciliana offices, where he suspected there would be bodies of murder victims. He was correct, but no one in the NYPD expected the extent of what they uncovered. The building, which became known as the "Murder Stable," concealed approximately 60 bodies. An exact count was impossible because most of the corpses had been cut up. Some body parts were missing, and it was difficult to piece them together. Lupo was arrested but later released because of a lack of evidence tying the bodies to him. Petrosino was frustrated but determined to bring the Black Hand to justice.

On April 14, 1903, the body of a man was found in a barrel in Manhattan. He had been stabbed to death, his body chopped to pieces, and his penis and testicles stuffed in his mouth. It was unknown who the victim was until Petrosino received an anonymous letter claiming the dead man was related to Giuseppe De Primo, who had recently been sent to prison for counterfeiting. Petrosino went to Sing Sing Prison to interview De Primo, who identified the victim as his brother-in-law, Benedetto Madonia, a member of the Black Hand from Buffalo. De Primo claimed his brother-in-law was murdered over a dispute about money in a counterfeiting deal. Petrosino and his men arrested Lupo, his underboss Joe Morello, Vito Cascioferro, and other gang members, but eventually, they were released for lack of evidence. However, during this investigation, Petrosino discovered that Cascioferro was wanted for murder in Italy and had fled to New York to avoid a murder charge. Petrosino tried to have Cascioferro deported, but he discovered what Petrosino's plans were and fled to New Orleans and later to Sicily.

In 1905, Petrosino was promoted to the rank of lieutenant and placed in charge of the Italian Squad, an elite corps of Italian American detectives assembled explicitly to deal with criminal activities of organizations like the Mafia. They were responsible for the deportation of over 500 Italian criminals.

One of New York's finest.

One of the Italians being extorted by the Black Hand was the famous opera singer Enrico Caruso. Caruso was at first given an ultimatum to pay $2,000 or be killed. Fearing for his life, he agreed to pay it. However, before he could pay it, he received another demand for $15,000. He turned to Petrosino for help. Petrosino supplied bodyguards for Caruso, and when two men showed up to collect, he arrested them and had them deported.

Among his high-profile exploits was the case of Angelo Carbone, who was convicted of murder and sentenced to death in the electric chair. Petrosino believed in Carbone's innocence and discovered who the real killer was, Allessandro Ciaramello, and began tracking him down. He tracked him through Delaware, Pennsylvania, and New Jersey before finally catching him in Baltimore. Petrosino delivered Ciaramello to authorities a week before Carbone's scheduled execution. Ciaramello admitted his guilt, provided the murder weapon, and agreed to return to New York. Carbone was released from Sing Sing prison.

Petrosino had neglected his personal life to focus on his job. That changed after the Italian Squad was formed. On April 7, 1907, he married Adelina Vinti in old St. Patrick's Cathedral. She was a 37-year-old childless widow who worked in her family's restaurant. On November 20, 1908, the couple had a baby girl, and he was delighted. He cut back on his work hours to spend more time at home.

In February 1909, the *New York Times* announced that "Police Commissioner Theodore Bingham has a secret service of his own at last." The newspaper report explained that Bingham had acquired private funding for the police organization and speculated that wealthy Italian businessmen or prominent industrialists like Andrew Carnegie and John D. Rockefeller might be footing the bill. "I have money and plenty of it," the commissioner boasted, "and it didn't come from the city." The paper noted that Petrosino was placed in charge of the new service and had not been seen in police headquarters for some weeks. When Bingham was questioned about this, he answered, "Why, he may be on the ocean, bound for Europe, for all I know."

Petrosino was, in fact, on his way to Sicily on a top-secret mission. A recently passed federal law allowed the government to deport any alien who had lived in the country for less than three years if that alien had been convicted of a crime in another country. Petrosino had a long list of known Italian criminals who had taken up residence in the States. He intended to collect their penal certificates and other evidence of their criminal pasts in Italy to aid their extradition from the United States. Bingham's announcement to the press was a mistake, and articles about the secret mission appeared in the press all over the U.S. and Europe.

On March 12, 1909, after arriving in Palermo, Petrosino received a message from someone claiming to be an informant. The sender requested that Petrosino meet him in the city's Piazza Marina, giving him

This tombstone keeps watch over Petrosino's grave.

Inscription of Petrosino's tombstone.

information that he wanted. While waiting for the informant, Petrosino was shot to death. Bullets hit him three times: once in the back, once in the throat, and once to the side of the head. The gunmen fled, and one dropped a handgun on his way from the piazza. Petrosino was unarmed. The next day the Italian Squad received an anonymous letter stating that the New York Black Hand had arranged the murder. Legend has it that Don Vito Cascioferro, who had become the most powerful Mafioso in Sicily after being run out of the United States by Petrosino's pursuit, had been told of Petrosino's location and dispatched someone to lure him into a trap. Cascioferro left a dinner party with top Palermo politicians, went to the piazza, murdered Petrosino himself, and returned to the dinner. He was arrested for Petrosino's murder but was released after an associate provided an alibi. Years later, he bragged about killing the police lieutenant, claiming it was the only time he killed someone with his own hands.

Petrosino's body was sent to New York aboard the steamship *Slavonia* arriving on April 9. On April 12, funeral rites were conducted at St. Patrick's Cathedral, with over 200,000 people taking part in the funeral procession. The only New York police officer to ever be killed exercising his duties overseas was laid to rest at Calvary Cemetery in Queens.

In 1987, the name of a small park in lower Manhattan was changed from Kenmare Square to Lieutenant Joseph Petrosino Square in his honor. Three biographical films have been made of Petrosino's Life: *The Adventures of Lieutenant Petrosino* (1912); *Pay or Die* (1960), starring Ernest Borgnine; and *The Black Hand* (1973), starring Lionel Stander. He has also been the subject of two Italian TV movies.

If You Go:

Ironically, Calvary Cemetery contains the graves of many organized crime notables. Very near the Petrosino grave are the Morello crime family's graves and the Terranova brothers he investigated in the famous Barrel Murder case.

Also buried near Petrosino in Calvary is **Ignatius "Lupo the Wolf" Lupo**. Lupo has been described as the most vicious of the Black Hand leaders. He was suspected of at least 60 murders and was never convicted

Terranova brothers' grave.

until 1910, when he was sentenced to 30 years for counterfeiting. He was granted parole in 1920. In 1921, President Warren Harding freed Lupo from the constraints of his parole by granting him a commutation of sentence. In 1936, President Franklin Roosevelt—acting on a petition of New York Governor Herbert Lehman that showed Lupo was shaking down the New York City Bakers Union—signed an arrest warrant for Lupo. He was sent back to prison. He was released in a few years in bad health and died in Brooklyn in 1947 at 69.

Tombstone of five-year-old Joseph Varotta who was a victim of the gang known as the Black Hand.

Also buried in Calvary Cemetery is a victim of the Black Hand gang. In 1921, **Joseph Varotta** was kidnapped from in front of his home in Manhattan. The Gang demanded $2,500 for his return, but the money could not be raised. A few weeks later, Varotta's body was found in the Hudson River near Piermont. His headstone reads: "Here rests the remains of Joseph Varotta, age five years, who was kidnapped by the Blackhands at 354 East 13th St., New York, May 24, 1921, was found June 11, 1921, at Piermont New York." Three members of the Black Hand Gang were tried and convicted of the murder and sentenced to death. New York Governor **Alfred E. Smith** (See Chapter 21) commuted their death sentences to life in prison.

17

"Granny"

Grantland Rice

County: Bronx • Town: New York
Buried at Woodlawn Cemetery
517 East 233rd Street

As told by Charles Fountain in his book *Sportswriter,* it was in 1953 when four men who had known each other for decades got together for lunch in New York. The quartet talked about the old days before one of them brought everybody back to the present by addressing the oldest man at the table. He said, ". . . you conferred an immortality on us that gold could never buy. Let's face it. We were good, sure. But we'd have been just as dead two years after graduation as any other backfield if you hadn't painted that tag line on us. It's 29 years since we played. Each year we run faster, block better, score more TDs than ever! The older we are, the younger we become—in legend." Don Miller, who spoke those words, was there with two of his teammates Jim Crowley (see *Keystone Tombstones Volume 1*) and Elmer Layden. The trio made up three-quarters of the famous Notre Dame backfield that will forever be known as the Four Horsemen. The comments were addressed to the man who had so christened them, the most accomplished sportswriter of his time Grantland Rice.

Henry Grantland Rice was born on November 1, 1880, in Murfreesboro, Tennessee. His father, Boiling Hendon Rice, was a cotton dealer. His mother was Mary Beulah (Grantland) Rice. His maternal grandfather Henry Grantland had fought on the Confederate side under General Braxton Bragg in the Civil War. Based on stories he heard from

Grantland Rice

his grandfather, his boyhood hero was General Nathan Bedford Forest, who Robert E. Lee had called "my finest general."

When Rice was eight years of age, his family moved to West Nashville. He attended school at the Wallace University School, an institution whose goal was to prepare students to attend college. The headmaster of the school was Clarence B. Wallace, who left a lasting impression on the young Rice. In his book, Fountain recounts that when Rice came to be known nationwide for his writing skills, he sent Wallace a letter which stated, "If I have gained any measure of success in writing, I owe it all to you." Wallace's reply to America's best-known sportswriter was short and succinct, "Now right there's the best piece of writing you ever did."

Like many of Wallace's graduates, Rice enrolled at Vanderbilt University. The young Rice had developed a love of competitive sports. As a six-foot-tall 130-pound sixteen-year-old freshman, he didn't look like a football player, but he was determined to make the Vanderbilt squad. He was not chosen for the varsity, so he contented himself by starting at the freshman team's left end. That team played but one game, winning 10-6. He continued to play football for the rest of his college career, for which he was rewarded with a broken collarbone, a broken arm, a broken shoulder blade, and the wonderful experience of having four ribs torn from his spinal column.

Rice also played baseball at Vanderbilt and was elected team captain in his senior year. He had more success on the baseball diamond, and it is believed (though not documented) that Rice was offered a contract with the Nashville minor league team after he graduated. Any chance of Rice signing said contract was squelched by his father and grandfather, who saw no advantage nor reason for any respectable young man to make a living as a professional baseball player.

Rice began working in a dry goods store and soon found himself unhappy with the job. He went to his father and told him that he wanted to give journalism a go. The elder Rice voiced no objections because his son applied for a job as the newspaper's sports editor for the *Nashville Daily News.* He was offered a job covering and writing stories emanating from the state capitol and told he could write about sports on the side. He jumped at the chance.

Rice's early career as a sportswriter took him from Nashville to Atlanta, where in 1902, he became the sports editor for the *Atlanta Journal.* It was in Atlanta that he began to hit his stride as a writer. People took notice of his coverage of minor league baseball. In 1904, he received an anonymous telegram telling him to watch out for a terrific young player, Tyrus Raymond Cobb. Rice dismissed the message, but as the season wore on, he heard more and more about Cobb. He was receiving postcards from around the South from people who said they had seen Cobb play and that he was indeed fantastic. Rice eventually saw Cobb play in the minors, and he approached the young ballplayer telling him that he'd been hearing about his prowess and said, "My name is Rice. I write baseball for the *Journal.*" Cobb replied that he had heard of Rice as well. More than 40 years later, Cobb would tell Rice that he'd been the one sending all those postcards.

It was around this time that Rice met a 22-year-old Atlanta beauty named Katherine Hollis. The two began seeing each other regularly despite her family's reservations about young Kate hanging around with a sportswriter. On April 11, 1906, Rice and Hollis tied the knot. They would be together for the next 48 years, and the union produced a daughter Florence. Florence Rice would go into acting to succeed in Hollywood, appearing in almost 50 films in the '30s and early '40s.

By 1907, Rice could have found a job working for any newspaper in the country. He decided to head home, and he went to work for the *Nashville Tennessean.* He went back to covering Southern League baseball and Vanderbilt football. He had become known for including a poetic verse in his columns, and he continued this practice in his new position. Rice never stopped writing poems, and throughout his lifetime, he wrote six books of poetry. These were well received by the critics of his day, but later readers have not been as kind. Perhaps in anticipation, Rice wrote the following verse:

> Let the critics slip their tether,
> Light on us like sloppy weather
> All us poets, linked together,
> Simply scribble all the more
> If Bill Shakespeare's stuff was hooted,
> Wordsworth as a bard refuted,
> If old Burns and Keats were booted,
> Tell me, why should I get sore?

America's premier sportswriter at work.

He also began predicting the outcome of college football games. His predictions became an important part of his column, and readers anxiously sought them out weekly. They would do so for the next 45 years.

In 1911, Rice moved to New York, where he accepted a position with the *Evening Mail.* He was now in the major leagues covering the city's beloved New York Giants and the far less successful Yankees. In 1913, the most prominent sports story was that the great athlete Jim Thorpe (See *Keystone Tombstones Volume 1*) had been paid to play baseball in a summer league and, as a result, would be stripped of his Olympic medals. Rice had already declared Thorpe the greatest living athlete, and he was one of the few to come to his defense. Rice wrote of other amateur athletes he knew about who had also been paid for their services. His view was that Thorpe's actions were a minor violation at best, writing, "the best definition of an amateur is one who can get away with it and not be nicked with the goods." The treatment of Thorpe was something he never forgot. In 1954, the last year of his life, he wrote, "The act that so barred Thorpe could never be justified. What right did the AAU (Amateur Athletic Union) have to Thorpe's private gifts, fairly won in those 1912 Olympics? They merely robbed the Indian in cold-blooded fashion."

In 1914, Rice moved to the *New York Herald Tribune.* The paper offered him more in the way of salary, but there was another attraction. A syndicated column that would result in his musings on sports appearing in newspapers all across America. While writing for the *Tribune*, he covered the 1916 U.S. Amateur Golf Championship held at the Merion Country Club outside of Philadelphia. Here he first saw a 14-year-old Bobby Jones who advanced to the quarter-finals of the event. Rice wrote of Jones in glowing terms and was instrumental in bringing the man who would become the first to win golf's grand slam to the American public's attention.

Then came World War I. In 1917, Rice was almost 37 years old and therefore beyond draft age, which was 21 to 30. Also, he was married and had a 10-year-old daughter. Rice enlisted and served on the front lines as an artilleryman. He counted himself among the lucky ones who were able to return home after the armistice. Before he had left for Europe, he had entrusted his life savings of about $75,000 to a friend. The money was gone due to a series of poor investments, and his friend had committed suicide. Rice would make monthly contributions to help support the man's widow for the next 30 years.

After the war, the one thing that stayed with Rice as he covered the sports world were those able-bodied athletes who had managed to avoid answering their country's call. For example, after Jack Dempsey won the heavyweight boxing championship in 1919, Rice noted that Dempsey was a champion boxer and not a champion fighter. In Rice's view, calling

Dempsey (who it should be pointed out had a legitimate deferment) a fighter was an insult to all those who had fought in the Great War. As time went on, the two would iron out their differences and become great friends.

The 1920s has become known as the Golden Age of Sports. Rice certainly had a hand in making it so, as he set out to make heroes of those in the sporting world who made an impression on him on the field of play. In addition to Dempsey, among those he singled out were Babe Ruth (see Chapter 19), Bill Tilden (See *Keystone Tombstones Volume 1*), Babe Didrikson Zaharias, Knute Rockne, and Red Grange, who Rice nicknamed the Galloping Ghost.

Rice is best known for the beginning of a story he wrote after covering the 1924 Army-Notre Dame football game at the Polo Grounds in New York. Rice wrote, "Outlined against a blue-gray October sky; the Four Horsemen rode again. In dramatic lore, they are known as famine, pestilence, destruction, and death. These are only aliases. Their real names are Stuhldreher, Miller, Crowley, and Layden. They formed a crest of the South Bend cyclone before which another fighting Army team was swept over the precipice at the Polo Grounds this afternoon as 55,000 spectators peered down upon the bewildering panorama spread out upon the green plain below." So powerful was the image Rice created that one can purchase Notre Dame shirts that carry the image of the Four Horseman to this day. This author attended a banquet where one of the Horsemen, Jim Crowley, was the main speaker. Crowley said it never mattered what he did in life after college; he was always identified as one of the Four Horsemen. He stated that he believed he could have been governor of a state, and he would have still been introduced as one of the Four Horsemen.

By the end of the decade, Rice was being called the "Dean of American Sportswriters." He was known and recognized throughout the country. This fact seemed to have passed Rice by. In the 1940s, as recounted by his biographer, Fountain, Rice arrived at the stadium to cover a World Series game to discover he had forgotten his press pass. He was about to head back to the street to buy a ticket when another writer,

Final resting place of the man who christened Notre Dame's Four Horsemen.

Frank Graham, told the guard what had happened. The guard quickly spoke up, "Please, Mr. Rice, come in. You don't need a press card." Rice believed that Graham had somehow pulled a fast one and asked, "How'd you do that?" as the two headed to the press box.

Over the years, the one thing that Rice has been criticized for is how he wrote of black athletes. He referred to Jack Johnson as "The Chocolate Champ." He said that the skills exhibited by Joe Louis were a matter of instinct as he believed was the case with most great Negro fighters. He called Jesse Owens "a wild Zulu running amuck." Also, his All-American Football teams are strikingly white. His defenders point out that it may be unfair to judge a man's whose actions took place in the past by contemporary standards. Not to mention that his contemporaries' accounts are entirely consistent with those written by Rice when it comes to the treatment of black athletes. We will leave it to the reader to decide.

Rice covered the major sporting events for the rest of his life, including the World Series, the Kentucky Derby, the Olympics, and the major golf tournaments. He was instrumental in creating the heroes that sprang from these events. He was by far the most widely read sportswriter in the nation. Only his talented young friend Red Smith, who referred to Rice as Granny, would come close to matching his popularity.

During his later years, Rice cast an impressive and imposing shadow upon those around him. The very cocky and quite sure of himself young writer Jimmy Breslin would later admit that he was in awe of Grantland Rice. Notre Dame's first Heisman Trophy winner Angelo Bertelli said that sitting at the same table with Rice during the award ceremony was a bigger thrill than accepting the coveted trophy.

Rice died at the age of 73 in 1954, after suffering a stroke. It is a fact that those who knew him best, his closest friends, and those he influenced couldn't say a bad word about him. Red Smith wrote the following after Rice passed away: "Grantland Rice was the greatest man I have known, the greatest talent, the greatest gentleman. The most treasured privilege I have had in this world was knowing him and going about with him as his friend. I shall be grateful all my life. I do not mourn for him, who welcomed peace. I mourn for us."

Rice was laid to rest in Woodlawn Cemetery. He may have composed his epitaph with a verse from a poem called "Alumnus Football:"

> For when the great scorer comes
> To mark against your name,
> He writes, not that you won or lost,
> But how you played the game.

If You Go:

Rice might be happy to know that he shares the cemetery with the well-known sports artist **Leroy Neiman**. For further information, see chapters 3, 5, 13, 15, 22 on **Nellie Bly**, **George M. Cohan**, **Bat Masterson**, **Robert Moses,** and **Elizabeth Stanton** in this volume.

18

"42"

Jackie Robinson

County: Brooklyn • Town: New York
Buried at Cypress Hills Cemetery
833 Jamaica Avenue

Jackie Robinson is perhaps the most historically significant baseball player ever.

It is hard to find any American who does not know the name. When he took the field for the Brooklyn Dodgers on April 15, 1947, he ended more than 60 years of racial segregation in Major League Baseball. Robinson's display of his character, his use of non-violence, and his unquestionable talent changed the way many Americans thought and challenged the traditional basis of segregation. He made a significant contribution to the Civil Rights movement.

In addition to his cultural impact, Robinson had an exceptional baseball career. He was the first black player to win a batting title (.342 in 1949), the first black player to win the Most Valuable Player award (1949), and the first black player to be inducted into the Baseball Hall of Fame. He was selected for six consecutive All-Star Games and was the recipient of Major League Baseball's first Rookie-of-the-Year Award in 1947.

The words on Robinson's headstone read: "A life is not important except in the impact it has on other lives." It is hard to argue that any player had a greater impact on baseball than Babe Ruth (*see* Chapter 19). Ruth changed how the game was played, from a game based on speed to one based on power, and gave those who had turned away from baseball after the 1919 Black Sox scandal reason to love the game again. But Jackie Robinson changed more than just baseball. He helped change America.

Jackie Robinson

Jack Roosevelt Robinson was born to impoverished sharecroppers in Cairo, Georgia, on January 31, 1919. He was the youngest of five children born to Jerry and Mallie Robinson. His middle name was in honor of former President Theodore Roosevelt, who died shortly before Jackie was born. Jackie's father left the family in 1920, and Jackie's mother moved herself and the children to Pasadena, California, where she worked as a domestic. Her family's diet often consisted of leftovers from the kitchens of families for whom she worked.

In 1935, Jackie graduated from Washington Junior High School and enrolled in John Muir High School (Muir Tech). There he starred in baseball, basketball, football, track, and tennis. After Muir Tech, Robinson attended Pasadena Junior College, where he continued his athletic career by participating in basketball, football, baseball, and track. He played quarterback and safety on the football team, shortstop and leadoff hitter on the baseball team, and broke the school's broad-jump record in track.

Robinson transferred to UCLA after graduating from Pasadena JC in the spring of 1939. He soon gained national recognition by becoming the school's first athlete to win varsity letters in four sports: baseball, basketball, football, and track. He was the Bruins baseball team's regular shortstop, on the gridiron averaged 11 yards per carry as a running back, on the basketball court led the Pacific Coast Conference in scoring in both his junior and senior years, and won the 1940 NCAA Men's Track and Field Championship in the long jump. He almost surely would have gone to the 1940 Olympics in the long jump had the games not been canceled because of the war. He has to be considered one of the most versatile college athletes in history.

In his senior year, Robinson met his future wife, Rachel Isum, a freshman at UCLA. In the spring of 1941, financial problems forced Robinson to leave college just a few credits short of graduation. He accepted a job as an athletic coach for the National Youth Administration and played semi-pro football for the Los Angeles Bulldogs. After the National Youth Administration ceased operations, Robinson signed to play pro football with the Honolulu Bears in the fall of 1941.

Shortly after the Japanese attack on Pearl Harbor, Robinson was drafted and assigned to a segregated Army cavalry unit in Fort Riley, Kansas. Having the required qualifications, Robinson applied for admission to an Officer Candidate School (OCS) but was initially denied admission. One of Robinson's fellow soldiers stationed at Fort Riley was Joe Louis, the world boxing heavyweight champion. Louis befriended Jackie. As fortune would have it, Louis's lawyer, Truman Gibson, was

Robinson's modest Brooklyn home.

an advisor to the Secretary of War, Henry Stimson. Louis contacted Gibson on Jackie's behalf. Shortly after that, the denial of Jackie's OCS application was overturned. Robinson was commissioned as a second

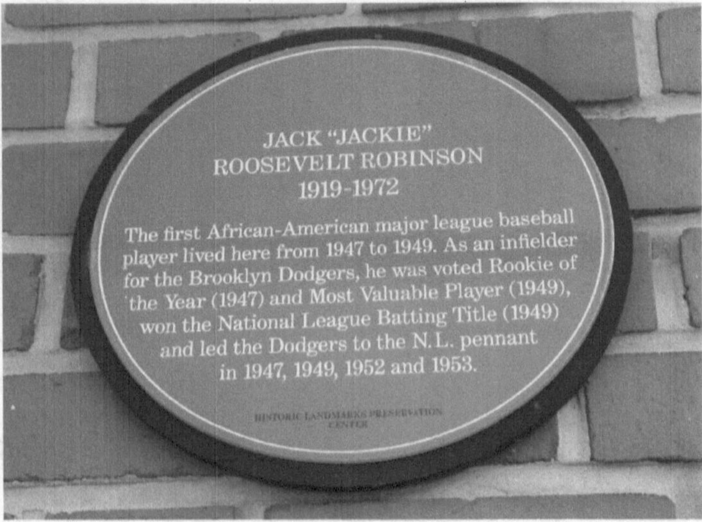

Plaque found at Robinson's home.

lieutenant in January 1943. He and Louis would remain friends for the rest of their lives.

After receiving his commission, Jackie was reassigned to Fort Hood, Texas. On July 6, 1944, he boarded a bus and was ordered by the bus driver to move to the back. Robinson refused. The driver summoned the military police, who took Robinson into custody and charged him with multiple offenses. At the subsequent court-martial in August, Robinson was acquitted by an all-white panel of nine officers. His unit, the 761st Tank Battalion, became the first black unit to see combat, but Robinson's court-martial proceedings prevented him from being deployed. He never saw combat and ultimately was honorably discharged in November 1944.

In early 1945, Robinson accepted a contract to play for the Kansas City Monarchs in the Negro Baseball Leagues. The contract was for $400 a month. He hit .387 and appeared in the Negro League All-Star Game.

At that time, Branch Rickey, the president and general manager of the Brooklyn Dodgers, was scouting the Negro leagues for possible additions. His scouts were compiling a list of candidates to break the major league's color barrier. Rickey was looking for a man with the talent to excel and the character to withstand the inevitable racial abuse that would be directed at him. When Rickey considered Robinson, he saw a man who fit that description. Robinson was extremely talented. He had played with and against white players. He had faced big crowds and the media. He had been an officer in the Army, was well-spoken, personable, did not smoke or drink, and was not a womanizer.

In a now-famous three-hour meeting on August 28, 1945, Rickey and Robinson discussed the situation, and Rickey obtained a commitment from Robinson to "turn the other cheek" to racial antagonism. Robinson signed a contract for $600 a month. It was formally announced on October 23, and Robinson was assigned to the Dodgers' top minor league team, the Montreal Royals. A few months later, he married Rachel Isum.

In the spring of 1946, Robinson's reporting for spring training in Daytona Beach caused quite a stir. He was not allowed to stay with his teammates at the team hotel and instead stayed at a local black politician's home. Many cities in Florida threatened to cancel games (and some did) if Robinson was to play. When the Montreal Royals opened the season on April 18, 1946, against the Jersey City Giants at Roosevelt Stadium in Jersey City, New Jersey, Robinson played second base. Robinson banged out four hits in front of a packed house and scored four times to lead Montreal to a 14-1 victory. He hit a three-run homer, stole two bases, and drove the pitcher so crazy while leading off of third base that he scored twice on balks.

Robinson proceeded to lead the Triple-A International League in hitting (.349) and in runs scored (113), stole 40 bases, and led the league in fielding for second basemen. He was named the league's Most Valuable Player. The Royals established a new attendance record along the way, and their road attendance almost tripled over the previous year.

It seemed evident that Robinson would open the 1947 season with the Dodgers. Rickey tried to ease the way for Robinson in several ways. First, rather than have the Dodgers train in Florida as they had done in previous years, Rickey set up spring training camp in Havana, Cuba, to avoid the racial attitudes in the American South. Next, Rickey assigned Robinson to the Royals roster to minimize the initial reaction. He hoped that the Dodgers' veterans would get used to Robinson and see for themselves what an asset he would be for the team. Rickey scheduled a seven-game exhibition series between the Dodgers and the Royals to showcase Jackie's skills. He hit .625 in those games. A crisis arose, however, when a group of players began to circulate a petition against Robinson. The petition insinuated that the signers would sit rather than play alongside Robinson. Dodger management took a stand and ended the brewing storm. Dodgers' manager Leo Durocher informed the team:

> I do not care if the guy is yellow or black or if he has stripes like a fucking zebra. I'm the manager of this team, and I say he plays. What's more, I say he can make us all rich. And if any of you cannot use the money, I will see that you are all traded!

Rickey also determined that Robinson would be switched to first base since the Dodgers were set at both the second and the short with Eddie Stanky and Pee Wee Reese.

Then, on April 15, 1947, at Ebbets Field in Brooklyn, Jackie Robinson made his historic major league debut at 28. He failed to get a hit but walked and scored in a 5-3 victory over the Boston Braves. Success would soon follow, and Robinson would win the MLB's inaugural Rookie of the Year award. He played in 151 games that season, finishing with a batting average of .297, 12 homers, 48 RBI, and leading the league in sacrifice hits (28) and stolen bases (29).

His personal experiences were quite different. Rickey was correct about the racism Robinson would face, which made his on-field performance all that much more impressive. He was the target of racial epithets, flying cleats, hate letters, and death threats. Fans hurled bottles and invectives at him while opposing players deliberately threw at him and spiked him whenever the opportunity presented itself. When players on the St. Louis Cardinals threatened to strike if Robinson took the field, MLB Commissioner Ford Frick quashed it by threatening to suspend any player who did so.

The ugly remarks, death threats, and Jim Crow laws forbidding a black player from staying in hotels or eating in restaurants with the

A Jackie Robinson baseball card.

rest of the team made Robinson's groundbreaking experience a bleak one. For example, he received death threats when the Dodgers visited Cincinnati in May 1947. During the first game of the series against the Reds, heckling from the crowd towards Robinson became intense. Dodger captain Pee Wee Reese, from neighboring Kentucky, left his position on the field and put his arm around Robinson in solidarity. The two became lifelong friends.

Robinson learned how to exercise self-control and kept his promise to Rickey. He answered insults, violence, and injustice with silence. He was a model of unselfish team play and earned the respect of his teammates and, eventually, the opposition.

In 1949, Robinson won the Most Valuable Player Award while leading the Dodgers to the National League pennant for the second time in three years. He won the batting title with a .342 average and led the major leagues in stolen bases with 37—the highest total in the National League in 19 years. He also drove in 124 runs, scored 122 runs, and was voted as the starting second baseman for the 1949 All-Star Game. Robinson had been switched to second base after Stanky was traded in 1948.

During the 1949 season, Robinson had to deal with another unwanted distraction. In July, he was called to testify before the House of Representatives Committee on Un-American Activities concerning statements made by actor and athlete Paul Robeson, who had made a speech implying that blacks would not support the United States in a war with the Soviet Union due to continued second-class status under U.S. law. Robinson was reluctant to testify, but he eventually agreed to do so, fearing that it might negatively affect his career and future integration of professional athletics if he declined. His testimony was a major media event, with his carefully worded statement appearing on the *New York Times*' front page. In the statement, Robinson said that Robeson "has the right to his personal views and if he wants to sound silly when he expresses them in public that is his business and not mine . . ." He also stated that "the fact that it is a Communist who denounces injustice in the courts, police brutality, and lynching when it happens doesn't change the truth of his charges."

Robinson played ten seasons in the major leagues, all with the Dodgers. Statistics only scratch the surface in evaluating him as a ballplayer because racism kept him from playing in the major leagues until he was 28. He played in six World Series and six All-Star Games and had a career batting average of .311. He stole 197 bases, including 19 steals of home. It was on the basepaths where his star shone the brightest. He took long leads and threatened to steal on every pitch.

After the 1956 season, Robinson was traded to the arch-rival New York Giants. However, he declined the trade, effectively retired from baseball, and accepted a position with the Chock-Full-o-Nuts coffee company. He engaged in politics and civil rights activism after retirement. He made appearances with Martin Luther King, Jr. He once served as a Special Assistant for Community Affairs when Nelson Rockefeller was re-elected governor of New York in 1966.

In 1962, Robinson was elected to the National Baseball Hall of Fame. It was his first year of eligibility, and he was the first black player to be inducted.

He served as an analyst for ABC's Major League Baseball "Game of the Week" in 1965 and was a member of the NAACP's Board of Directors from 1957 until 1967. He helped found Freedom National Bank and served as its first Chairman. In 1970, Robinson established the Jackie Robinson Construction Company to build housing for low-income families. *The New York Times* reported that the company built over 1,600 units.

Robinson's eldest son, Jackie Jr., served in Vietnam and was wounded in action on November 19, 1965. After his discharge, he struggled with drug problems, completed rehab, and became a counselor at Daytop Village in Seymour, Connecticut. In June 1971, at the age of 24, Jackie Jr. was killed in an automobile accident.

Robinson himself had struggled with diabetes. The disease had weakened him and made him almost blind. On October 24, 1972, he died of a heart attack in his home at 53.

More than 2,500 people attended his funeral at Riverside Church on Manhattan's Upper West Side. Many former teammates and famous players served as pallbearers, and Reverend Jesse Jackson gave the eulogy. Tens of thousands lined the streets of Harlem and Bedford-Stuyvesant to watch the parade of his funeral procession. He was buried at Cypress Hills Cemetery in Brooklyn along with his mother-in-law, Zellee Isum, and his son Jackie Jr. A parkway once called the Interboro Parkway runs through the cemetery. It is now called the Jackie Robinson Parkway.

Shortly after his death, his wife founded the Jackie Robinson Foundation, which still operates today. The Foundation's mission is to perpetuate Jackie's memory by advancing higher education among underserved populations.

On July 4, 1972, Jackie's number "42" was retired in a ceremony at Dodger Stadium (the Dodgers had moved from Brooklyn to Los Angeles after the 1957 season) along with Roy Campanella's number "39" and Sandy Koufax's number "32." His autobiography, *I Never Had It Made: An Autobiography of Jackie Robinson*, was published on October 28, 1972—a mere four days after his death—and is still available today (as are many other biographies about his life). In 1976, his home at 5224 Tilden

As evidennced by the grave goods Robinson's fans have not forgotten him.

Avenue in Brooklyn was declared a National Historic Landmark. The U.S. Postal Service issued commemorative Jackie Robinson stamps in 1982, 1999, and 2000. President Ronald Reagan posthumously awarded Robinson the Presidential Medal of Freedom on March 26, 1984.

In 1987, 40 years after Robinson broke the color barrier and won the inaugural Rookie of the Year award, Major League Baseball honored Jackie by renaming the award the "Jackie Robinson Award." Ten years later, in 1997, his number "42" was retired throughout Major League Baseball. In 2004, MLB declared April 15 as "Jackie Robinson Day," commemorating his MLB debut anniversary. For Jackie Robinson Day in 2007, the MLB invited all players to wear the number 42 during that day's games. The response was so great that in 2009 the MLB decided that from that point forward, all players, coaches, and umpires would wear number "42" every April 15th.

In 1997, the U.S. Treasury issued a commemorative silver dollar. In 1999, *Time* magazine named him one of the 100 most influential people of the 20th century. The New York Mets' stadium, Citi Field, has a memorial in its "Jackie Robinson Rotunda," and there is a Jackie Robinson Middle School in Brooklyn.

There is little doubt of the impact Robinson made on the lives of others.

The City of Pasadena, California, where Jackie grew up, has also recognized him in several ways, including a Jackie Robinson Field, a Jackie Robinson Community Center, and a bronze sculpture outside Pasadena City Hall.

Robinson has been portrayed many times in movies. The most noteworthy films are *The Jackie Robinson Story* (1950), in which Jackie plays himself, *The Court-Martial of Jackie Robinson* (1990) starring Andre Braugher, and most recently *42* (2013), which stars Chadwick Boseman as Jackie and Harrison Ford as Branch Rickey.

The great Hank Aaron once said of Robinson that he:

> . . . had to be bigger than life. He had to be bigger than the Brooklyn teammates who got up a petition to keep him off the ball club; bigger than the pitchers who threw at him, bigger than the bench jockeys who hollered for him to carry their bags and shine their shoes; bigger than the so-called fans who mocked him with mops on their heads and wrote him death threats. He was a fighter—the proudest, most competitive person I've ever seen.

"Robinson could hit and bunt and steal and run," Roger Kahn wrote in *The Boys of Summer*, adding that:

> He had intimidation skills, and he burned with a dark fire. He wanted passionately to win. He bore the burden of a pioneer, and the weight made him stronger. If one can be certain of anything in baseball, it is that we shall not look upon his like again.

If You Go:

Cypress Hills Cemetery is a vast and historic cemetery, having over 400,000 graves. It occupies both Brooklyn and Queens and is divided by the Jackie Robinson Parkway. In 1862, a section of the cemetery was designated as a military burial ground for soldiers of the American Civil War and dubbed "Cypress Hills National Cemetery." In 1941, it received the bodies of 235 Confederate prisoners who died on the Bronx's Hart Island.

Cypress Hills Cemetery also has the graves of legendary entertainer and actress **Mae West** and boxer **James "Gentleman Jim" Corbett**, a member of the International Boxing Hall of Fame and heavyweight champion of the world from 1892 to 1897.

Also buried in Cypress Hills is folk and blues singer, songwriter, actor, and civil rights activist **Josh White**. White was born in 1908 and overcame seemingly insurmountable obstacles to become an actor and radio/cabaret star. He was a groundbreaking performer of powerful protest songs and became an intimate friend of Franklin and Eleanor Roosevelt. He performed and recorded with **Billie Holiday** (see Chapter 9), Woody Guthrie, and Pete Seeger. White was blacklisted at the peak of his career during the 1950s after appearing before the House Un-American Activities Committee. He died in 1969 of heart disease at the age of 61.

The famous jazz musician, composer, and lyricist **Eubie Blake** is also buried in Cypress Hills. He was born in Baltimore in 1883 to former slaves and identified as a musical genius early in life. He was a pioneer ragtime pianist and composer. He wrote such hits as “Charleston Rag,” “Love Will Find a Way,” and “I’m Just Wild About Harry.” His collective works were featured in the hit Broadway musical *Eubie!* In 1981, he was awarded the Presidential Medal of Freedom by President Reagan. He died in Brooklyn on February 12, 1983, at the age of 100.

19

"The Sultan of Swat"

George Herman "Babe" Ruth

County: Westchester • Town: Hawthorne
Buried at Gate of Heaven Cemetery
10 West Stevens Road

He was considered the greatest baseball player of his time; many still believe of all time. He started as a pitcher, and a very good one at that, but soon became the most prodigious slugger baseball had ever seen. His record of 60 home runs in a single season stood for 34 years. He changed the way baseball was played by turning it into a game of power as opposed to speed. His career slugging percentage of .690 is a record that still stands today. Many believe that his popularity saved the game after the Black Sox scandal. In his words, "I swing big, with everything I've got. I hit big, or I miss big. I like to live as big as I can." When he retired from baseball, he was the career record holder in home runs, runs batted in, total bases, walks, strikeouts, on-base percentage, and slugging percentage. He was named George Herman, but the world came to know him as Babe. In 1993 almost 100 years since his birth, the *Associated Press* reported that Ruth was tied with Muhammad Ali as the most recognized athletes in America

On February 6, 1895, Ruth was born in what was considered a very rough neighborhood in Baltimore. After working a series of jobs, Ruth's father settled in to running a combination grocery store and tavern. Ruth's mother was often sick and always tired and was busy taking care of his younger sister Mamie. Of the couple's eight children, Ruth and Mamie were the only ones to survive infancy. With both parents involved in running the business, they had little time to spend on their young

Babe Ruth

boy. As a result, he took to the streets with the neighborhood toughs. By the age of eight, he had already chewed tobacco and drank whiskey. He hated school and avoided it at all costs. He later recalled, "I was a bum when I was a kid."

On June 13, 1902, when he was about eight and a half, his parents sent Ruth to St. Mary's Industrial School for Boys. The school was very much like a reform school, which it later became. When Ruth arrived, it was a school for orphans, boys from broken homes, and poor boys whose family found it impossible to care for. When Ruth entered the school, he was listed as "incorrigible," a description he never took issue with as he grew older. The school would serve as his primary home for the majority of his next twelve years.

St. Mary's was run by a Catholic order known as the Xaverian Brothers. For all the non-Catholics out there, it is worth noting that brothers are not priests though they wear similar clothing. They do take religious vows and are often involved in teaching and nursing. They cannot say mass, nor can they take your confession. Some have said they can best be described as male nuns.

At St. Mary's, there were about twenty or so brothers in charge of hundreds of boys (at times as many as 800). They were strict disciplinarians. There was a set schedule: you were up by six and in bed by eight. School began at 7:30 sharp, always after mass. The rest of the day was spent in class or workshops with a short break for lunch. Before supper, there was about an hour of free time. After supper, it was back to the dorms to prepare for the same regimen the next day. When a boy turned twelve, more time was devoted to learning a trade. Ruth worked as a tailor and also at carpentry. Later in life, even after he was famous, Ruth would work on his shirts rather than using a tailor.

Of all the brothers, Ruth grew to admire one named Brother Mathias, who, of all things, was in charge of discipline. Ruth would later call him the greatest man he had ever known. Ruth credited Matthias with developing his running and hitting styles. According to Ruth's biographer, Robert W. Creamer, "Ruth caught Brother Matthias' attention early, and the calm, considerate attention the big man gave the young hellraiser from the waterfront struck a spark of response in the boy's soul. The spark did not seem to do much in the way of making Ruth into a polished soft-spoken gentleman, but it may have pulled some of the sharper claws and blunted a few of the more savage teeth in the gross man whom I have heard at least a half-dozen of his baseball contemporaries describe with admiring awe and wonder as 'an animal.'"

One of the things the boys at St. Mary's did was play baseball. Ruth would later claim that he played about 200 games a year while at the school. Ruth played several positions but was primarily used as a left-handed catcher. The school teams took the names of major league teams, and Ruth played for the Red Sox. He quickly became known as the best player in the school. During one game when the Red Sox were getting beat rather badly, Ruth began laughing at his pitcher. Brother Matthias demanded to know what was so funny, and Ruth said it was the pitching. Matthias responded by sending Ruth in to pitch. He did, and he soon became known as the best pitcher at St. Mary's. By the time he turned 18, Ruth was allowed to leave St. Mary's on weekends to play for local teams. Stories about his hitting and pitching skills began to appear in the Baltimore newspapers.

There are various stories about how Ruth came to be a professional ballplayer. One of those involves Mount St. Joseph's College, located in Baltimore and run by the Xaverians. The St. Joseph's varsity baseball team was quite competitive, playing college teams like Seton Hall and Villanova. In 1913, the star of the team was a right-handed pitcher by the name of Bill Morrisette. That year he had already pitched a one-hitter against Western Maryland. The baseball coach at St. Joseph's was Brother Gilbert, and he was not shy about bragging up his team, and young Mr. Morrisette in particular. When word of this reached the brothers at St. Mary's, they arranged a game that would match Ruth against Morrisette.

During this period, the owner of the Baltimore Orioles (then a minor league team) was a man named Jack Dunn. Back in those days, most minor league squads were independently owned and made a good deal of money by selling their players to major league squads. As a result, Dunn was always on the lookout for young talent and had already signed Morrisette to a contract. He had heard about Ruth as well.

According to legend, shortly before the big game was scheduled to be played, Ruth ran away from school. After a few days, Ruth was back, and the official word was that he had returned voluntarily. However, the boys were aware that the school had sent a search party into Baltimore to locate Ruth. Many at the school didn't believe the official version, but all were glad to have their pitcher back.

On the day of the game, a huge crowd that included Dunn gathered to witness the proceedings. Ruth was spectacular striking out 22 batters in leading St. Mary's to a comfortable 6–0 win. As the story goes, Dunn then met with Ruth for about two hours, and a few months later signed him to a professional contract. Whether or not this story is true is up for debate as there are others out there. For instance, in his autobiography, Ruth recalled working out for Dunn for about a half-hour before signing a contract that would pay him $250 per month.

Ruth's first trip out of Baltimore would be by train to Fayetteville, North Carolina, where the Orioles would begin their spring training. He was twenty at the time and in terrific shape weighing in at about 180 pounds. Ruth's first appearance as a professional was in an intrasquad game. He pitched two innings, and his team won 15–9, but what had everyone in the town talking was what he did at the plate. In the second inning, Ruth hit a ball that carried so far to right field that he could walk around the bases before it could be retrieved. The locals were amazed by the hit as for years they told the story of a homer that Jim Thorpe had walloped, which was easily the longest ball they had ever seen clouted. Now they agreed that Ruth's homer had traveled at least sixty feet further than the ball hit by Thorpe.

It was around this time that Ruth acquired his nickname. The veteran players on the club took to calling him Dunnie's Babe. The name seemed to fit better than George, and soon that's what the Baltimore papers were calling him, and then the fans followed. Before his career would end, Ruth would earn other nicknames such as the Great Bambino, the Colossus of Clout, and the Sultan of Swat.

When the regular season started, both Ruth and the Orioles did well. However, the attention of baseball fans in Baltimore was drawn elsewhere. That year saw the start of a third major league, the Federal League, and Baltimore was represented by the Terrapins. Baltimore hadn't had a major league baseball team since 1902, and that's who the folks in the city went to see. After exploring other avenues that didn't work out, Dunn's only option was to sell some of his better players to major league clubs to balance the books.

On July 4th, Ruth pitched the opening game of a doubleheader and won 4–1. In a few days, he would come in as a relief pitcher and win yet again, giving him a record of 14–6. That stint in relief proved to be Ruth's last appearance as a Baltimore pitcher. Meanwhile, Dunn left town to meet with Joseph J. Lannin, the Boston Red Sox owner. A few days later, the announcement came that Ruth and two other Orioles had been sold to the Red Sox. It is worth noting that Dunn had offered Ruth to Connie Mack before meeting with Lannin, but Mack was looking to unload his star players rather than buy new ones. One manager who was interested in Ruth was the New York Giants skipper, John McGraw. Dunn and McGraw were old friends, but that friendship came to an end when Dunn failed to contact McGraw about Ruth. McGraw was an Irishman who could hold a grudge, and it came back to bite him. Ten years later, Dunn had Lefty Grove on the market and would have been happy to sell him to McGraw, but the Giant manager would have none of it. As a result, Grove was purchased by Connie Mack and the Athletics. Grove would be a vital piece in leading the Athletics to three pennants.

It was July 11, 1914, when Ruth arrived in Boston to begin his major league career. Ruth and the two other Orioles reported to Bill Carrigan, a catcher who was also the Red Sox manager. Carrigan was quiet and well-mannered off the baseball field, but he was hard, aggressive and supremely sure of himself on it. His playing style had earned him the name Rough Carrigan. Ruth would play for several managers throughout his career, including Miller Huggins, Ed Barrow, Bill McKechnie, and Joe McCarthy. All of these managers were elected to the Baseball Hall of Fame, but as far as Ruth was concerned, the best manager he ever played for was Bill Carrigan.

The first day that Ruth donned a Red Sox uniform, he was named the starting pitcher. He would go up against the last-place Cleveland Indians. Ruth pitched seven innings and was taken out for a pinch hitter when the Red Sox came to bat in their half of that inning. When Ruth left the game, the score was tied at three, but Boston scored one

Young Ruth as a member of the Boston Red Sox.

in their half, and the game ended 4–3, giving Ruth had his first major league win. In his second start, the Detroit Tigers knocked him out in the fourth inning. He was credited with the defeat and suddenly found himself benched and out of the rotation.

While his career had its ups and downs, his love life was doing just fine. He made it a point to eat breakfast every day at Lander's coffee shop. It wasn't the food that kept bringing him back. It was a sixteen-year-old waitress by the name of Helen Woodford. It appears that Ruth had fallen in love, and it wasn't with bacon and eggs, though the truth is he was quite fond of those as well.

Carrigan continued to keep Ruth on the bench. In four weeks, he had pitched only twice, and these appearances were in exhibition games. Why was Ruth not playing? According to one story, Carrigan spotted a habit Ruth had of poking his tongue into his cheek before throwing a curveball. Based on this, Ruth was benched until he could correct this habit of telegraphing his pitches. Ruth's biographers don't buy this story. The majority believe that poor behavior was responsible for the benching. Ruth finished the 1914 season back in the minor leagues. He was sent down to Providence to help that team win the International League pennant. They did.

Ruth's relatively quiet rookie season was over, and as he prepared to head back to Baltimore for the winter months, he couldn't get Helen Woodford out of his mind. Though they had known each other for under three months, he headed to the coffee shop where he proposed. Helen agreed, and in a couple of days, the two left for Baltimore as a soon to be married couple. Because Ruth was not yet 21, he persuaded his father to write a note granting his permission for the couple to wed. When they went to get their license, Helen lied about her age, saying she was 18 (she was a year younger) and about where she was from, reporting that she hailed from Galveston, Texas rather than Boston. On Saturday, October the 17th, they were married by a Catholic priest in Ellicott City rather than in Baltimore. Some believe they made this choice because Ruth feared that word of the wedding would reach the brothers' ears at St. Mary's and that they would not be happy about it. Brother Paul was still Ruth's legal guardian. None of that mattered as the two were wed and spent the winter living with Ruth's father above his saloon.

No longer a rookie in March of 1915, Ruth reported for spring training in Hot Springs, Arkansas. The Red Sox already had two superb left-handed pitchers in Dutch Leonard and twenty game winner Ray Collins. As a result, Ruth was not guaranteed a spot in the rotation. However, when the regular season started, Leonard was ill and unable to pitch, and

Collins didn't have his best stuff. Carrigan used Ruth in relief, and he performed well. Based on this, Ruth was given a start, which he won 9–2. It would be another ten days, due to five games being called because of rain before Ruth was sent to the mound again. Pitching against the New York Yankees, he went 13 innings but lost 4–3. Despite the loss, he had impressed Carrigan, earning a spot in the starting rotation. The game was also noteworthy because when Ruth came to bat in the third inning, he sent one into the right-field stands. It was the first home run he ever hit in the major leagues.

The Red Sox and Ruth got off to a rocky start in 1915. By May 29th, the Sox, who had been favored to win the pennant, found themselves with a record below the .500 mark, and they were trailing both the White Sox and the Tigers, who seemed to be in a daily fight for first place. It was at this point that Boston went on a modest five-game winning streak. Ruth won the fifth game 7–1, again beating the New York Yankees and hitting a home run. This one caused a New York sportswriter to comment, "All left-handers are peculiar, and Babe is no exception because he can also bat." The man who would become known as the Sultan of Swat was beginning to be noticed.

Ruth and the Red Sox continued to play well. The team won the pennant, and Ruth finished the season with a record of 18–8. Also, he had batted .315 and hit four home runs. One of the home runs that he hit in Saint Louis sailed out of the ballpark and across a street where it broke a car dealership window. It was the longest home run ever hit in that stadium.

The Red Sox would meet the Philadelphia Phillies in the 1915 World Series. The Phillies had bragged that they could beat any lefthander anywhere. It appears that Carrigan took them seriously in that he intended to throw nothing but right-handed pitchers at the National League champs. Ruth only made one appearance in the series, and that was as a pinch hitter in the last inning of Game 1. He grounded out, and the Red Sox lost. Overall, Carrigan's strategy worked as the Sox emerged from the series the World Champions.

Suffice it to say that Ruth was having a great time during the 1915 season—so much so that his off the field behavior (a sign of things to come) became a problem for his manager. Ruth, who was making $3,500 a year, felt like he was rolling in money, and it appears that the brothers back at St. Mary's hadn't done a very good job of teaching him how to handle it. This began a period in Ruth's life where he wanted to explore everything, including drinking, eating to excess, and spending his money as fast as possible. To keep an eye on his young star, Carrigan arranged to make sure his room was next to Ruth's when the team was on the road.

At the end of the 1915 season, the Federal League folded. Major league owners, including the Red Sox's Joseph Lannin, found themselves holding a competitive advantage with the demise of the one other professional league. In 1916, Ruth was not affected because he was in the third year of a three-year contract. Other players were not so fortunate. Take Tris Speaker, for example. He was the star of the World Champions and their only .300 hitter, and Lannin offered him a contract that included a 60 percent cut in salary. Speaker reported to spring training but refused to sign a contract. His holdout continued until shortly before the start of the season when Lannin did the unthinkable and sold his star player to the Cleveland Indians for $50,000.

Even without Speaker, the Red Sox were a formidable team. They had great pitching and fielding; they just needed to find a way to score a few runs. They did, and Ruth had quite a year highlighted by his numerous pitching duels with the great Walter Johnson of the Washington Senators. Ruth and Johnson met five times during the year, and Ruth won four of those contests. In Johnson's only win, Ruth did not figure in the decision. That year Ruth posted a record of 23–12 with an ERA of 1.75. The young lefthander had also hurled nine shutouts, a record that would stand until 1978 when Ron Guidry tied it. The Red Sox won the pennant and the World Series again, and this time Ruth won game two 2–1 in fourteen innings. That performance remains the longest postseason complete-game victory in baseball history. By this time, many viewed Ruth as the best pitcher in baseball. In the Ken Burns documentary *Baseball* author Dan Okrent said Ruth was the best left-handed pitcher of that era in the American League.

At the end of the 1916 season, the Red Sox organization saw a few major changes. Carrigan retired as both a player and a manager. Jack Barry was hired to replace him. Finally, Lannin sold the team to a group of men led by Harry Frazee, a New York City theatrical promoter.

In 1917, five days before opening day, the United States entered World War I by declaring war on Germany. The declaration of war made those involved in professional baseball very nervous. After all, the patriotic feeling was riding high, and the majority of players in the major leagues were of draft age. The War Department took the position, or baseball said it had, that the department would leave undisturbed in their current employment those men who were receiving military instruction. Baseball teams formed military drill teams to comply with this directive.

The season started well for both Ruth and the Red Sox. As May ended, the Sox were first, and Ruth had a record of 10–1. On June 23rd, Ruth was involved, for a very short time, in what would become a very memorable game. He was the starting pitcher that day against Washington. The first batter stepped to the plate, and Ruth delivered the first pitch, and the umpire called it a ball. Ruth immediately complained about the call. On the second pitch, the same thing happened. Ruth was growing angry now as he delivered pitch number three, which the umpire called ball three. Ruth screamed at the umpire, instructing him to open up his eyes; the umpire responded in turn, telling Ruth to shut up and pitch. When he delivered the next pitch, and the ump called it ball four, Ruth lost it. He ran toward the plate, complaining about the umpire's seeing problem. The umpire told him to start pitching, or he'd toss him out of the game. Ruth then threatened to punch the umpire if he was ejected, which is precisely what happened. Ruth charged the umpire. The catcher blocked Ruth's path, but he still got in a shot that caught the umpire in the back. Finally, an angry Ruth was led off the field by a policeman.

Ruth was replaced in the game by Ernie Shore. When Shore threw his first pitch, the runner on first tried to steal and was thrown out.

The Bambino shows off his pitching prowess.

Shore went on to retire the next 26 batters he faced. He had pitched a perfect game, and that is how it went down in the record books. Some questioned calling it a perfect game because a runner had reached first. In 1991, the Major League Baseball Committee on Statistical Accuracy (who knew there was such a thing) determined that it was a combined no-hitter.

The next day, Ban Johnson, the league president, had suspended Ruth indefinitely (while his first, this would not be his last suspension). Only Frazee's intervention caused Johnson to lift the ban after ten days. Johnson claimed he lifted the suspension because of how close the pennant race was at the time. When he returned, Ruth lost his first two starts, but he was hitting well: his average was .325 with two home runs for the season. As a pitcher, he went 24–13 with six shutouts, but the Red Sox finished second to the Chicago White Sox, a team that would become known as the Black Sox in two years.

After the 1917 season, Jack Barry, who had enlisted in the reserves, was called up and ordered to report for active duty. As a result, Jack Frazee was once again looking for a manager. In addition to managing, Frazee wanted someone who could take over some of his day-to-day responsibilities in running the Red Sox. Frazee brought this up in a discussion he was having with Ban Johnson, and the league president, eager to help, suggested that Ed Barrow, the current president of the International League, just might be the right man for the job. Though Barrow had been in baseball for 30 years, he had little experience as a manager. Frazee hired him anyway. In the meantime, Frazee had signed Ruth to a $7,000 contract (Ruth had wanted $10,000), which amounted to a 40 percent raise.

The year 1918 was the first that Ruth played consistently at a position other than pitcher. Harry Hooper was a Red Sox player who also advised Barrow on game strategy, and he urged Barrow to play Ruth at other positions when he wasn't pitching. Hooper argued that the team could use Ruth's bat and that besides that, people were coming to the ballpark to watch Ruth hit. Early in the season, Barrow gave in and began using Ruth in the outfield. Ruth didn't disappoint, hitting .300 and knocking out 11 home runs, which tied him for that year's home run title. As a pitcher, he went 13–7 with an ERA of 2.22, and Boston once again won the pennant.

The 1918 World Series began early on September 5th due to the war-shortened regular season. Ruth and the Red Sox would face the Chicago Cubs with the first three games played in Chicago. The Cubs, because of Ruth, decided they would rely on their left-handed pitchers in the series. Two lefty's Jim Vaughn and Lefty Tyler pitched all but two innings for Chicago in the six-game series.

Ruth started the first game for Boston and won by a score of 1–0. Ruth didn't pitch again until game four with the Red Sox up 2 games to 1. In the fourth inning, he hit a triple, driving in two runs and giving Boston the lead. The Cubs didn't score until the 8th, when they tied the game at two. In their half, the Red Sox scored to retake the lead at 3–2. Ruth gave up a hit and a walk in the 9th before being relieved. The game ended 3–2, and Boston took a 3–1 lead in the series. Two days later, they would win it all and become World Champions yet again. When the series ended, Ruth had pitched 29 and 2/3 scoreless innings in succession in World Series play. It was a record that wouldn't be broken until 1961 by Whitey Ford when he hurled 33 and 2/3 innings without allowing a run.

World War I came to an end two months after the World Series ended. By this time, Ruth was well aware of the attraction he was at the box office and intended to cash in. Also, he needed the money since his lifestyle had him spending more and more on things like his wife, other girls, partying, and new automobiles. He frequently left his young wife Helen alone on a farm he had purchased outside Boston during this time.

Entering the new season, Ruth wanted his salary raised from $7,000 to $15,000. At the time, there was only one player in the majors who made more than that, Ty Cobb. Besides that, Ruth was demanding a two-year contract or, looking at it another way, $30,000 over two years. Frazee said no way, and Ruth held out. Frazee found himself in a bind. He knew how vital Ruth was to his team, but he had lost money on the Red Sox for the past two years, even with the team's success. As a result, he began selling some of his players.

The standoff between Ruth and Frazee continued, and Ruth told the press that he just might quit baseball. He also said that he didn't think he was out of line with his demands, adding that he only wanted to be paid what he was worth. Frazee countered with an offer of $8,500. When the Red Sox left for spring training without Ruth, Frazee felt he had to do something. He contacted Ruth and set up a meeting with him in New York. The two reached an agreement Ruth would be paid $10,000 per year for the next three years. By this time, Ruth had let it be known that he no longer wanted to pitch; he wanted to be an everyday player.

Ruth got his wish but not for the reasons he would have liked. The Red Sox opened the 1919 season against the Yankees, and yet again, Boston was favored to win the pennant. Their opening day performance reinforced that prognostication when they pummeled the Yanks 10–0 with Ruth collecting two hits, including a home run. The rest of the opening series was canceled because of rain, so Boston continued their road trip in Washington, where they won two more with Ruth continuing to hit well, belting two doubles and a triple. One would have thought that everything was fine, but there was more going on after the games. It seems that while on the road, Ruth had decided it was time to party. After their third win of the season, Barrow had decided to wait up for Ruth in the hotel lobby.

When the clock hit 4 AM, he gave up and headed for bed. The next day Ruth didn't get a hit, and the Red Sox lost their first game of the season. That night, Barrow paid a hotel porter to come to his room and wake him up when Ruth got back to the hotel. When the porter woke Barrow up, it was six in the morning. Barrow went to the door of Ruth's room, and when he knocked, he noticed that the light went out. The door was unlocked, so he walked in and turned on the light. Ruth was in bed under the covers. Barrow approached the bed and pulled the covers back to find Ruth fully dressed. The angry manager told Ruth he would see him later and left the room.

The more Ruth thought about the incident, the madder he got, and by the time he reached the ballpark, he was literally beside himself. When Barrow arrived, Ruth yelled out, "if you ever come into my room like that again, you son of a bitch, I'll punch you right in the nose." Barrow sent all the players but Ruth out of the locker room, saying he would give the young man a chance to punch him in the face. Two assistant coaches intervened, and Ruth could get out of the locker room and onto the field. When the two met in the dugout, Ruth asked Barrow if he was playing today. Barrow told him no and added that he was suspended indefinitely. The Red Sox won that day without Ruth, and after the game, the very contrite outfielder apologized to Barrow, who lifted the suspension, providing Ruth would change his ways.

As mentioned previously, this was the year Ruth got his wish to be more of an everyday player. He only pitched in 17 games, finishing 8–5, and his pitching appearances were early in the season when Barrow still believed a pennant was winnable. By the end of June, the Red Sox were out of the race, and Barrow was more than happy to use Ruth every day because people came to the ballpark to see the slugger. By mid-July, Ruth had already tied his season-high total of 11 home runs. On July 29th, he hit number 16, which tied the American League record for the most homers hit in a single season. By the end of the season, he had hit 29, setting a new major league record. Ruth was a national sensation on a ball club that finished sixth.

Once again, Ruth felt that he was being underpaid. He was threatening to sit out the year if his salary wasn't doubled to $20,000. This demand came at a bad time for Frazee, who still owed Lannin a substantial amount for the Red Sox purchase. Some say this led to the sale of Ruth to the Yankees. Also, there is another story that Frazee needed money to finance the Broadway musical *No, No, Nanette*. This popular belief has no basis. *No, No, Nanette* opened on Broadway years after Frazee sold Ruth to the Yankees. As a matter of fact, by the time the play opened, Frazee no longer owned the Red Sox.

Meanwhile, in New York, the Yankees had hired a new manager by the name of Miller Huggins. The principal owner of the New York team, Jacob Ruppert, asked Huggins what the Yankees needed to succeed. Huggins, who was reportedly aware of Frazee's money problems, said, "Get Ruth from Boston." Ruppert was more than interested in acquiring Ruth and had made an offer two years previously to Frazee to buy Ruth, but at the time, Frazee showed no interest. However, Ruppert had financial concerns of his own. One of the sources of Ruppert's wealth was his Manhattan brewery, and with prohibition about to take effect, he knew his income was about to decline. The Yankees had also obtained permission from John McGraw and the New York Giants to play their games in the Polo Grounds. Ruppert worried that McGraw would cancel that arrangement were Ruth to join the Yankees, which would result in the Yankees being forced to build their own ballpark.

The two sides met and were able to hammer out a deal. Frazee sold Ruth to the Yankees for $100,000, an amount that was double the largest amount ever paid for a baseball player. In addition to the purchase price, Ruppert agreed to loan Frazee $300,000. By the time all was said and done, the Yankees had put up more than $400,000 to obtain Ruth. The deal included a clause that Ruth had to sign a new contract with the Yankees. He did so, agreeing to fulfill the remaining years on his current contract in return for receiving a $20,000 bonus.

Shortly after making the deal, Frazee broke the news to Barrow. Barrow told him he was making a mistake, and Frazee admitted that might be the case, but he insisted that his financial position left him no other choice. Looking back, it appears that Barrow was right. Between 1903 and 1919, the Red Sox had won five World Series championships. After Ruth was sold, they wouldn't win a pennant until 1946, nor would they win a World Series until 2004. The drought became known as the "Curse of the Bambino." Meanwhile, the Yankees, who had never even won a pennant before obtaining Ruth, would begin a dynasty that, as of this writing, would see the team capture 40 pennants and 27 World Series titles.

The New York press was thrilled with the trade. In a banner headline on its sports page, the *New York Times* reported that the deal constituted the highest amount ever paid for a player. The body of the story didn't offer one criticism of the price. Instead, it proclaimed that Ruth's feat of hitting 29 home runs in a single season would stand for many years unless he broke it himself. The article said that considering the short porch in right field at the Polo Grounds (Yankee stadium had yet to be built), that was a distinct possibility. The article also included a prediction by a Yankee pitcher Bob Shawkey that with Ruth, the Yankees would win the pennant.

The game of baseball was changing, and Ruth was the man responsible for it. Before the twenties, pitching ruled in the major leagues, and low scoring games were the rule. Now hitting and scoring runs in batches became more the norm. For example, before 1920, if two or three men in the majors drove in more than 100 runs, it was considered a rare feat. In 1921, fifteen players did it. Before 1920, the average annual earned run average for pitchers was about 2.85, but in the twenties, it stayed above 4.00. However, earned run averages weren't the only thing increasing, so was attendance. In 1920, every major league team attracted more fans to the park except Detroit and Boston. The Yankees became the first major league club to attract more than a million fans in a single season.

Ruth himself didn't even wait until he arrived in New York to start his partying. His roommate during spring training was a player named Ping Bodie. The two got along well and often ate together and were pals who would clown around together on the field. Hotels were a different story. During the spring, as the team made its way north, they would stop at different hotels, and their luggage would be left in the lobby for the players to claim. Ruth usually headed right into town rather than go to the hotel, and Bodie would pick up his own and Ruth's bag and take them to their room. He would also return Ruth's bag to the lobby when it was time to leave. According to one of Ruth's biographers, a reporter asked Bodie what Ruth was like at one stop. Bodie responded by saying he didn't know anything about Ruth. The newspaperman didn't buy the answer and asked again, you room with him what's he like? Bodie responded, "I don't room with him; I room with his suitcase."

When the regular season started, Ruth, who was now an outfielder, started slowly, and so did the Yankees. By the end of April, the Yankees were 4–7, and Ruth had yet to hit a home run. That's how it was on May 1, with Boston in town to play the second game of a series. That day Ruth hit his first homer, a memorable one that left the ballpark, and the Yankees won 6–0. The New York team would win two of the next three, and Ruth began to hit. By the end of May, he hit 11 more homers and followed that by hitting a dozen more in June. By July 15th, Ruth had tied his home run record from the previous year, and on the 19th, he broke it when he hit homers in both games of a doubleheader. Opposing teams became reluctant to pitch to him, as evidenced by the fact that he walked 148 times in the 142 games he played in 1920.

The Yankees stayed in the pennant race into August when they went into a slump. While the team finished third, Ruth had a phenomenal year hitting .376, belting out 54 home runs, scoring 158 runs, and batting in 137 more. Ruth's slugging percentage of .847 stood as a major league record until 2001 when Barry Bonds broke it during the steroid era. To give you an idea of how good Ruth was in 1920 (and it wasn't

Babe watches one leave the park.

because of a juiced-up baseball), his 54 home runs topped the number hit by every other team in Major League Baseball except the Philadelphia Phillies who hit 64. The runner-up in the American League hit 19 that year, and the National League leader Cy Williams knocked a total of 15 out of the park. Frankly, Ruth's performance that year defies explanation.

Before the start of the 1921 season, the Yankees acquired a couple of more players from Boston, including catcher Wally Schang and a young pitcher named Waite Hoyt. When the club reported for spring training, they were an optimistic bunch. When the season began, Ruth started strong, hitting five home runs in April. On July 18th, he hit the 139th home run of his career, making him the all-time leader in major league history. It was a record he would hold for more than five decades. Ruth would hit 575 more home runs after taking the career lead. Since then, only nine players have hit that many in their entire careers and four of those are believed to have used steroids.

Meanwhile, the Yankees found themselves in a two-team pennant race with the Cleveland Indians. The lead went back and forth. On September 15th, Ruth hit his 55th home run breaking his record, and the Yankees were in the lead. The next day Cleveland regained control, but for only one day. So, it went until September 23rd, when the Indians arrived in New York for a four-game series with the Yankees clutching to the slimmest of leads just two percentage points.

In game one, Ruth hit three doubles and crossed the plate three times as the Yankees won 4–2. The following day Cleveland came out strong and overwhelmed the New York team 9–0. Game three was played on Sunday before a capacity crowd, and the home team prevailed by a score of 21–7. The Indians needed a win badly in the fourth game to stay in the race, but Ruth wouldn't have it. He hit two home runs, numbers 57 and 58, slammed a double, and walked in the Yankees 8–7 win. A few days later, the Yanks clinched the pennant.

The year 1921 proved to be quite an encore for Ruth. His 59 home runs set a new record. His batting average was .378. He scored 177 runs and batted in 170. His slugging percentage was.846, just one point lower than in 1920. He finished the year with 204 hits and 144 walks. It was better than even money that he would end up on base every time he came to the plate.

It would be a subway series with the Yankees facing John McGraw's New York Giants. The Yankees were confident, and it seemed that the confidence was justified when they won the first two games by the identical scores of 3–0. In Game Three, things seemed to be going the Yankees' way when they took an early 4–0 lead. However, the Giants staged a rally and won 13–5, making it two games to one in the best of nine series.

Before Game Four could be played, it was announced that Ruth was injured. He had scraped an elbow while sliding, and the wound had become infected. The Yankees announced that their star was out for the remainder of the series. Ruth was in uniform for Game Four, but he took no batting practice. However, when the team left the dugout to take the field, Ruth was with them. His arm was bandaged, and he was in obvious discomfort but still managed a single and his first World Series home run. It wasn't enough as the Giants won, evening the series. The next day he played again, and he surprised the Giants by laying down a bunt single in the fourth inning. He eventually scored what became the winning run in the Yankees 3–1 victory. The Yanks now led the series, but Ruth's condition worsened, and he didn't even dress for the next two games, and the Yankees lost both. With his team trailing four games to three, Ruth was in uniform for Game Eight. In the ninth inning, with the Giants ahead 1-0, Miller Huggins sent Ruth in as a pinch hitter. The slugger grounded out, and the Giants went on to win the World Championship.

After the series, Ruth's arm healed, and he was determined to hit the barnstorming circuit with a team called The Babe Ruth All-Stars (his teammates Bob Meusel and Bill Piercy were on the rooster.) Ruth was anxious to go on this tour because he expected to make about $25,000. The problem was that Major League Baseball had a rule at the time that didn't allow players from World Series teams to appear in exhibitions. Ruth got the Yankee organization's permission to make the trip, but that wasn't enough to satisfy the new High Commissioner of baseball Judge Kenesaw Mountain Landis.

Landis let it be known that he was against the tour. Ruth decided to go ahead with it anyway. Shortly before the team's scheduled departure date, a couple of players, who had met with Landis, told Ruth they were backing out. They also informed Ruth that Landis wanted to speak with him. Also, other people advised Ruth that the commissioner wanted to see him. Ruth took his time before calling Landis, waiting until the day before playing an exhibition in Buffalo. Already angered over the delay, Landis told Ruth to come and see him immediately. Ruth replied that he had a previous engagement and added that he was playing in the first game on the tour the next day. Landis exploded, to put it lightly, telling Ruth he'd be sorry if he did before slamming down the phone. A sportswriter who was with Landis at the time recalled Landis pacing the room, muttering, "Who does that big monkey think he is?"

Ruth went on the tour, and Landis let it be known that the case was in his hands, and he would decide, in his own good time, how to resolve it. As it happened, the crowds for the exhibitions were disappointing, and Ruth decided to end the tour early. That wasn't enough to satisfy Landis. On December 5th, the Commissioner fined both Ruth and Meusel their entire World Series shares of $3,362, and he suspended the duo for the first six weeks of the 1922 season.

Ruth's original contract with the Yankees had expired, and he was ready to negotiate a new one. The slugging outfielder knew what a draw he was, so he expected considerably more than the Yankees were currently paying him. The word was that he was first offered $40,000, which he turned down. Then the Yankees offered him a five-year deal at $50,000 a year. Ruth countered, saying he wanted $52,000 per season. The Yankees agreed but wondered why the odd amount. Ruth answered that there are 52 weeks in a year, and he always wanted to make $1,000 per week. The agreement represented the highest amount ever paid to a ballplayer, and it made up 40 percent of the team's total payroll.

Even without Ruth and Meusel, the Yankees got off to a strong start in 1922. They stayed in first place in April and May. Some people thought, who needs Ruth? Still, there was excitement about his return. It took place on May 20, versus the Saint Louis Browns, and Ruth struck out once while going 0 for 4. By the end of the game, he was being booed by the 40,000 fans who had come to see his return. The slump continued, and he was hitting all of .093 when he came to bat on May 25th in the third inning. He found a pitch he liked and sent it to center for a single, but when the centerfielder mishandled the ball, he tried for second and was thrown out. Hearing the umpire's call, he rose to his feet and threw a handful of dirt into the umpire's face. He was thrown out of the game, and as he walked to the bench, he was booed and hissed. He went up into the stands after one fan who heckled him. Later that day, American League President Ban Johnson announced that Ruth would be suspended pending an investigation.

The Yankees were scheduled to leave New York to begin a road trip in Washington. Clark Griffith, who owned the Washington team, and had been selling tickets based on Ruth coming to town, got in touch with Johnson and asked him to lift the suspension. He did so after one game. Before the season was over, Ruth would be suspended five times. Ruth played in just 110 games in 1922. His batting average was .315. He hit 35 home runs and drove in 99. Through it all, the Yankees managed to win the pennant and earned the chance to face John McGraw's Giants in the World Series for the second consecutive year. The only difference in the outcome was that the Giants swept the series 4–0.

By this time, Ruth had hired a man named Christy Walsh to handle his business affairs. After the 1922 season, Walsh was worried about Ruth's public image. With this in mind, he set up a dinner party at the Elks Club in New York to which he invited sportswriters and well-known New Yorkers, among them an up-and-coming politician by the name of Jimmy Walker. The dinner was designed to be no holds barred, and the guests were invited to take their best shots at Ruth. Many did. Jimmy Walker, who was known to be a great speaker, used Ruth's fondness for children to get to him. Walker described the children, including the dirty-faced kids who idolized the great hitter, and finished his speech by asking Ruth, "Are you going to keep on letting those kids down?" Ruth responded by admitting his past mistakes and promising to work hard and straighten out. He finished to great applause when he predicted he would set a new home run record in 1923.

During the 1922 season, Charles Stoneham, owner of the Giants and the Polo Grounds, announced that the Yankees' lease to play on the grounds would not be renewed. The Yankees' owners, Jake Ruppert and Tillinghast Huston, had thought about building a new stadium. Now they had no choice. Yankee Stadium was completed in time for the home opener of the 1923 season. It became known as "the House that Ruth Built," and it was designed with him in mind. The new stadium's right-field fence was only 295 feet from home plate favoring left-handed hitters such as Ruth, so much so that the right-field bleachers became known as "Ruthville." Also, the stadium was designed so that left field was the sun field. During a game the previous year, Ruth had lost a ball in the sun. From that day on, he refused to play a sun field again. That's why Ruth always played right field at Yankee Stadium, but when the team was on the road, he sometimes played left.

For Ruth, it was a relatively quiet year. The Yankees were at the top of the league standings for most of the year and won the pennant by 17 games. While Ruth didn't break the home run record, he was a unanimous choice for the Most Valuable Player Award in the American League. His batting average of .393 was the highest of his career, he hit 41 homers (as did Cy Williams in the National League), and he led the league in runs scored and runs batted in.

For the third straight year, it was the Yankees versus the Giants in the World Series. This time the outcome was different, with the Yankees capturing their first world title 4 games to 2. Ruth had a superb series walking eight times, batting .368, and pounding out three home runs. The Giants won both their games on home runs hit by Casey Stengel (Stengel became the first player to hit a Yankee Stadium home during a World Series game). After his second homer, Stengel thumbed his nose at the Yankee bench as he rounded the bases. Asked about it later, Ruth said he didn't mind adding, "Casey's a lot of fun."

In 1924 Ruth continued to play well, but his teammates were aging and showing it. Injuries beset the team for much of the year. Ruth led the league in hitting with a .378 average and 46 home runs, but the Yankees finished the season second to the Washington Senators. Ruth got it done on the field, but 1924 saw the return of his less-than-perfect off-the-field behavior. Feeling that he had made up for his previous mistakes, he began going out every night drinking. He ignored the rules manager Miller Huggins (Ruth referred to Huggins as the flea) had laid down for the team.

In 1925, things only got worse. Ruth's behavior was as bad as ever, and his marriage was on the rocks. His wife, Helen, couldn't deal with him and the all too steady flow of rumors concerning his sexual exploits. The two argued and separated before a priest got involved and brought the couple back together for what would be a short reconciliation. By this time, Ruth had met a beautiful woman by the name of Claire Merritt Hodgson. She represented something that Ruth wasn't used to in that his fame failed to overwhelm her. The two began seeing each other regularly, and it was always on her terms.

Before starting spring training in 1925, Ruth, as was his custom, headed to Hot Springs, Arkansas, where he planned to exercise to get into playing shape. By this time, his weight had ballooned to about 260 pounds, and for every hour he exercised, he spent two partying. He came down with the flu, and as spring training began, he couldn't shake it. As the team headed north, they were scheduled to stop in Asheville, North Carolina. When Ruth got off the train, he collapsed. Teammates managed to get him to the hotel where the Yankees stayed, and a doctor was summoned. The doctor said Ruth had the flu and had suffered an intestinal attack. He said that Ruth needed to do nothing but rest.

Against the doctor's advice, the Yankees decided to send Ruth back to New York. While he was on the train ride, the rumor spread that he had died. Newspapers in England ran his obituary. The train stopped in Washington, where a Yankee scout, who was assigned to stay with Ruth on the trip, put an end to the rumor. Ruth's wife was waiting for him in New York when the train arrived. When the ill slugger failed to appear on the platform, she rushed onto the train. Ruth was obviously in a bad way, and an ambulance was summoned. He had to be sedated twice before he could be loaded into the waiting emergency vehicle. He was taken to Saint Vincent's Hospital.

During this period, a newspaperman wrote a story claiming that Ruth's ailment occurred because he had gorged himself on hot dogs and soda. Based on this story, the illness was called "the bellyache heard round the world." The doctors at Saint Vincent's saw it differently, concluding that Ruth's condition resulted from his failure to take care of himself. Whatever the cause, it landed Ruth in the hospital from April 9th to May 26th. During his stay, he underwent surgery to address an intestinal abscess.

In the meantime, the Yankees were having a terrible year, and Ruth's return didn't help. He managed to play in 98 games, hitting .290 with 25 home runs. The team finished next to last in the American League with a record of 69–85. The Yankees wouldn't have another losing record until 1965. However, by the end of 1925, Ruth was 31 years old, and many thought he was finished as a ballplayer. Ruth wasn't one of them.

In 1926, Helen moved out and headed back to Boston, and this time there would be no reconciliation. Meanwhile, Ruth was avidly courting Claire Hodgson spending more and more time with her and her daughter Julia, ten years old. That, however, did not stop the slugger from seeking other women. His exploits in this regard were well known. As told by one of his biographers, Ruth was roasted in song by a sportswriter named Rud Rennie. Playing the role of Miller Huggins, Rennie sang:

I wonder where my Babe Ruth is tonight.
He grabbed his hat and coat and ducked from sight.
I wonder where he'll be
At half-past two or three?
He may be at a dance or in a fight.
He may be at some cozy roadside inn,
He may be drinking tea or maybe—gin.
I know he's with a dame,
I wonder what's her name.
I wonder where my Babe Ruth is tonight.

While Ruth may have been serious about securing a lot of women's services, he was also serious about getting back in shape. He put himself through regular workouts at the Artie McGovern gym, and he reported for spring training in the best shape he had been in since his early days in the major leagues. Meanwhile, the Yankee front office had been rebuilding the team by securing future stars like Lou Gehrig and Tony Lazzeri.

Based on the team's play in spring training, when the 1926 season started, many were picking last year's 7th place team to win the pennant. By the middle of June, the Yankees had a ten-game lead. Although they failed to maintain that margin, they won the American League championship by three games. Ruth had a great season hitting .372 and sending

47 homers into the seats. Along the way, he managed to lead the league in walks, runs scored, and slugging percentage.

The Yankees faced the Saint Louis Cardinals in that year's World Series. The underdog Cardinals surprised virtually everyone by winning two of the first three games. Ruth stepped to the plate in Game Four in the first inning. Thus far, he had but two singles in the series. He sent the first pitch into the seats for a home run. In the third inning, he did the same thing. In the sixth inning, he blasted one deep into the center field bleachers with a full count. It marked the first time anyone had hit three homers in a World Series game. The Yankees won that day and the next, but the Cardinals won Game Six to tie the series at 3–3.

Game Seven was one for the ages. In mid-season, the Cardinals had acquired the now 39-year-old pitching legend Grover Cleveland Alexander. By this time, Alexander's best days were behind him, and he was known to have a severe drinking problem. He had already beaten the Yankees in Game Two of the series and again in Game Six. After the latter victory, Alexander, thinking his work in the series was over, celebrated by having more than his fair share of drinks. Nursing a hangover, he watched Game Seven from the bullpen.

The Cardinals had a 3–2 lead in the seventh inning when the Yankees loaded the bases with two outs and the dangerous Tony Lazzeri approaching the plate. The Cardinal skipper, Rogers Hornsby, came to the mound and motioned his bullpen. He wanted Alexander. After taking a strike, Lazzeri lofted Alexander's second offering into the left-field stands, just a few feet foul. On the next pitch, Alexander got out of the jam by striking Lazzeri out. Alexander then retired the side in the 8th and the first two batters in the 9th, which brought Ruth to the plate. Alexander sent Ruth to first on a base on balls. The talented Meusel was the next batter, and the ever-dangerous Gehrig was on deck. Alexander pitched to Meusel, and Ruth took off for second, where a throw from the catcher cut him down, ending the series. Ruth's decision to attempt to steal has been debated for years, and many considered it a bad play. Ruth wasn't among them. He always felt that attempting to put himself in scoring position was the right move at the time.

Okay, just say it, the 1927 Yankees. What does it bring to mind? Is it Murderer's Row? Is it the team that won a then-record of 110 games while clinching the pennant on Labor Day? Is it the recurring question of whether this squad was the greatest baseball team to take the field? Or do 60 home runs come to mind? Whatever the answer is, no one can deny that even now, almost a century later, that team's accomplishments remain a legendary part of Major League Baseball history.

Based on the Yankees' total domination, there was little interest in the 1927 American League pennant race. No, fans packed ballparks to witness the pursuit of the single-season home run record of 59. However, Ruth was not alone in his pursuit of the record. His teammate Lou Gehrig was right there with him until early September. As a matter of fact, through August, the two Yankees were never more than two home runs apart. However, Gehrig slowed down in September (finishing the year with 47), while Ruth never did. Still, with four games to go in the season, Ruth's total stood at 56. In the first of those games, he pounded out number 57, a grand slam. In the next game, he hit two more, bringing his total to 59. On September 30th, with two days to go, Ruth stepped to the plate to face Tom Zachary of the Washington Senators. The score was tied at 2 in the eighth when Ruth caught one and sent it, just inside the foul pole, into the right-field stands. Zachary screamed that the ball was foul and argued with the umpire to no avail. After the game in the clubhouse, Ruth exclaimed, "Sixty! Let's see some son of a bitch try to top that." Years later, Ruth would meet Zachary and ask him, "Do you still think that ball was foul?"

It should be noted that Ruth did more than hit sixty home runs in 1927. His batting average was .356, and he drove in 164 runs. To show how good the Yankees were that year, Gehrig had a higher batting average (.373) and drove in more runs (175). Gehrig was named the league's Most Valuable Player over Ruth and his home run record.

At the season's end, the Yankees headed to Pittsburgh to take on the Pirates in the World Series. In a practice session, one day before the series was scheduled to begin, Ruth and his teammates sent pitch after pitch over the fences in Forbes Field. The Pirates were on hand to watch, and so was Wilbert Robinson, the manager of the Brooklyn Dodgers. After viewing the hitting demonstration, Robison, referring to the Pirates, said, "They're beaten already." Indeed, they were as the Yankees swept four straight games to claim the World Championship.

The 1928 season started very well for the Yankees, and by July 1, they led the league by 13 and 1/2 games. Then multiple injuries began to take their toll, and the Washington Senators took advantage of it, actually moving ahead of the Yankees by a half-game on September 8th. That set the stage for a four-game series scheduled to start between the two clubs the very next day with a doubleheader. Yankee Stadium was filled to the brim, and thousands of fans were turned away at the gates. The New York team swept the doubleheader and then took game three when Ruth broke a tie by blasting a two-run homer in the 8th inning. A couple of weeks later, the Yankees clinched the pennant in Detroit. Ruth had another great year hitting 54 homers as compared to Gehrig, who finished second with 27.

When the Yankee players returned to their hotel, they found that Ruth had rented four rooms connected by doors and threw a party to celebrate. When the hotel explained that they did not have a piano they could supply, Ruth purchased one. Waiters were on hand with plenty of food and, of course, bootleg liquor. According to one biographer Ruth, never known for his subtlety, climbed atop a chair and proclaimed, "Any girl who doesn't want to fuck can leave now." The story has been told that very few of them left.

As in 1926, the Saint Louis Cardinals provided the opposition in the World Series. Much like the year before, the series proved to be no contest as the Yankees won four straight games. Ruth had a great series hitting an incredible .625, and Gehrig wasn't far behind with a .545 average. The New York Yankees had won back-to-back World Championships.

On January 11, 1929, a fire started in a home located at 47 Quincy Street in Watertown, Massachusetts. The owner of the home, Dr. Edward Kinder, wasn't home at the time. Firemen asked neighbors if anyone was in the house. The neighbors said that, in all probability, Mrs. Kinder was. Once the fire was somewhat subdued, a fireman by the name of John

Kelly entered the home. In a second-floor bedroom, he found a woman on the floor. With help, he got the woman out of the building, efforts to revive her failed.

The next day Boston newspapers reported that the dead woman was Helen Kinder, the doctor's wife. Dr. Kinder knew better. He had been living with the woman for two years: she was Helen Ruth. Still stunned, Dr. Kinder had enough of his wits about him to know that Babe Ruth would need to be informed of the death. Kinder decided to travel to New York to deliver the news himself. How Ruth got the word is unclear, but he decided he needed to go to Boston once he did.

In the meantime, the truth became public, and Helen's death made headlines. Aside from a short, prepared statement, Ruth remained silent. Ruth attended the funeral, and Helen was laid to rest. She was 31 years old. Ruth and Helen had adopted a daughter named Dorothy in 1921. Dorothy would later write a book in which she claimed to be Ruth's biological daughter by one of Ruth's girlfriends named Juanita Jennings.

Ruth, a Catholic, had told Claire that he couldn't get a divorce. With Helen's death, the path to marriage was cleared. On April 17, 1929, the two were wed, and Ruth adopted Claire's daughter, Julia, while Claire adopted Dorothy. April 17th happened to be opening day, but the game was postponed due to rain.

Claire had influenced Ruth from the day they met. Now that they were married, her influence increased. She took control of his diet, supervising his eating habits when he was home. She also managed to get him to cut down on his drinking. She saw that he wasn't able to spend time with old drinking buddies, and she began to accompany him on road trips. She also assumed control over the couple's finances. Ruth would have to go to her when he needed money.

As for the 1929 season, the Yankees started fast, winning 13 of their first 17 games, but they soon learned they were in for a real battle with an excellent Philadelphia Athletic team that had been put together by the Tall Tactician, Connie Mack. In 1929, Mack's team boasted four future Hall of Famers: Lefty Grove, Mickey Cochrane, Jimmie Foxx, and Al Simmons. In mid-May, the Yankees went into a slump, and the Athletics took advantage, seizing first place. They would go on to beat the Yankees by 18 games.

Ruth finished the season with 46 home runs even though he missed 17 days with an illness severe enough to warrant hospital admission. Despite Ruth and Gehrig, who hit 37 homers that year, the Yankees were not the team they used to be. Meusel's best days were behind him, and Pennock and Hoyt could no longer be counted on to deliver consistent pitching efforts. During the season, Miller Huggins grew gravely ill. On September 20, he entered the hospital, and five days later, he died. A coach by the name of Art Fletcher managed the Yankees for the rest of the season. Barrow (now the general manager) offered Fletcher the job permanently, but he turned it down. Ruth wanted to be named player-manager, but Barrow chose a former Yankee pitcher, Bob Shawkey, for the job.

While Ruth liked Shawkey, he still wasn't happy with the choice. Since his contract was up, he decided that if he weren't going to be the manager, he would get more money. Once again, he worked out hard in the offseason to get into shape. Before reporting to spring training, he informed the Yankees that he wanted $100,000. The team responded with an offer of $75,000, which Ruth promptly turned down. Ruth's business manager wrote a letter that Ruth signed and sent to both the Yankees and newspapers where he noted that he could quit baseball today and be very well off. The Yankees ignored the letter while the newspapers gave it some play. During spring training, the negotiations continued. On the day the exhibition season began, Ruth signed a two-year contract for $80,000 a year. President Herbert Hoover was making $75,000 a year, and as the oft-times repeated story goes, Ruth was asked if he thought it was right for him to be paid more than the president. Ruth supposedly replied, "Why not, I had a better year than he did."

Ruth had another good year in 1930, once again leading the league in home runs with 49 while hitting .359 and driving in 153 runs. For the fourth straight year, Gehrig finished second in home runs. Still, despite the efforts of the two sluggers, the Yankees struggled. There were quarrels between the new manager, Shawkey, and some players. The pitching was at best inconsistent, and numerous players couldn't fill the holes left behind by the departure of players like Dugan and Meusel. As a result, the Yankees finished a disappointing third. When the season ended, the Yankees hired Joe McCarthy as manager before they fired Shawkey. Years later, Shawkey would describe the situation as a dirty deal. Shawkey wasn't the only person upset. Ruth once again felt that the manager's job should have been his. However, in Barrow's opinion, Ruth couldn't even manage himself, much less a whole team, but to soothe the slugger's feelings, he was told that the Yankees didn't believe in player-managers.

Ruth never respected McCarthy, and he wasn't above showing it. On the other hand, McCarthy was smart enough to know that he would never be able to win Ruth over, and as a result, he concentrated his efforts on the other players. Though he was a strict disciplinarian, he made sure he hit it off with Gehrig and Lazzeri and a young catcher who became a regular on the team in 1929 by the name of Bill Dickey. In a short time, McCarthy made it clear that this was his team.

The Yankees were a better team in 1931, but they were still no match for Connie Mack's Athletics, who won the league by 13 and 1/2 games. Ruth hit .373, and he and Gehrig tied for the league lead in homers with 46. At the end of the season, Ruth's contract had run out, and the Yankees offered him $70,000, which represented a $10,000 cut. Ruth wanted another two-year contract for the same $80,000 he had been making. The two sides finally agreed on a one-year contract that would pay $75,000.

In 1932 the Yankees showed they were back. Behind strong pitching and consistent hitting, they won the pennant easily. Ruth had a good year, but at age 38, he was slowing down, and he often left games in the late innings. He hit 41 home runs, which was second in the league, but nowhere near Jimmie Foxx's total of 59. He batted .341 and drove in 137 runs. All very good statistics though the numbers were below those of his glory days.

The 1932 World Series featured the Yankees versus the Chicago Cubs. The Cubs were a solid team, as evidenced by the fact that they won four pennants between 1928 and 1938. The Yankees, led by Gehrig's hot bat, won the first two games in New York. The series then moved to Chicago, where a woman spit on Ruth and his wife as they were entering their hotel.

Game Three began with Ruth hitting a three-run homer in the first inning before the Yankees had made an out. By the fifth inning, the score was tied at four with the Yankees coming to bat. Ruth stepped to the plate to a chorus of boos and taunting from the Cubs bench. The Chicago pitcher, Charlie Root, delivered a called strike, which brought cheers from the home crowd. With a big grin on his face, Ruth looked at the Cub bench holding up one finger on his right hand. The next two pitches were called balls, but the fourth pitch was another called strike. The crowd cheered, and some of the Cubs left the dugout and came on to the field to razz Ruth who looked over at them and held up two fingers while saying, "it only takes one to hit it." From the mound, Root yelled something at Ruth, and according to Gehrig, waiting on deck, Ruth yelled back while pointing at the pitcher, saying that he was going to hit the next pitch right down the pitcher's throat. What he did was hit it deep into the center-field seats. This became known as the called shot home run. Arguments about whether Ruth called it raged for years. Charlie Root refused to play himself in the movie about Ruth's life because the script had Ruth calling the shot. Root went to his grave, maintaining that Ruth had never pointed to the spot where he hit the home run. Still, the fact remains that the homer put the Yanks ahead to stay, and the next day they beat the Cubs again, sweeping the series.

Heading into the 1933 season, Ruth expected to take a salary cut, but he was more than surprised when the Yankees offered him $50,000, which cut his yearly paycheck by more than 30 percent. Ruth publicly announced that he would never sign for that amount. By the spring, Ruth countered the Yankee offer saying he would sign for $60,000. The Yankees turned him down. They announced that if he didn't sign by March 29th, the offer would be lowered. A few days later, Ruth gave in and signed.

That year Ruth remained productive, hitting .301 with 34 home runs and 103 runs batted in, and he led the league in walks. He was selected to play in the first All-Star game and hit the first homer ever in that contest. The Yankees themselves finished second that year seven games back. During the final game of the season, as a publicity stunt, Ruth started the game as a pitcher. He pitched a complete game and won, finishing his pitching career with 94 wins and 46 losses.

The year 1934 was Ruth's final full season in the majors. He took another salary cut though he was still the top paid player in baseball. The Yankees finished second again, and Ruth seldom played an entire game. He finished the season with a batting average of .288, and he hit 22 home runs. The Yankees viewed him as a hindrance and not a help. He openly defied his manager, and he had a falling out with his old friend Gehrig to the point that the two no longer spoke to each other. Ruth still wanted to manage, but the Yankees informed him that McCarthy was their man and the team began looking for teams that would be willing to take Ruth on as a player, a manager, or both.

By this time, Ruth was adamant about wanting to stay in baseball and manage. The Boston Braves were interested in Ruth as a gate attraction and not as a manager. In February of 1935, the Yankees traded Ruth to the Braves, and it was announced that in addition to playing, when he wanted, Ruth would be the club's assistant manager. The arrangement did not work. Ruth was in such poor condition that he could no longer run the bases. His fielding was so bad that his pitchers refused to take the mound if he was in the lineup. Also, he found that he was an assistant manager in name only and that most of his duties in that regard involved signing autographs.

On May 25, 1935, Ruth had his last big day at the plate. Against the Pirates at Forbes Field, he went 4 for 4 and belted three home runs, one of which left the ballpark after being blasted over the upper deck in right field. In a perfect world, Ruth would have retired right then and there, but he had promised the Braves that he would play through Memorial Day. About a week later, he retired from the game. Counting the six he hit in 1935; he finished with 714 career home runs.

Ruth was once asked what he planned to do once his playing days were over. His response was, "take life easy." He may have meant it since one of the first things he did after retiring was call the sportswriter

Grantland Rice (See Chapter 17), telling him, "Get out your golf clubs. I'm ready for you now." The truth was Ruth still hoped to manage, but the opportunity never came. He returned to the majors in 1938 as the first base coach for the Brooklyn Dodgers, who made it a point to state that Ruth would not be considered for the manager's job should it become available. His wife Claire maintained after the great ballplayer passed away that the owners had blacklisted him. After the 1938 season, he was never again to work in baseball.

On July 4, 1939, Ruth returned to Yankee Stadium on Lou Gehrig Appreciation Day, which was held to honor the star forced to retire and struck by the disease that bears his name and would kill him two years later. Ruth gave a brief speech and then embraced Gehrig before the sold-out crowd. The following week he traveled to Cooperstown, New York, to open the Baseball Hall of Fame. As baseball games became popular radio broadcasts, he sought a job in that field without success.

When World War II broke out, he made many public appearances to support the war effort. One of those was as a player to benefit the Army-Navy relief fund. He hit a ball into the stands that just curved foul, and he circled the bases anyway, waving to the crowd. He made his last effort to get back into baseball in 1946 when he contacted the Yankees, who sent him a letter turning him down.

Late in that same year, Ruth began experiencing pain over his left eye. He entered the hospital, where he was diagnosed with an inoperable tumor at the base of his skull. He was not told he had cancer because those close to him feared he might harm himself. The doctors attempted to treat his condition with experimental drugs and radiation. Ruth may have been one of the first cancer patients to have their condition treated in such a manner. He left the hospital in February of 1947 and headed to Florida to regain his strength (he had lost 80 pounds).

In April, the Commissioner of baseball, Happy Chandler, declared that Sunday, April 27th, would be Babe Ruth Day throughout the major leagues. Ruth returned to the house he had built for the ceremony. He stepped to the microphone and, in a hardly recognizable voice, said, "Thank you very much, ladies and gentlemen. You know how bad my

Ruth's grave decorated with numerous grave goods left by his admirers.

voice sounds; well, it feels just as bad. You know, this game of baseball of ours comes up from the youth. That means the boys. And after you've been a boy and grow up to know how to play ball, then you come to see the boys representing themselves today in our national pastime. The only real game in the world, I think, is baseball. As a rule, some people think that if you give them a football or a baseball or something like that, naturally, they're athletes right away. But you can't do that in baseball.

Just some of the items left by fans to honor the Yankee slugger.

You've got to start from way down, at the bottom, when you're six or seven years old. You can't wait until you're fifteen or sixteen. You've got to let it grow up with you, and if you're successful and you try hard enough, you're bound to come out on top, just like these boys have come to the top now. There's been so many lovely things said about me, I'm glad I had the opportunity to thank everybody." Ruth then waved to the crowd who had filled his house on his day and ambled to the Yankee dugout listening to their cheers.

The tumor continued to grow, and the pain worsened. The only relief was found in morphine. In June, the doctors tried treating Ruth with a new drug, and he improved, but it was only temporary. On August 16, 1948, Babe Ruth died in his sleep. He was 53 years old. His casket was taken to Yankee Stadium, where more than 70,000 people filed by to pay their respects for two days. The greatest Yankee of them all was laid to rest in the Gate of Heaven Cemetery in Hawthorne, New York.

The great sportswriter Red Smith noted Ruth's passing in a column titled *News Aboard Ship,* which is where he was when he got the news. Smith ended the column this way:

Now that Babe is gone, what's to be said that hasn't been said? Nothing, when you come down to it. Just that he was Babe Ruth. Which tells it all, for there was never another and never will be. Probably he was the greatest ballplayer who ever lived, Ty Cobb and Honus Wagner and the rest notwithstanding.

It's a typically shabby trick on history's part that, as time goes by, he will be remembered merely for his home runs. He was also, remember, a genuinely great pitcher, a genuinely great outfielder, a genuinely great competitor, a truly great personality.

Merely by being part of the game, he wrought lasting changes in its strategy, its financial standards, its social position, and the public conception of it. Somebody else will come along to hit sixty home runs, probably very soon. That won't make somebody else a second Babe Ruth. Never another like him.

If You Go:

See Chapters 4 and 6 on **James Cagney** and **James Farley**.

20

"A Pie in the Face™"

Soupy Sales

County: Westchester • Town: Valhalla
Buried at Kensico Cemetery
273 Lakeview Avenue

When you hear about Soupy Sales' early life, you suspect it's one of his numerous pranks. He was born Milton Supman in Franklinton, North Carolina, to Irving and Sadie Supman, the only Jewish family in town. He was born on January 28, 1926, and had two brothers, Leonard and Jack. The family name was often mispronounced as "Soupman" and his parents had nicknamed his brothers "Hambone" and "Chicken Bone." They gave Milton the nickname "Soupbone," which eventually became just "Soupy."

Sales' father ran a dry goods store in Franklinton, and Soupy often joked that local Ku Klux Klan members bought their sheets from his father's store. His father died when he was five, and the family moved to Huntington, West Virginia. Soupy acted in school plays and was voted the most popular boy. He graduated in 1944 from Huntington High School and enlisted in the United States Navy, where he served on the USS *Randall* in the South Pacific during World War II. He sometimes entertained his shipmates by telling jokes and playing crazy characters over the ship's public address system. One of the characters he created was "White Fang," a large dog that played outrageous jokes on the seamen. Surely the humor was a blessing as the USS *Randall* navigated the South Pacific and participated in the Battle of Okinawa.

After the war, Sales returned home and entered Marshall College to study journalism. While attending Marshall, he performed in nightclubs

Soupy Sales

as a comedian, singer, and dancer. He graduated in 1949 and went to work for a radio station in Huntington as a scriptwriter, while he continued to do stand-up comedy in nightclubs and worked as a disc jockey. Later that year, he moved to Cincinnati to work as a morning deejay. He developed the stage name "Soupy Hines." Later he would change the "Hines," deciding it was too close to Heinz Soup Company, to "Sales" in honor of Chic Sale, a vaudeville comedian of some note. In Cincinnati,

Sales began his television career on WKRC-TV with a show called *Soupy's Soda Shop*. It was the first teenage dance television show program, beating Dick Clark's *American Bandstand* by two years. He also had a late-night comedy/variety program called *Club Nothing*.

After a couple of years, WKRC canceled his shows, and Sales moved to Cleveland, where he hosted radio and TV shows and continued his nightclub act. The late-night comedy/variety show was called *Soupy's On,* and it was a skit on that show where he got his first pie in the face.

In 1953, Sales left Cleveland "for health reasons" (he claimed "they got sick of me") and moved to Detroit for a job with WXYZ-TV. He launched a daily live children's show called *Soupy Sales Comics,* which caught on and led to his nighttime show *Soupy's On*. In 1955, the noontime show's name was changed to *Lunch with Soupy,* and it began to be broadcast nationally on the ABC television network. He hosted 11 hours of TV time each week, and *Lunch with Soupy* was the first non-cartoon Saturday morning program on the ABC network. The show was improvised and slapstick in nature, full of comedy sketches, gags, and puns, almost all of which resulted in Sales receiving a pie in the face, which became his trademark.

Sales developed pie-throwing into an art form. He took pies from all angles and multiple pies in rapid succession and countless variations. He bantered with stagehands and with a gallery of puppets that included Pookie (a hipster lion), White Fang ("the meanest dog in the United States") who only grunted expressively and was seen as just a large furry paw, and Black Tooth ("the biggest and sweetest dog in the United States") who also was a furry paw that gave Sales slurpy off-screen kisses. Other characters included his irrepressible girlfriend Peaches, the vivacious Marilyn Monwolf, and a bloodthirsty neighbor, the Count, who touted an album titled "Love in Vein."

Guest stars like Frank Sinatra, Burt Lancaster, Shirley MacLaine, and Sammy Davis, Jr. would come on the show and get plastered with a pie in the face. One show featured Sinatra, Sammy Davis, Jr., and Trini Lopez, all getting pied together. While meant for kids, the show developed a cult following among adults. Meanwhile, *Soup's On* was thriving on its

If you were close to Soupy you were in danger of taking one to the face.

own. It was on at 11 o'clock, and the guest star was always a musician (frequently a jazz musician). His show seemed to help sustain jazz in Detroit as artists would regularly sell out their club shows after appearing on *Soup's On*. Coleman Hawkins, Louis Armstrong, Duke Ellington, Billie Holiday, Charlie Parker, and Stan Getz were among the guests on the show, and Miles Davis made six appearances.

In 1960, Sales moved his show to the ABC-TV Studios in Los Angeles. However, ABC dropped the show from the network schedule in March 1961 while continuing the series as a local program until January 1962. The show went back on the network as a late-night fill-in for *The Steve Allen Show* in 1962 but was canceled after only three months.

During this time in Los Angeles, Sales started a sporadic film career that lasted more than 40 years. His movie debut was in *The Two Little Bears* (1961), which starred Eddie Albert, Jane Wyatt, and Nancy Kulp. He made his debut in a starring role in 1966 in *Birds Do It,* which also starred Tab Hunter and Arthur O'Connell. His last movie was *Angels with Angles* in 2005, in which he appeared with Frank Gorshin, Rodney Dangerfield, and Adam West.

In September 1964, Sales took his show to WNEW-TV in New York City, where it soon became the biggest show of its kind in local television. Screen Gems syndicated 263 episodes, and soon the show was seen throughout the U.S., Canada, Australia, and New Zealand. This show marked the height of his popularity. He was able to attract guest appearances by stars such as Frank Sinatra, Tony Curtis, Jerry Lewis, Sammy Davis, Jr., Judy Garland, and musical acts like The Shangri-Las, The Supremes, and The Temptations. Sales performed musical numbers on the show, often using his jazz collection and adapted popular jazz numbers as themes for his puppet characters. Frank Nastasi played White Fang, Black Tooth, Pookie, and all the "guy at the door" characters.

For notoriety, nothing beat the show that aired live on January 1, 1965. Sales was somewhat miffed at working on New Year's Day and had a few minutes to kill at the end of his program. Ad-libbing, Sales looked into the camera and delivered a request to his young viewers to sneak some "little green pieces of paper" out of their parents' wallets and send them to him. (No tape of the show exists, so a verbatim transcription of what Sales said is not available.) Complaints from outraged parents came fast and furious. Sales' show was suspended, prompting fans to swamp the station's switchboard with protest calls, mostly from high school and college students who demanded that Soupy be put back on. Within two weeks, he was. The uproar only increased his popularity. Sales described the incident in his autobiography *Soupy Sez! My Life and Zany Times* (2001).

Later that year, Sales invented a dance called The Mouse, a loony version of The Twist in which Sales bared his upper teeth, raised his hands to his ears, and wiggled his fingers while chewing in time to the music. He performed The Mouse on the *Ed Sullivan Show* in September 1965, just before The Beatles' segment of the broadcast (which would turn out to be the band's last live appearance on the show). While appearing on the Sullivan show, he met dancer Trudy Carson and married her in 1980 (less than a year after he and his first wife, Barbara Fox, got divorced after 29 years of marriage).

In the late '60s, animation took over children's programming, and shows like Sales' and Shari Lewis' lost their appeal. In 1966, his show was not renewed in New York and went into syndication. The show did make a brief comeback as *The New Soupy Sales Show* in 1978 in Los Angeles.

It ran for one season live and then was syndicated.

Soupy during his heyday.

One of Sales' biggest fans was Frank Sinatra. When Sinatra started his record label, Reprise Records, he signed Sales to a recording contract for which Sales produced two albums: *The Soupy Sales Show* in 1961 and *Up in the Air* in 1962. He also recorded a single—"Muck-Arty Park" (a play on "MacArthur Park")—and an album, *A Bag of Soup*, for Motown Records in 1969.

Soupy Sales was everywhere. He did Broadway, dinner theater, comedy clubs, loads of radio, television, and film. In 1968 he joined the panel on *What's My Line?* and went on to record 1,500 shows in his seven-year run. He was also a panelist on the revival of *To Tell the Truth,* and a frequent guest on *Match Game*, *The Gong Show*, *Hollywood Squares,* and *Pyramid,* as well as a featured performer in the musical variety show *Sha Na Na*.

For two years in the mid-'80s, Sales emceed a radio show on WNBC in New York, sandwiched between the drive-time shows of Don Imus in the morning and Howard Stern in the afternoon. The relationship between them was rocky. Stern and Imus gave Sales a hard time. After Sales died, Stern admitted it on the air and claims he apologized to Sales some years before his death. He praised Sales, claiming he was his childhood hero and expressed regret over his harsh words towards Soupy. When Sales' show was not renewed in 1987, he lost his temper on the air and began to speak frankly about how he had been treated poorly by the station. When the show went to commercial, Sales was off the air and never returned.

Sales kept up club appearances through the 1990s, remaining popular with baby boomers. He died of cancer on October 22, 2009, at Calvary Hospice in the Bronx at 83. He is buried in a modest grave at Kensico Cemetery in Valhalla, New York.

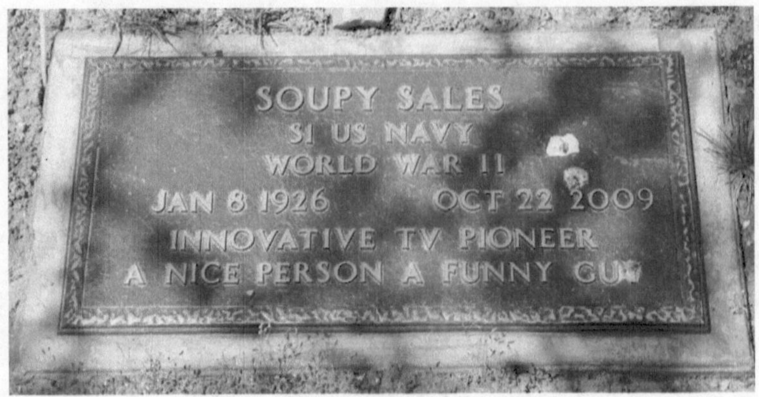

The modest grave of a funny man.

If You Go:

Kensico is a large, beautiful cemetery containing many notable graves, including **Anne Bancroft** (1931–2005) (see Chapter 2), **Lou Gehrig** (1903–1941), and **Danny Kaye** (1911–1987).

Two other notable graves at Kensico are **David Sarnoff's** (1891–1971) and **Florenz Ziegfeld** (1867–1932).

Sarnoff was an American businessman and pioneer of American radio and television. He was the founder of NBC and led RCA from its founding in 1919 until his retirement in 1970. At the onset of World War II, Sarnoff served on Eisenhower's communications staff, and in December 1945, he received a brigadier general's star and, after that, was known as General Sarnoff. The star which he proudly and frequently wore was buried with him. He died the year after he retired at the age of 80.

Ziegfeld—popularly known as "Flo"—was an American Broadway impresario, notable for his series of theatrical revues, the Ziegfeld Follies, and his production of the musical *Show Boat.* He is a member of the American Theater Hall of Fame. The Follies featured many famous names such as Fanny Brice, W.C. Fields, and Will Rogers. Ziegfeld died in 1932 at the age of 65.

21

"The Happy Warrior"

Al Smith

County: Queens • Town: New York
Buried at Calvary Cemetery
4902 Laurel Hill Boulevard

One could say he was a born politician who lived his entire life in New York City's Fourth Ward. He was a leading reformer of his time but remained a firm supporter of the Tammany Hall machine that was notorious for its graft and dishonesty. He first made his mark as a member of the New York State Legislature, but he is most remembered for his four terms as Governor of the empire state. In 1928, he became the first Roman Catholic to be nominated for the Presidency by a major party. While he was Governor, he counted Franklin D. Roosevelt as a friend and supporter. After Roosevelt became President, he became a vocal opponent of New Deal policies. He was baptized Alfred Emanuel Smith, but in time everyone came to know him as Al.

Al Smith made his earthly debut on December 30, 1873. His father, for whom he was named, made his living as a teamster, meaning someone who carted goods in the neighborhood. This occupation required hard work and long hours. Smith would later recall his father leaving the house for work at daybreak and not returning home until after dark. The elder Smith lived by the code that a man who can't do a friend a favor is not a man. He was unswerving in his loyalty to his friends, who would often accompany him home when they needed a meal. Smith's father was an active member of the political organization that his son would be closely associated with, Tammany Hall.

Al Smith

While Smith's father was Italian, his mother, Catherine Mulvihill, was as Irish as they come, and her boy remained close to her for as long as she lived. She significantly influenced Smith as he developed the values that would guide him through his adult life. Some have even described her as his moral compass. As a man, Smith seldom spoke about his father.

It was his mother who raised him and bestowed upon him his Irish heritage, which he embraced.

A button favored by Smith supporters.

The fourth ward, where Al grew up, was a hodgepodge of ethnicity. Author Robert Slayton in his excellent biography of Smith quotes Robert Moses (See Chapter 15) speaking in memory of the man who would give him his start in government "within a radius of five miles Alfred E. Smith could see . . . Neapolitans who brought into Little Italy the colors and passions of the Mediterranean; refugees from the knout in Russia, sturdy Germans of the *turnverein saengerfest*, pre-Nazi variety; old Americans being elbowed aside by new Irishmen who understood the air of reconciling before the League of Nations and the Dumbarton Oaks were thought of." The neighborhood described by some as the wickedest ward in New York City after 1850, housed more than its share of very cheap lodging houses, pawnshops, and saloons. The great Jimmy Durante recalled performing at some of what he referred to as joints in the area. He said, "Some were worse than others, but they were all pretty bad." However, Al Smith found a brighter, cleaner side of his neighborhood, which would shape his thinking for years to come. What the fourth ward created in Smith was a man who was free of prejudice. In his view, most Americans were as well; it was a belief that would come back to haunt him.

Smith, a Roman Catholic, worshipped at Saint James Church and was educated at the parish school. He was both a student and an altar boy. There is no surviving record as to how well Smith performed in school. He did show a command of the English language, as evidenced by his selection to represent Saint James at an elocution contest that included the other local parochial schools. Smith did well enough in the event to win a silver medal.

Anyone who has ever attended a parochial school knows how much importance and time was given to the teaching of religion. This author attended parochial school for 12 years, and his first class every day, every year, was religion. Smith had much the same experience at Saint James, and it had a profound effect on how he would live his life. His grandson Arthur Smith, who became a priest, recalled that his grandfather never brought religion up in a conversation, but "he lived it."

When Smith was 11 years old, his father's hard work began to take its toll daily. The elder Smith was forced to hire help to load his wagon as he was physically unable to perform the task. To make ends meet, he took on the added burden of working a second job as a night watchman. Within a year, even these tasks were too much, and Smith's father was so weak he was confined to his bed. His condition forced him to sell his horses and his wagon. When Election Day came in 1886, a Tammany Hall official helped the elder Smith to the polls. After casting his vote, he had to be carried up the steps to his bed. A few days later, he died, leaving his 12-year-old namesake fatherless.

As the family's bills began piling up, Smith was faced with a tough decision, and he made it, quitting school before graduating grade school to go to work. Smith valued education, and when he was older, he proved it through the positions he took and his actions as a chief executive. Smith would later state that "There are two great functions the state performs for our people. One is the education of our children, and the other is the preservation of health."

Smith worked a few jobs that paid under ten dollars a week. Then he landed a position with John Feeney and Company where he made twelve dollars a week working out of Gotham's Fulton Fish Market. Working for Feeney, Smith performed multiple duties, including selling, cleaning, and wrapping the fish. In addition to his wages, Smith was permitted to take home any fish he could carry. Suffice it to say that the Smiths ate quite a bit of produce from the market in those days.

This is not to say that Smith's life was filled with nothing but work. Once again, through Saint James Church, the young man became involved in something that would prove quite beneficial during his political life: acting. There was a stage in the church basement and a group to which Smith belonged, the Saint James Players, which put on multiple

Al Smith

shows. Smith appeared in many of these productions, often cast as the villain. He was at ease in front of audiences, he developed an excellent memory, and he learned how to use language to deliver a message. In time he would put all these talents to good use.

After four years at the fish market, Smith accepted a position that paid a little more when he went to work for the Davidson Steam Pump Works located in Brooklyn. While his compensation increased, Smith had little interest in the work itself, which involved checking pipes manufactured by the company. During this period, what did grab Smith's attention was an Irish lass named Catherine Dunn, who lived in the Bronx. In 1894, Smith first met Dunn when he took a trip to the Bronx with a friend of his. He courted her steadily for six years before the pair married on May 6, 1900. The couple would have five children.

As mentioned previously, Smith's father had been an active member of Tammany Hall, though, in Manhattan, the institution was generally referred to as "The Hall." It was a New York City political organization founded in 1786. Aaron Burr is often credited with being the driving force behind the group's founding, who envisioned it as an instrument that could counter Alexander Hamilton's (See Chapter 8) Society of the Cincinnati. Burr used Tammany in the presidential election of 1800, in which he was elected vice president. Many historians believe that minus Tammany's efforts, John Adams would have captured New York's electoral votes and won reelection.

As "The Hall" evolved, its political power was provided mainly by immigrants. Those newly arrived at the American shore found much-needed assistance in Tammany. These immigrants generally lived in extreme poverty, and the government at the time offered little in the way of assistance. Tammany filled this void, providing food, coal, money for rent, and in some cases, a job to those in need of assistance. As an example, in one day, a Tammany ward leader might assist the victims of a house fire; intervene with a judge for people from his ward who had been arrested; provide rent money to a family facing eviction or food for another without the means to acquire it; find jobs for a few able-bodied men in search of work; attend a few funerals and perhaps a Bar Mitzvah. All that Tammany asked in return was your vote for the candidates supported by "The Hall" come Election Day. The society wasn't doing all this good work for nothing. With its handpicked candidates in power, Tammany Hall served as a foundation for graft and political corruption.

Tom Foley, an important Tammany officer, would become Smith's mentor. A saloon owner, Foley stayed close to the people he represented in parts of Manhattan. According to the *Tammany Times* in 1911, Foley, who was known for giving special attention to the poor, invited everyone in his district to a picnic. There the people enjoyed movies and vaudeville acts. The picnickers also consumed sandwiches as well as cakes and ice cream. They were also able to refresh themselves by drinking soda and lemonade, all provided by their host Tom Foley.

Smith joined the Foley organization, and through loyalty and hard work, he soon became one of Foley's most trusted aides. It was Foley who decided that Smith should run for a seat in the state legislature. With Foley's and "The Hall's" backing, he did so and easily won the election garnering over 75 percent of the vote. He would serve as a member of the statehouse from 1904 through 1915.

Smith's initial legislative session began in January of 1904. His legislative baptism was not a pleasant experience. He wielded very little influence as the Republicans controlled the chamber. He was put on the bank committee and the committee on public lands and forestry. Smith would later note that at the time, he had little knowledge of either. He said that he knew nothing when it came to banking laws and that he had never even seen a forest. His votes reflected total loyalty to Tammany Hall.

Tom Foley had advised Smith not to make a speech during a legislative session until he had something worthwhile to say. Smith followed this advice, given that he never sought the floor to make a statement in his first two years as a representative. In these early years, Smith did excel at responding to constituent requests and making sure that he campaigned in person during elections. These actions were enough for the voters who continued, yearly at the time, to send him back to Albany as their representative.

However, two years into his career as a representative, Smith gave serious thought to calling it quits before deciding to hang on for one more year. He threw himself into the work of the legislature, thoroughly examining every bill, even the voluminous appropriations bill. Through hard work and a bit of luck, he became a legislator on the rise.

As is often the case, it could be said that Smith made his own luck. In 1904, James Wadsworth, Jr. was elected to the assembly. His family had an illustrious history in America that dated back to 1634. Wordsworth was a Republican who took a liking to Smith and was impressed by his abilities. When the speaker of the statehouse passed away in 1905, a coalition of forces came together and elected the then 28-year-old Wadsworth the new speaker of the assembly. The new speaker had tremendous clout when it came to committee assignments on both sides of the aisle. Wadsworth was aware that traditionally the speaker would accept the recommendations of the Democratic leadership when it came to the assignments of the members of their party. Wadsworth followed this tradition with a lone exception. When he was informed of the recommendations regarding Smith, he told the Democrats, "I can't stand for this." As a result, for the first time in 1906, Smith was placed on important committees.

Smith made the most of his new and improved situation. He began introducing bills of his own, and now that he had something to say, he would take to the floor in legislative sessions and say it. It was in doing the latter that he put his old acting skills to use. He used his memory to compile numbers and facts on the issues he was advancing, and he leaned heavily on humor. For example, as detailed in Slayton's biography, Smith was involved in a floor debate with three upstate New York Republican representatives. In turn, to enhance their credentials, each of these men touted their educations, noting that they had graduated from Cornell, Harvard, and the U. of M. Not to be outdone, Smith proudly announced that he was an F. F. M. man. One of those in the assembly yelled out, "What is that Al?" Smith responded, "Fulton Fish Market. Let's proceed with the debate."

In 1910, the New York State Republican Party was rocked with corruption charges. As a result, the Democrats won resounding victories in the yearly elections and became the majority party in both houses of the legislature. Not only was Smith named Majority Leader, but he was also made the chairman of the powerful Ways and Means Committee, which gave him control over the flow of all proposed legislation. Smith didn't rest on his laurels; he introduced 72 bills and championed the fight for the first Workmen's Compensation Law to be passed by any state in the union. It was during this period that he began to earn the reputation of a political reformer.

One might wonder how a city machine politician, a Tammany Man, could come to be regarded as a reformer. The truth be told, it probably wouldn't have been possible had "The Hall" been headed by any of the leaders previous to that of the man in charge at the time, Charles Francis Murphy. This is not to say that Murphy did not have Tammany's best interests foremost in his mind. He certainly did. Evidence of this is seen in his opposition to a direct primary system. This proposal was more democratic than the traditional manner of having party bosses name the nominees. No, what made Murphy so effective a Tammany leader was his ability to recognize that the political game involved considerably more than graft. For example, Murphy believed that it was essential to have competent people in charge when it came to public health or to matters like education that you couldn't rely on political hacks.

On the other hand, he fully expected that the kickbacks from contractors working in both areas would continue unimpeded. As a result, Tammany began supporting reform in certain areas of government. Therefore, Smith was not only able to fight for reforms in many instances, but he had Tammany's support in these fights when it came to issues benefiting the public.

On March 25, 1911, at approximately 4:40 on a Saturday afternoon, a fire broke out in a building located close to Washington Square, including the Triangle Shirtwaist Company. That company occupied floors eight through ten in the ten-story building. The fire began on the eighth floor, perhaps sparked by a discarded cigarette, and it quickly rose to the floors above. Almost all of Triangle's employees were immigrant teenage girls working 12 hours a day in what can only be described as a sweatshop. Many of these young women were trapped by the blaze. Of the four elevators, only one was fully operational. Of the two stairways that led to the street, one was locked to prevent theft, and the other could only open inwards. The building's overloaded fire escape collapsed during the fire, and the fire trucks that arrived on the scene had ladders that could only reach the sixth floor. It was all over in 18 minutes. The fire killed a total of 146 people. Some of the dead had either suffocated or been burned to death. Others were found lying in an elevator shaft, and more than 50 died jumping from the building's windows to escape the flames. Two of the victims who escaped the building died later due to their injuries.

A monument erected to remember the victims of the factory fire that claimed over a hundred lives.

The tragedy sparked outrage throughout the city. There were numerous protests, and reformers demanded a government investigation. These reformers approached Smith, urging that a commission to investigate the tragedy be formed that would include the best and brightest New York had to offer. Smith advised the reformers to push for a legislative committee instead of arguing that the legislature would have to approve any changes to the state code.

On June 11, 1911, New York's Governor signed a bill creating the Factory Investigating Commission. The legislation went beyond fire safety, as it was written in such a manner that allowed the Commission to investigate industrial work's general conditions. At its initial meeting, Robert Wagner was elected chairman, and Smith was chosen to serve as vice-chairman.

The Commission worked for a year and a half visiting factories, meeting with workers, and holding public hearings. The Commission's findings resulted in the enactment of more than 30 laws aimed at securing the health and safety of workers. The work of the Commission would serve as a model for other states throughout the country to follow. As for Smith, his personal experience on the committee served as an eye-opener. His meetings with workers in their homes had touched him deeply. As chronicled in the Slayton biography from that point on, he had little time for those who favored, among other things, night work for women. Facing these folks, Smith would respond, "You can't tell me. I've seen these women. I've seen their faces. I've seen them!"

In 1912, Teddy Roosevelt split the Republican Party when he decided, after failing to secure the Republican nomination, to run for president as the standard-bearer for the Progressive or the Bull Moose Party as it was commonly known. The split resulted in the election of a Democrat, Woodrow Wilson, and in New York, Democrats won the Governorship and both houses in the legislature. Smith, who had already emerged as a Democratic Party leader, was elected Speaker of the Assembly. Smith took the job seriously, and he hoped to use his newfound power to advance the people's interests, but Tammany was about to interfere with his plans.

The new governor of New York was William Sulzer. He had been handpicked and supported by "The Hall" mainly because he had always been loyal to that organization. Once in office, he began to change his tune, supporting, among other things, the direct primary. He went even further, denying patronage positions to Tammany and awarding state contracts to those not in bed with Tammany. These actions infuriated Charles Murphy, who managed to get the legislature to appoint an investigative committee to look into the governor's campaign tactics. The committee turned up slight irregularities about fundraising. Further inquiries resulted when Sulzer refused to cooperate, and these turned up serious charges relating to the governor's use of campaign funds to speculate on the stock exchange.

Acting on Murphy's orders, the Assembly voted to impeach the governor. As Speaker, Smith had no choice but to lead the charge in this regard, and his actions made him appear as little more than a puppet held on the end of strings controlled by Tammany. Some newspapers reported that Smith was urging Murphy, apparently without success, to let the matter end. While the impeachment proved successful, there is little doubt that the proceedings damaged Smith's image and the Democratic Party. In the elections of 1913, the Republicans regained control, and Smith found himself the minority leader. Smith would serve in this position until 1915 when he was elected Sheriff of New York County.

Enter William Randolph Hearst. The very wealthy and flamboyant newspaper magnate let it be known that, despite the many sacrifices he would have to make, he was willing to be the Democratic candidate for the office of Governor of New York in 1918. Charles Murphy had no desire to see Hearst take up residence in Albany. Murphy wanted a man that Tammany could count on, and with that in mind, he used his influence to get Smith the nomination. Hearst was persuaded to support Smith in return for the endorsement of the municipal ownership of public utilities, which was an issue close to the publisher's heart.

The 1917 campaign marked the first time that Smith had to face an issue that would dog him throughout his political life: prohibition. The anti-saloon league looked into Smith's legislative history and decided that a Smith win equated a loss for prohibition proponents. The election marked the first, though most assuredly not the last, time that the dry forces would attack Smith.

The election was also the first time women would vote in a New York State election. Belle Moskowitz joined the campaign and guided Smith on how to approach women's issues. By the end of the campaign, she had impressed Smith to the point that she would remain one of his closest and most trusted advisors throughout his public life.

When the votes were counted, Smith prevailed by less than 15,000 votes. His margins in the city boroughs proved to be the difference. In the end, he had been elected by city dwellers and immigrants who had formed the opinion, based on his record, that Smith was someone on whom they could count. Ethnic groups supported him en masse (particularly the Irish), and the young lad from the fourth Ward now found himself to be the chief executive of the largest state in the union.

When Smith took the oath of office to begin his first term as governor, he had no idea that he would repeat it three more times. His closest advisors, all of whom happened to be descendants of German Jews, were the aforementioned Belle Moskowitz, Robert Moses (See Chapter 15), and Joseph Proskauer, who had made a name for himself as a judge. The one trait the three shared was a genuine admiration for Smith, the man. Proskauer's daughter would later recall that, while her father looked up to very few men, he idolized Smith.

Smith had taken office after both World War I and the Russian revolution. The entire country was going through a "Red Scare," and the New York legislature passed a series of bills in response. The lawmakers wanted to create a police agency to chase down and prosecute radical elements. They wished to allow the courts to strike any name from the ballot if they deemed that person subversive. They wanted a loyalty test for teachers and private schools' licensing based on the institutions' abilities to teach and foster American values. Finally, they created Americanization classes for immigrants.

Smith vetoed every measure. He and Proskauer prepared statements supporting the vetoes. Smith pointedly criticized creating a secret police force; he said that the loyalty measure would deprive teachers of their freedom to think. Further, it would eliminate from the teaching ranks those with the courage to question existing institutions. Smith summed up his position by stating, "It is a confession of the weakness of our own faith in the righteousness of our cause, when we attempt to suppress by laws those who do not agree with us." It would be an understatement to say that Smith was disappointed in the performance of the legislature in his initial term. While he may have vetoed their attacks on civil liberties, they had failed to pass any of the reform measures proposed by his administration.

In 1920, a presidential election year, Smith would stand for reelection. However, before he could concentrate on that, he had to prepare for the National Democratic Convention, held in San Francisco. Smith would head the delegation from what was then the largest state in the union. For the first time, his name was placed in nomination for the highest office in the land. The Democrats knew that they had little chance to win in 1920, and they nominated James Cox from Ohio for president and a young New Yorker, Franklin Delano Roosevelt as his running mate.

In the Empire State, Smith found himself in a tough race against the Republican nominee, Nathan Miller. Smith, as was his habit, tried to run on his record. Miller would have none of it as he campaigned against the Wilson administration and Smith's ties to it as a fellow Democrat. Smith lost by 74,000 votes while the Democratic presidential candidate, Cox, lost New York by more than a million votes. In New York City, Cox had managed to pull in a mere 40 percent of the vote while Smith captured 71 percent. As a result, despite the Republican landslide, Smith was still viewed as a significant asset to the Democratic Party.

By 1922, William Randolph Hearst was back in the picture. He and Smith were by now bitter enemies. During Smith's initial administration, the founder of yellow journalism had accused Smith of starving New York City's children by not reducing milk prices. Even though Governor Smith had little authority when it came to the cost to the public of agricultural commodities, Heart's papers had gone so far as to publish cartoons showing Smith climbing over children's tombstones to reach the governor's chair. At the time, Smith gave a speech where he described Hearst as "a man as mean and low as I can picture." Well, in 1922, that man was pushing hard to secure the gubernatorial nomination.

Smith didn't want to run for office again. He was now the chief operating officer of a trucking company and was doing very well financially. Murphy, who still ran Tammany Hall, tried to convince Smith to run for United States Senator on a Hearst ticket. Smith refused to consider teaming up with Hearst. What finally drew Smith into the race for governor was realizing that Hearst would be the nominee if he didn't enter the contest.

Once he announced his intentions, it was clear that Smith would get the party's nod. However, Murphy remained concerned about the influence of the Hearst forces. He now decided that Hearst should be the Senate candidate. Nobody had any objections to this except Smith, who took the position that if Hearst was on the ticket, he was off. Murphy was forced to settle on nominating a Hearst supporter for senator. In the end, that was enough to get the Hearst papers to endorse Smith, though only as the lesser of two evils.

In the general election, Nathan Miller no longer had Woodrow Wilson to run against, and he made more than a few mistakes. For instance, during a speech to the League of Women Voters, he described the organization as a menace to representative government. On Election Day, Smith surged to victory, winning by the largest margin in the state's history. The size of the victory made Smith one of the most important Democratic politicians in the country.

During his second term as governor, Smith championed the idea of administrative reform to modernize how New York State was governed. It would be an understatement to characterize the Empire State's governance as archaic in 1922. For example, there were over 150 department heads, but only a few reported to the Governor. Each of these departments played their hand in making an annual budget, which was maddening. Smith knew things had to change if the Governor was going to be in charge of running the state. He stated publicly that the reorganization of state government was his top goal because "in its present dislocated, disorganized and scattered form," it could not possibly "render the services it should, nor even be brought in harmony with the needs and desires of the people."

Smith worked with Moskowitz and Moses to reach this goal. Eventually, 189 state offices were combined into a cabinet-level series of departments. Changes to the budget system came with the governor creating a budget and submitting it to the legislature for approval. Years later, a Republican governor named Thomas Dewey would state, "We are indebted to Governor Alfred E. Smith more than any other man for the modern framework of government."

Then there was Prohibition. Suffice it to say that Smith was never a big fan of the 18th amendment. When the amendment became part of the constitution, its advocates fully expected that states would play a big part in enforcing the measure. In New York, a law known as the Mullin-Gage Act gave the state the authority to pursue liquor violations. In May of 1923, on the last day they were in session, the legislature repealed the Mullin-Gage Act. Smith had 30 days to act on the repeal. He knew that if he signed the repeal, his anti-prohibition action would make national news. At the same time, he also knew that repealing the law would make him appear to be a hypocrite considering his publicly stated views on the subject.

Smith was under pressure from both sides. The anti-saloon league claimed a repeal could result in a constitutional crisis. On the other hand, old and powerful supporters like Charles Murphy (who had owned a saloon or two) pressured Smith to uphold the repeal. Smith worked long hours with Proskauer and Moskowitz, preparing his response to the repeal. On June 1, 1923, Smith signed the repeal. Smith's critics have pointed to this action as proof that as late as 1923, Smith was still in Tammany Hall's pocket. In his autobiography, Smith would record that he signed the repeal by allowing his conscience to be his guide. The authors don't buy the arguments that Smith bowed to Tammany pressures. They believe that he took action to be consistent with his past statements on the subject and because he thought it was the right thing to do.

The repeal did receive national attention. As detailed by Robert Slayton in his Smith biography, no less a personage than William Jennings Bryan, a three-time Democratic candidate for president, denounced Smith for the repeal. Bryan, by now an old workhorse, stated, "When the governor of the largest state in the Union boldly raises the black flag and offers to lead the representatives of the outlawed liquor traffic in their assault upon the nation's honor and the people's welfare, he must expect resistance from the defenders of the home, the school, and the Church." Bryan then issued a warning saying, "If the wets expect to obtain control of the Democratic Party and make it the mouthpiece of the underworld, they must prepare for such a struggle as they never had before."

Against this backdrop, Smith entered 1924 as an acknowledged contender for the Democratic nomination for president. No less a politician than Jim Farley (See Chapter 6), who would manage Franklin Roosevelt's first two presidential campaigns, wrote Smith expressing his view that the governor would be the nominee. One has to look no further than the rising opposition to a Smith candidacy, from a group growing in power known as the Ku Klux Klan, to see how serious his critics viewed his potential for success.

Smith supporters, led by Proskauer and Moscowitz, set up a campaign team with Franklin D. Roosevelt as the campaign manager. Smith received another positive bump when it was announced that the Democratic Convention would be held in New York City's Madison Square Garden. When the convention opened on June 24th, the Smith supporters were in high spirits. Smith's name would be placed in nomination two days later, and there was some debate within the campaign as to who should deliver the nominating speech. Proskauer's choice of Franklin Roosevelt prevailed though Smith himself questioned the choice. Proskauer explained the choice to Smith by telling him, "... you're a Bowery mick, and he's a Protestant patrician, and he'd take some of the curse off of you."

The appearance was Roosevelt's first since being stricken by polio. All of Madison Square Garden was silent as Roosevelt, assisted by his son James, made his way to the podium.

Though the microphone was only a few feet away, by the time he reached it, Roosevelt's face was covered in sweat, a testimony to the effort he had exerted. The speech, composed by Proskauer, called attention to the fact that Smith had transformed the politics of the nation's premier state and that he was ready to do the same for the entire nation. Then he delivered the line that would forever be associated with Smith, "He is the Happy Warrior of the political battlefield . . . Alfred E. Smith." A tremendous demonstration followed led by multiple bands playing different songs as the Smith supporters took to their feet to march between the aisles as a bank of fire sirens were started at the same time to accompany them.

On June 30th, the last scheduled day of the convention, the delegates began casting their votes. It would take 732 votes to nominate, and on the first ballot, William McAdoo led the way with 431 and 1/2 while Smith received 231. The day ended without naming a nominee. So, it went on day after day. Though they tried, neither candidate could break the deadlock and garner the necessary votes to secure the nomination. Days went by, and many delegates left and had to be replaced by alternates. As the balloting continued, Will Rogers offered some levity saying that years from now, children would ask their fathers if they were in the big war and that the response they would get was "no, but I went through the 1924 Democratic convention."

Finally, exhausted delegates decided on July 9th to nominate a compromise candidate John W. Davis on the 103rd ballot. Davis would go on to be overwhelmed by Calvin Coolidge in the general election. Meanwhile, Smith was re-elected Governor of New York as he would be again in 1926.

Thus, Smith served four two-year terms as governor of New York. By the time his fourth term expired in 1928, he could point to several accomplishments beyond modernizing state government. He created the Council of State Parks and made Robert Moses its chairman. Together they built the nation's first state park system. The state park system was not popular with many of New York's wealthy citizens. One of them told Smith that the new parks would result in his town being "overrun with rabble from the city." Smith replied in anger, "Rabble! That's me you're talking about." When the millionaire tried to change the mood by jokingly asking where a rich man should go when he wishes to be alone, Smith suggested he visit an institution for the mentally insane.

Also, under Smith, New York's civil service system was reformed. As the number of automobiles on the road increased dramatically, more than 3,000 miles of highways were constructed during his administration. He had earned a national reputation as a politician who had made government more efficient, effective, and responsive in meeting social needs. Laws governing workman's compensation were strengthened until they became a model for the nation. In addition, with the help of Frances Perkins (who would become Labor Secretary under Franklin Roosevelt), laws were put in place to protect women and children in the workplace. Perhaps his most outstanding achievement as governor was that he had grasped the reins of power and administered the government to the public's benefit in a fair manner.

The year 1928 was a presidential election year. President Coolidge had announced that he would not seek another term. So, both Republicans and Democrats were searching for candidates. The Republicans nominated

Herbert Hoover on the first ballot, and it was up to the Democrats to provide the opposition.

The party of Jefferson had decided to hold their convention in Houston, Texas, becoming the first major party to meet in a Southern state since the Civil War. Smith was the acknowledged front runner as the convention began on June 26th, though there were those in Houston who were clearly in the anti-Smith camp. For example, women supporting prohibition called for a season of prayer so that a drunkard would not lead the Democratic Party.

Once again, Smith's name was placed in nomination by Franklin Roosevelt. By now, speaking on behalf of Smith had become a Roosevelt habit, and he rose to the occasion. He went down a list reciting the things that people looked for in a leader and explained how, not only did Smith possess those qualities, but he had also put them into practice. His voice, climbing and growing stronger with each word, he finished by stating, "We offer one who has the will to win, who not only deserves success but demands it. Victory is his habit, the happy warrior, Alfred E. Smith." The speech, which was followed by the traditional parade of delegates, was universally praised.

The balloting began with Smith and close friends gathered around a radio back in Albany. By the conclusion of the first ballot, Smith was ten votes shy of the magic number needed to be nominated. With that, Senator Atlee Pomerene of Ohio was recognized by the convention chairman. Standing before the convention, he announced that all of Ohio's 45 votes should be recorded in favor of Al Smith. He had become the first Roman Catholic to be nominated for the highest office in the land by a major party. Back in Albany, Belle Moscowitz told Bob Moses, "Bob, it's over." She was wrong; it was just beginning.

While some states followed Ohio's lead and switched their votes to Smith, others did not. Notably, several southern states, including Texas and Virginia, had failed to endorse Smith. Many believed their reluctance to support Smith stemmed from their view that Smith was anti-prohibition. If that was the case, it didn't take long for the candidate to confirm their fears. The following day Smith sent a telegram to the convention to accept the nomination. He promised to stand by the platform, which as a means of avoiding directly confronting the prohibition issue, pledged to uphold and enforce the Constitution. Smith's telegram didn't stop there as it when on to state that it was common knowledge "that I believe there should be fundamental changes in . . . national prohibition." Smith added that in his view, his duty as a leader required him to ". . . point the way which, in my opinion, leads to a sane, sensible solution of a condition which . . . is entirely unsatisfactory to the great mass of our people." To put it lightly, the telegram was viewed by the drys in the Democratic Party as a declaration of war.

The campaign began, and Smith soon found that he was up against more than Herbert Hoover. Smith had to deal with the religious question even more so than another Catholic candidate who would be nominated in 1960. In 1928, many Americans were convinced that a Smith victory would result in the Pope running The United States. The Ku Klux Klan, far more influential and powerful than they would be three decades later, warned that the Pope planned to move to America once Smith was elected. Some estimate that the Klan spent more than two million dollars sending anti-Smith literature nationwide. When Smith headed west on his campaign train, he was greeted by burning crosses placed on the hills along the route. This both angered and disappointed the candidate, who was prone to give all Americans more credit than deserved. Trying to make light of the matter after seeing the crosses, he said to Joseph Proskauer, "Joe, how did they know that you were on the train?"

But it wasn't just extreme groups like the Klan that opposed Smith. Established and well-regarded Protestant ministers and publications came out against Smith. One magazine, *Christian Century*, said that "a real issue exists between Catholicism and American Institutions." A Methodist Bishop wrote that Smith's very nomination signaled the rising of the "unassimilated elements" in the nation's cities against the ideals set forth by the founding fathers. The bishop concluded that Smith was un-American. Protestant ministers preached to their congregations, telling them that if Smith became president, their marriages would be annulled, and their children would be labeled illegitimate. Some told their flock that a vote for Smith would send them straight to hell. One Florida school board voted to have a note placed in each child's lunch pail warning that you would not be allowed to read or own a Bible under a Smith presidency. To top it off, pictures of the then under construction Holland Tunnel were distributed, describing it as a pathway to the Vatican basement in Rome.

Faced with these and other ridiculous charges, Smith did what he could to respond. He said, "If there were any conflict between religious loyalty to the Catholic faith and patriotic loyalty to the United States, I, of all men, could not have escaped it, because I have not been a silent man, but a battler for social and political reform. These battles would, in their very nature, disclose this conflict, if there were any." He also said that he did not want any catholic to vote for him based on his religion, stating that anyone who felt that Mister Hoover could do more for the country should cast their vote accordingly.

On Election Day, the feelings in the Smith camp were mixed. Frances Perkins felt that religious prejudice was so deeply rooted that the campaign was in trouble. Belle Moscowitz, on the other hand, felt that things were going well and remained optimistic. On the day votes were cast, Smith's wife Katie was celebrating a birthday, and she confidently predicted that she was going to get the one present she wanted.

It was over early, and it wasn't close. Hoover won with over 58 percent of the popular vote and amassed 444 electoral votes. The hardest blow for Smith to endure was losing New York by just over 100,000 votes. Also, Hoover won in Virginia, North Carolina, and Florida as for the first time since the Civil War, the South failed to remain solidly Democratic. Even the Southern states that went for Smith did so by smaller margins than Democrats had enjoyed in previous elections.

The analysis of the election began shortly after the official results were announced. The common conclusion was that Hoover had won because of the booming economy. Hoover himself agreed, claiming that the issue of religion did not affect the results. Democratic leaders did not share this belief throughout the country. Franklin Roosevelt, who was elected Smith's successor as New York Governor, polled his party's leaders. The

Al Smith's grave which looks out over the city he loved.

Stone that notes Smith's service as the Governor of the state of New York.

results indicated that more than 55 percent believed that religion led to Smith's defeat; less than two percent felt that the economy turned the election. One Catholic reacting to the election stated that he was satisfied that a Catholic could not be elected president while the present generation still lived. In Oklahoma City, a prominent Democrat named Ross Lillard summed it up: "they wiped us off the face of the earth down here because of religion, do not let anybody tell you different, that is what did it, and this question needs to be settled someday . . . or the nation cannot stand." Smith, who had once said the following about the Klan, "The Negroes can stand it, the Jews can stand it, the Catholics can stand it, it's the United States that can't stand it," had learned that the country had not come along as far as his neighbors in the old fourth ward.

After the election, Smith expressed that he did not expect to run for public office ever again. For a time, he took up authoring a book titled *Up to Now,* which sold reasonably well. He became the president of Empire State Inc., the corporation that built the Empire State Building, where he worked out of a top-floor office. The job turned into a nightmare for Smith once the depression hit and many floors of the storied building remained empty.

Meanwhile, Smith's relationship with his successor began to take a turn for the worse. Roosevelt, who believed he had to make his name as governor, did consult Smith on occasion, but that was not enough to satisfy the now ex-governor. There is evidence that Smith early on did not support Roosevelt to succeed him. According to James Farley, it was Smith's view that Roosevelt, due to his physical condition, couldn't be expected to meet the office's demands. The truth be told, Smith liked Roosevelt, but he vastly underestimated him.

The year 1932 was another presidential election year, and as Smith viewed the political landscape, he concluded that things, in light of the Great Depression, looked promising for the Democrats. Smith probably enjoyed a joke that was going around at the time involving an immigrant applying for citizenship. During his examination, the judge asked who the president of the United States is. The immigrant responds, "Al Smith." Hearing the reply, the judge repeats the question and gets the same answer. Finally, the judge asks, "why do you keep saying Al Smith?" The immigrant responds, "Well, the Republicans said that if Smith was elected, we'd have a stock market crash, unemployment, and bread lines . . . so Al must be president."

Having caught the presidential bug, Smith decided to try for the nomination once again. Ironically, Smith's most formidable opponent was none other than Franklin Roosevelt. At the Democratic convention, Smith worked with both of his old enemies, William McAdoo and William Randolph Hearst, to stop Roosevelt. For three ballots, the stop Roosevelt coalition had its way as Roosevelt's vote total failed to reach the number needed to seal the nomination. The convention then adjourned until the following day.

James Farley, Roosevelt's campaign manager, went to work. Farley and another Roosevelt supporter named Joseph Kennedy convinced Hearst that blocking Roosevelt would lead to a deadlocked convention that would probably turn to either Smith or Newton Baker as the nominee. Hearst couldn't bear the thought of either man being nominated and agreed to accept Roosevelt. The next day on the fourth ballot, Roosevelt won easily. It took some time for the wounds to heal. Still, Smith eventually supported the Democratic ticket and was one of the first to congratulate Roosevelt when he won the general election, taking, incidentally, those Southern states that had gone for Hoover in 1928.

Smith would break with Roosevelt again over New Deal programs and expand the power of the federal government. Smith supported the Republicans in both the 1936 and the 1940 Presidential elections. It would take the rise of fascism to bring Smith and Roosevelt back together. When it came to opposing Hitler, Smith said that Roosevelt spoke for the nation and that no right-thinking American could oppose him. Shortly before his death, someone asked Smith what he thought of Roosevelt. Smith replied, "He's the kindest man who ever lived, but don't get in his way."

On May 4, 1944, Smith's wife died after a bout with cancer. Five months later, on October 4th, at the age of 70, Smith suffered a heart attack and joined her. As in life, the two were laid to rest side by side in Calvary Cemetery in Queens, New York.

If You Go:

Several other prominent people call Calvary their final resting place. Among them is the librettist **Lorenzo de Ponte** who provided the lyrics for Mozart's most famous operas. While his exact burial location on the grounds is unknown, you can still visit a memorial within the cemetery.

Tombstone of Martin Sheridan

Baseball great and Hall of Famer **William Henry "Wee Willie" Keeler** is also buried at Calvary. Known for his slogan "hit 'em where they ain't," the baseball star's 44-game hitting streak was only surpassed by one man: Joe DiMaggio.

The well-known character actor **Joe Spinell** is at Calvary as well. He is best known for his roles as Mafioso Willie Cicci in *The Godfather* and *The Godfather Part II*. Also, he played the loan shark who employed Rocky Balboa as a collector in *Rocky* and *Rocky II*.

Finally, not far from Al Smith's grave, you can find the final resting place of four-time Olympic gold medal winner **Martin John Sheridan**.

22

"The Solitude of Self"

Elizabeth Stanton

County: Bronx • Town: New York
Buried at Woodlawn Cemetery
517 East 233rd Street

Elizabeth Cady Stanton was a woman suffragist and writer who pushed the envelope as a social activist by advocating issues beyond voting rights. She cared about women's custody and parental rights, property rights, divorce law, and birth control. She attracted a lot of attention and used the spotlight to further her ideas for more than 50 years.

She was born on November 12, 1815, in Johnstown, New York, the daughter of Margaret Livingston and Daniel Cady, a distinguished lawyer, state assemblyman, and congressman. She was the eighth of eleven children; five of her siblings died in early childhood or infancy. Later on, her father, Daniel, would become a circuit court judge, a justice of New York's Supreme Court (a trial-level court of general jurisdiction), and an *ex officio* judge on the state's highest tribunal, the New York Court of Appeals, in 1849.

Elizabeth received her education at the Johnstown Academy and at Emma Willard's Troy Female Seminary, where she graduated in 1832. Her early exposure to the law at home and at dinners with New York's legal establishment and the many young men who came to study with her father caused Stanton to realize how the law favored men. Married women had virtually no property, income, employment, or even custody rights over their children.

Slavery was legal in New York until 1827, and like many men at the time, Stanton's father owned a slave. His name was Peter Teabout, and

Elizabeth Cody Stanton

he took care of Stanton and her sister, Margaret, when they were young. Teabout is remembered fondly in Stanton's memoir *Eighty Years and More* and may have influenced her later work in the anti-slavery movement.

As Elizabeth entered her 20s, she became close to her cousin, Gerrit Smith, and through him was introduced to Henry Brewster Stanton.

Stanton was an agent for the American Anti-Slavery Society and an eloquent speaker for the immediate abolition of slavery. Elizabeth was quite taken with Henry Stanton, and she married him in 1840 against her parents' wishes. She requested, and it came to be, that the phrase "promise to obey" be removed from the wedding vows. After the wedding in Johnstown, the Stantons sailed to England to attend the World's Anti-Slavery Convention. The convention refused to seat American female delegates, including Lucretia Mott. This controversy took up most of the first day of the convention, and Stanton later claimed that it was there and then that the American women's rights movement began.

Soon after returning to the United States, Henry agreed to complete his legal training with his father-in-law in Johnstown. In 1843, the Stantons moved to Boston, where Henry joined a law firm. The couple would have seven children between 1842 and 1859. Elizabeth enjoyed Boston's intellectual and social stimulation and the constant exposure to the abolitionist movement with such people as Frederick Douglass, Louisa May Alcott, and Ralph Waldo Emerson. She also maintained her friendship with Lucretia Mott and her circle of anti-slavery advocates.

In 1847, the Stantons moved from Boston to Seneca Falls, New York. Although she assumed primary responsibility for the children and enjoyed being a mother, she found herself bored and even depressed by the lack of stimulation found in upstate New York. She felt fully and firmly committed to the women's rights movement and was ready to become involved in the struggle to secure those rights.

Stanton, Lucretia Mott, and a handful of other women organized the Seneca Falls Convention, held July 19-20, 1848. At this meeting, the group of attendees (numbering more than 300) drew up its "Declaration of Sentiments" and took the lead in proposing that women be granted the right to vote. They argued that consistency with the American Revolution's fundamental principles required an end to women's taxation without representation and government without their consent. The final resolutions, which included voting rights for women, were passed with Frederick Douglass's support, who attended and informally spoke at the convention.

Soon after the convention, Stanton was invited to speak at a second women's rights convention in Rochester, New York, solidifying her role as a movement leader. After these events in New York, women's rights advocates' conventions became commonplace from New England to Indiana. Two publications for women became popular: *The Lily*, which was the first women's newspaper; and *Una*, which was a women's rights periodical. Stanton was a frequent contributor to both publications. In her articles, she embraced a wide range of changes that women of her generation were pursuing, such as entering medical schools, wearing short hair, experimenting with more rational dress, writing novels, and taking jobs unusual for women to have.

Stanton met Susan B. Anthony in Seneca Falls in 1851, and as a result, her participation in the women's rights movement intensified. Anthony was an activist in the temperance movement, and with Stanton, they helped found the Women's State Temperance Society in New York. Stanton presided as the society's president until she was voted out of office because of her views on equal rights and her conviction that women needed the right to divorce. Stanton alienated many supporters by suggesting that drunkenness be made sufficient cause for divorce.

In 1854, Stanton and Anthony launched their first campaign to change specific laws regarding women. They worked well as a team. Stanton was tied down with children and a frequently absent husband who traveled a lot on business and abolitionist activities. Anthony's greater mobility was an asset and allowed Stanton to craft the arguments that she would then take to meetings and conferences and lobby the legislature. Single and having no children, Anthony had the time to do the speaking and traveling. Stanton scripted many of Anthony's speeches. Stanton's interests were broader than Anthony's (whose primary focus was suffrage), but the two remained close friends and colleagues until death some 50 years after they met.

While both Elizabeth and Henry Stanton considered their marriage of 47 years a success, it was not without its tensions and disagreements. Henry disagreed with the idea of women's suffrage, as did Elizabeth's father. It's not

Stanton and Susan B. Anthony

hard to imagine some of the spirited arguments that must have taken place at family functions!

Stanton and Anthony's efforts bore some success in 1860, when they achieved a significant revision in New York state laws regarding married women's economic rights, mothers' custody rights, and rights for widows. In 1862, the Stantons moved to New York City following a federal appointment for Henry Stanton. A year later, Stanton and Anthony formed the Women's Loyal National League to campaign for a Constitutional amendment that would abolish slavery. In the largest petition drive in the nation's history up to that time, the League collected nearly 400,000 signatures in support of abolishing slavery and presented them to Congress. This drive significantly assisted the passage of the Thirteenth Amendment, which ended slavery in the United States. The League disbanded in August 1864 after it became clear the amendment would be approved. It was the first national women's political organization in the U.S.

Working for the right to vote.

When Congress opened the Fourteenth Amendment discussion at the end of 1865, Stanton joined the anti-slavery leadership in opposing educated suffrage or other restrictions on voting rights. Both Stanton and Anthony broke with their abolitionist backgrounds and lobbied against the Fourteenth and Fifteenth Amendments' ratification. They were angry that their former allies refused to demand that the amendments be changed to include women. Eventually, Stanton's oppositional rhetoric took on racial overtones and caused a rift between herself and many civil rights leaders, including Douglass.

In 1866, Stanton, Anthony, and several others drafted a universal suffrage petition demanding that the right to vote be given without considering sex or race. The petition was introduced and supported by Pennsylvania Congressman Thaddeus Stevens (see *Keystone Tombstones Volume 2).* The effort failed, however, and the Fourteenth Amendment was passed in 1868 without change.

In 1869, disagreement over the Fifteenth Amendment split the women's rights movement. The National Woman Suffrage Association (NWSA) was founded by Anthony and Stanton, the latter serving as its president for 21 years. The NWSA opposed the passage of the Fifteenth Amendment without changes to include females. The larger, more moderate American Woman Suffrage Association (AWSA) supported the amendment as written. The amendment passed as initially written in 1870.

In the following decade, both Stanton and Anthony took the position that the Fourteenth and Fifteenth Amendments did give women the right to vote by virtue of the definition of "citizen." This argument came to be called "the new departure" in women's rights circles. Anthony went to the polls and attempted to vote in 1872 and Stanton in 1880. It would not be until 1920—14 and 18 years after Anthony's and Stanton's deaths, respectively—that women obtained the right to vote throughout the United States.

In 1890, the two major women's rights organizations would merge into the National American Woman Suffrage Association (NAWSA), and Stanton would serve as its president for two years. In 1895, the NAWSA repudiated the ideas she published in her two-part book entitled *The Woman's Bible*, which argued that the Bible and organized religion played a role in denying women their rights.

Around that same time and getting on in her years, Stanton stopped touring the country as a lecturer, which she had done for 12 years. She moved out of her house in Tenafly, New Jersey, where she had lived since 1868, and after that lived chiefly with her children, sometimes in Europe. Her husband Henry died in 1887.

On January 18, 1892, Stanton appeared before the House Judiciary Committee in Washington, D.C., and delivered what many think was the most important speech of her career, "The Solitude of Self." Stanton opened with a summation of common arguments for women's rights, such as the right of all citizens to equal rights based on a concept of human beings as members of society. Then she turned these ideas on their head, basing her argument for women's rights on a concept of human beings as solitary, self-reliant individuals. According to Stanton, both men and women were destined to make the voyage of life alone. To succeed, both must be empowered with the necessary knowledge and skills. After nearly five decades of fighting for female suffrage, her last appearance was on the Washington stage.

In 1898, she published her autobiography, *Eighty Years and More*, a stirring depiction of American women's early struggles toward equality. Four years later, on October 26, 1902 (two weeks before her 87th birthday), Elizabeth Cady Stanton died of heart failure in the New York City apartment she shared at the time with two of her grown children.

Monument at Stanton's gravesite.

She left behind an unmailed letter to Theodore Roosevelt seeking his endorsement of woman suffrage.

At her funeral, the table where she wrote and signed the famous "Declaration of Sentiments" was placed beside her casket. It is now on display at the Smithsonian Museum of American History. She was interred in Woodlawn Cemetery in the Bronx.

The Nineteenth Amendment to the United States Constitution was ratified on August 18, 1920. It prohibits any U.S. citizen from being denied the right to vote based on sex. After its ratification, Stanton was commemorated along with Lucretia Mott and Susan B. Anthony in a sculpture by Adelaide Johnson unveiled in 1921. Initially kept in the crypt of the U.S. Capitol, the sculpture was moved in 1997 to its current, more prominent location in the Capitol rotunda.

Her houses in Seneca Falls and Tenafly have both been declared National Historic Landmarks. A World War II troop transport ship was named after her. The USS *Elizabeth C. Stanton* received five battle stars for service during the war.

If You Go:

Woodlawn Cemetery is a national treasure and has many famous and interesting graves. The "If You Go" portion of the chapter on **Nellie Bly** (Chapter 3) lists some more notable ones. Two others are:

- **James Bailey** (1847–1906), who along with Phineas Taylor "P.T." Barnum, founded the Barnum and Bailey Circus, which became known as "The Greatest Show on Earth." After Bailey's death, the circus became Ringling Brothers and Barnum and Bailey Circus, which still operates today.
- **Frank Winfield Woolworth** (1852–1919) is best known for founding the F.W. Woolworth Company, which operated as a chain of discount stores across the United States specializing in merchandise that cost five and ten cents. In 1913, he built his corporate headquarters on Broadway in Manhattan. When it opened, the Woolworth Building became the tallest building in the world at 60 stories/792 feet, a title it held until 1930 when two taller edifices opened within a month of each other: the 40 Wall Street building (71 stories/921 feet and known today as "The Trump Building"), and the Chrysler Building (at 77 stories/1,046 feet).

23

"The Toast of the Town"

Ed Sullivan

County: Westchester • Town: Hartsdale
Buried at Ferncliff Cemetery
280 Secor Road

Ed Sullivan is best remembered as the creator and host of the television variety program *Toast of the Town*, later officially renamed *The Ed Sullivan Show,* which set a record as the longest-running variety show in U.S. broadcast history. The basis for his massive appeal was a mystery to those who tried to analyze it. He was not witty, had no real talent, was bashful, clumsy, self-conscious, forgetful, and tongue-tied. The critics unmercifully panned him for these faults in the early years, and the *New York Times* said that "he was so honestly ill-at-ease that viewers came to be affectionately sorry for him."

In his early years, Sullivan suffered from camera-fright and rarely smiled. He became known as "The Great Stone Face." His stiff posture and large neck made many believe he suffered from various dire ailments. Despite all this, the bottom line was the public loved his show. He was an excellent judge of talent, and he stuck to being the master of ceremonies, i.e., introducing the acts, then getting out of the way.

Edward Vincent Sullivan was born in Harlem on September 28, 1901. His father, Peter, was a customs house employee of Irish descent. After the death of Edward's twin brother, Daniel, and younger sister, Elizabeth, the family moved to Port Chester, New York. There, young Sullivan attended St. Mary's Parochial School and Port Chester High School. He reportedly excelled in athletics, earning 12 letters. In 1917,

Ed Sullivan

he ran away from home to Chicago, where he tried to enlist in the U.S. Navy but was turned away because of his age.

He returned home, graduated from high school, and then worked for a short while as a reporter for the *Port Chester Daily Item*. In 1919, he landed a job as a sports reporter for the *New York Evening Mail* until the paper shut down in 1923. He continued to bounce around as a reporter from 1923 until 1927, when he joined the *New York Evening Graphic* as a sports reporter and then sports editor. In 1929, Walter Winchell, one of the original gossip columnists and the most powerful entertainment reporter of his day, left the *Evening Graphic* to join the Hearst syndicate's *Daily Mirror*. That opened the way for Sullivan, who took over for Winchell as the *Evening Graphic's* theatre columnist.

Sullivan wrote a column called *Little Old New York*, which focused on Broadway shows and gossip. He also did show business news broadcasts on radio. The New York Daily News later picked up his column, and soon thereafter, Sullivan became Winchell's main rival. He set up an unofficial headquarters in Manhattan's El Morocco nightclub, just as Winchell had his at the Stork Club. During these years as a columnist, Sullivan also produced vaudeville shows, often appearing in them as master of ceremonies. He would frequently organize a benefit revue for various causes, including two held at Madison Square Garden during World War II. He helped raise $226,000 for Army Emergency Relief and another $249,000 for the American Red Cross.

It was through emceeing that Sullivan broke into the new world of television. In 1947, he served as master of ceremonies for the Harvest Moon Ball, an annual event sponsored by the Daily News that began in the mid-1930s. It was one of the biggest amateur couples-dance contests held in the United States. The year that Sullivan emceed, the event was also carried on television by the Columbia Broadcasting System (CBS). A Columbia manager named Worthington Miner was so impressed by Sullivan's showmanship that he hired him to be master of ceremonies for the new television variety show *Toast of the Town*. The show debuted in June 1948 from the Maxine Elliott Theatre on West 39th Street. It featured Dean Martin and Jerry Lewis, singer Monica Lewis, and Broadway composers Richard Rodgers and Oscar Hammerstein II, who previewed the score of their then-new show *South Pacific*.

Television critics gave the new show—and particularly the host—poor reviews. Sponsors threatened to pull their advertising dollars unless CBS replaced Sullivan. Ed was a fighter, though, and battled hard to book the best talent he could. He also had the full backing of William Paley, the head of CBS at the time, who stood firmly behind him. Sullivan, on occasion, gave up some of his salary to pay for guests.

Harriet Van Horne, a well-known newspaper columnist and television critic for the *New York World-Telegram*, wrote of Sullivan: "He got where he is not by having a personality, but by having no personality—he is the commonest common denominator." In response, Sullivan wrote her a short note:

> *Dear Miss Van Horne,*
> *You bitch.*
> *Sincerely,*
> *Ed Sullivan*

When Alan King was asked about Ed Sullivan, he said, "Ed does nothing, but he does it better than anyone else in television."

Sullivan's sense of humor helped him survive the harsh criticism. He even encouraged impersonators such as John Byner, Frank Gorshin, Rich Little, and Will Jordan to imitate him on his show. Johnny Carson and Joan Rivers also did impressions of Sullivan. The impressionists exaggerated his stiffness, raised shoulders, and nasal voice in mocking some of his commonly used introductions such as: "And now, right here on this stage . . ."; "For all you youngsters out there . . ."; and "A really big shew . . ."

In January 1953, *The Ed Sullivan Show* moved to CBS-TV Studio 50 at Broadway and 53rd Street in mid-town Manhattan. That studio was renamed The Ed Sullivan Theater in 1967, which later became the home of *The Late Show with David Letterman* from 1993 until 2015, and as of this writing is the current home of *The Late Show with Stephen Colbert.*

One of the most important contributions Sullivan will be remembered for is how he bucked the system and embraced African American performers, often giving them their first television breaks. He was a respected star maker because of the number of performers who became big names after appearing on the show (which officially changed its name to *The Ed Sullivan Show* in 1955). He had a knack for identifying talent and paid a great deal of money to get that talent on his show. He supported performers with a passion regardless of race, introducing an audience to legends like Nat King Cole, Harry Bellefonte, Sammy Davis Jr., Ella Fitzgerald, and many others.

According to author Jerry Bowles (author of *A Thousand Sundays: The Story of the Ed Sullivan Show*), "Sullivan once had a Ford executive thrown out of the theater when he suggested that Sullivan stop booking so many black acts." In Cleveland, a Ford dealer objected to Sullivan embracing the tap dancer/actor Bill "Bojangles" Robinson at the end of his performance. "Sullivan had to be physically restrained from beating the man to a pulp," wrote Bowles. When Robinson later died penniless, it was Sullivan who paid for his Harlem funeral. It was just one of the many acts of quiet personal generosity for which Ed was known among his friends.

He was a close friend of Louis Armstrong (*see* Chapter 1). In the early to mid-1960s, Sullivan embraced Motown and presented many Motown acts, including The Supremes, who appeared 17 times. In 1969, Sullivan presented the Jackson 5 with their first single, "I Want You Back." He also helped break the comedy world's race barrier by presenting comedians such as Richard Pryor, Flip Wilson, and Bill Cosby.

Perhaps what Ed Sullivan is most remembered for is that he gave us two of the most memorable, iconic moments in television history: first with Elvis Presley's legendary appearance. Then eight years later, the live American debut of The Beatles.

When Elvis hit number one on the charts in 1956 with the song "Heartbreak Hotel," Sullivan insisted that his act was vulgar and distasteful and that he would never have him on his show. When Steve Allen had Elvis on in July of that year, it turned out to be a ratings blockbuster. The very next day, Sullivan booked Elvis for three appearances.

Presley made his first appearance on September 9, 1956, but Sullivan could not take part in the show's airing. He and his son-in-law were in a near-fatal car accident a few weeks before. The accident knocked out all his teeth and broke his ribs. He was watching from his hospital room when guest host Charles Laughton introduced Presley. At the time, Elvis was filming the movie *Love Me Tender* in Hollywood, and as a result, he could not perform at Sullivan's studio in New York City. Instead, the broadcast emanated from Los Angeles, where Presley sang from CBS Television City. Elvis did two segments on the show, singing "Don't Be Cruel" and "Love Me Tender" in the first and "Ready Teddy" and "Hound Dog" in the second. The show captured 82.6% of the TV audience.

It bothered Sullivan not to have been the first to present Elvis, and he was determined to be the one who grabbed the next big sensation. In November 1963, Sullivan witnessed Beatlemania firsthand while at London's Heathrow Airport as the band returned to England from Sweden. He immediately booked John, Paul, George, and Ringo. With Sullivan's now-iconic introduction "Ladies and gentlemen, The Beatles," the foursome made their live American debut on February 9, 1964, from within the girl-crazed, screaming confines of The Ed Sullivan Theater. It was the most-watched program in TV history to that point and remains one of the most-watched programs of all time.

The Beatles played two sets. They opened with "All My Loving," followed by "Till There Was You" and "She Loves You." They returned 35 minutes later with "I Saw Her Standing There" and the number one hit, "I Want To Hold Your Hand." The Beatles appeared on *The Ed Sullivan Show* three more times in person and later submitted several filmed performances.

Sullivan ran his show with an iron fist, and he was known to edit artists' routines when he saw fit. On January 15, 1967, he famously forced the Rolling Stones to change their lyrics from "let's spend the *night* together" to "let's spend some *time* together," much to the chagrin of Mick Jagger, who rolled his eyes directly into the camera each time he sang the revised line.

Sullivan was also quick to take offense if he felt he had been crossed. Eight months after the Rolling Stones incident, Jim Morrison and The Doors were asked to change the lyrics of their song "Light My Fire" and not sing the line "girl we couldn't get much higher" (which Sullivan believed to be a reference to smoking marijuana) during their September

Sullivan promising another really big show.

17, 1967, performance. Legend has it that in the Doors' dressing room that night before the show, Sullivan and a network executive paid a visit to "the boys" as they called the band members (a term which irked the band and got things off on a decidedly wrong foot). They proposed that the band change the lyric to "girl, we couldn't get much better," to which Morrison (half-joking and half-serious) reportedly suggested the alternative "girl you oughta bite my wire"—the humor of which was utterly lost on the stoic Sullivan, who commented that the band "ought to smile a little more." The Doors reluctantly agreed to avoid the word "higher," but when the time came for their live performance, Morrison kept the original lyrics, and Sullivan went ballistic. After the show, The Doors were informed in no uncertain terms, "we were going to book you boys for six more appearances, but now you'll never do the *Sullivan Show* again!" to which Morrison calmly replied, "Hey man, we just did the *Sullivan Show.*" Bo Diddley, Buddy Holly, and Jackie Mason were also objects of Sullivan's ire after clashing with him.

In May of 1963, Bob Dylan was just another aspiring young musician about to release his second album, *The Freewheelin' Bob Dylan*. He was slated to make his first nationwide television appearance on *The Ed Sullivan Show* on May 12. He decided to perform "Talkin' John Birch Paranoid Blues," a satirical blues number skewering the John Birch Society and the red-hunting paranoia associated with it. A few days before the show, Dylan auditioned the song for Sullivan himself, who seemed to have no issue with it. However, during the dress rehearsal on the day of the show, a CBS executive decided Dylan could not perform the song due to its controversial nature. When the show's producer, Bob Precht, informed Dylan of the decision and asked him if he wanted to do something else, he responded, "No, this is what I want to do. If I can't play my song, I'd rather not appear on the show." So instead of choosing another song to perform, a young Bob Dylan—just two weeks shy of his 22nd birthday—walked off the set of the country's highest-rated variety show.

The story received widespread media attention in the days that followed, causing even Sullivan to denounce the network's decision. The publicity from this event may have done more for Dylan's career than the actual appearance would have.

By 1971, the show's ratings were dropping, and CBS canceled it after a 23-year run. The show's cancellation so angered Sullivan that he refused to do a final show. He did, however, host a 25th anniversary special in June 1973.

His wife of 42 years, the former Sylvia Weinstein, died in 1973. He called Sylvia after every program to get her immediate critique.

Modest tomb of the man who brought The Beatles to America.

In September 1974, Sullivan was diagnosed with advanced esophageal cancer. He died on October 13, 1974, at New York's Lenox Hill Hospital. His funeral was attended by 3,000 at St. Patrick's Cathedral, and he is interred in a crypt at the Ferncliff Cemetery in Hartsdale, New York.

Many honors have been afforded to Ed Sullivan. In addition to the studio at Broadway and 53rd Street being named in his honor in 1967, a 44-cent commemorative postage stamp was issued in 2009, and he has a star on the Hollywood Walk of Fame.

If You Go:

Ferncliff Cemetery is well over 100 years old and offers lavish burial spaces. Its oldest mausoleum, "The Cathedral of Memories," houses not only Sullivan but also two legendary Hollywood stars, **Judy Garland** (1922–1969) and **Joan Crawford** (1905–1977).

"The Shrine of Memories" is its second mausoleum, and actor **Basil Rathbone** (1892–1967) is interred. Rathbone is best known for his portrayal of Sherlock Holmes in 14 Hollywood films between 1939 and 1946.

"Rosewood" is Ferncliff's most recent mausoleum and contains **Cab Calloway**'s (1907–1994) remains, one of the premier jazz entertainers. Calloway became nationally-known as a bandleader and star attraction at Harlem's famed Cotton Club. He went on to star on stage and screen for four decades.

A non-celebrity but equally noteworthy occupant of Ferncliff is **Jeffrey Glenn Miller** (1950–1970), one of four college students shot and killed by Ohio National Guardsmen at Kent State University on May 4, 1970. It is Miller's dead body that 14-year-old runaway Mary Ann Vecchio kneels over, screaming, in John Filo's Pulitzer Prize-winning photograph that appeared on the cover of *Newsweek* two weeks later, immediately becoming symbolic of not just Kent State but the entire anti-Vietnam War movement. Miller was cremated, and his ashes were placed in a mausoleum at Ferncliff.

Ferncliff is also known for its in-ground burials in sections located in front of the mausoleums. **Malcolm X** (1925–1965) and writer/activist **James Baldwin** (1924–1987) are two of the most famous ground burials.

24

"The Mayor of MacDougal Street"

Dave Van Ronk

County: Manhattan • City: New York
Buried at First Presbyterian Church
5th Avenue and West 12th Street

He was nicknamed "The Mayor of MacDougal Street." He was a singer-songwriter who played folk, ragtime, and the blues. He befriended and influenced Bob Dylan, Tom Paxton, Phil Ochs, Joni Mitchell, and many other musicians. He received a lifetime achievement award from the American Society of Composers, Authors, and Publishers. His name was Dave Van Ronk.

Van Ronk was born in Brooklyn on June 30, 1936. His family (despite the Dutch sounding name) was mostly Irish. His mother and father separated soon after he was born. He never met his father, so he was raised by his mother and several aunts. When his family moved to Queens, he was sent to catholic school. In his memoir *The Mayor of MacDougal Street*, he recalls an incident that took place when he was in the 7th grade. His teacher, who he claims was named Sister Attila Marie, gave the class an assignment to give a 15-minute presentation on what you want to be when you grow up. When Van Ronk's turn came, he went to the front of the class and began by saying, "What I want to be when I grow up is a migratory worker, which isn't just one thing. I want to travel from town to town doing odd jobs to make enough money to move on." That was as far as he got as Sister Attila Marie came charging at him from the back of the room screaming, "A bum! You want to be a bum." Suffice it to say that school and Van Ronk did not mix well together, and he dropped out when he was fifteen years of age.

Dave Von Ronk

After dropping out of high school, Van Ronk spent the next few years bumming around Lower Manhattan. On two occasions, he shipped out with the Merchant Marines. The life of a sailor could easily have been his chosen profession had fate not intervened. While hitchhiking back to New York after a trip to Chicago, Van Ronk lost his wallet and with it his seaman's papers. Rather than go through the considerable trouble it would take to get them replaced; Van Ronk decided to give the music business a try. His first jobs in music were in traditional jazz bands. He would later say, "We wanted to play traditional jazz in the worst way, and we did." However, as the jazz revival slowly died, Van Ronk began performing blues numbers that he had found while shopping for jazz 78s. One afternoon, as detailed in his memoir, he walked through Washington Square in Greenwich Village when he came upon a guy playing the guitar by fingerpicking. His thumb was picking out the bass notes while the rest of his fingers played the melody. As he watched the musician, he realized that this was something he had to learn. Van Ronk wanted to sing and fingerpick, as he saw it was an ideal way to accompany yourself. He would later credit the incident for beginning his shift to folk music. By 1956 he had become a regular playing in Washington Square.

There were regular Sunday music sessions at Washington Square dating back to the 1940s. By the time Van Ronk joined in, you had needed a permit to play in the square. The permit allowed you to sing and play from two to five as long as there were no drums. Van Ronk liked the no drums rule because it kept out the bongo players, and Van Ronk said that Greenwich Village had bongo players up the wazoo.

The Sunday sessions grew during the mid-fifties and became a tourist attraction. People would gather around the musicians as they performed. Van Ronk possessed a loud voice so he could always make himself heard. In his view, this led to him always drawing a pretty good crowd.

By 1958, Van Ronk was firmly committed to performing using a folk-blues style. He occasionally wrote his songs but, by and large, sang the work of earlier artists and those of his peers in the booming folk revival. He was considered a part of a folk-pop trio with Peter Yarrow, but that didn't work out, and the role went to Noel Paul Stookey, who became Paul in Peter, Paul, and Mary.

At this point, Van Ronk decided that he needed to make a record to get his career going. He had a friend by the name of Paul Clayton who had already recorded several albums. According to Van Ronk, Clayton would meet with Moe Asch from Folkways Records and say something like, "Moe, I was looking through your catalog, and I noticed you don't have a single album of Maine lumberjack ballads." Moe would respond, "I guess that's a pretty serious omission. Do you know anyone who can sing enough of those to make a record?" Clayton would reply, "Well, as it happens . . ."

As luck would have it, Folkways decided that Clayton should record a record with a group. Van Ronk was among the musicians he recruited. The group recorded an album titled *Fo'c'sle Songs and Chanties* by Paul

Clayton and the Fo'c'sle Singers. To his dying day, Van Ronk considered it one of the best records that he had been involved in making, though he admits that it attracted very little attention in his memoir.

Now Van Ronk wanted to make a record on his own. He knew producer Kenny Goldstein, who had worked with Clayton on a number of his Folkways albums. It took a while, but Van Ronk eventually succeeded in convincing Goldstein to record him. While Van Rock wasn't happy with the finished product, the fact that he had made a record for Folkways made it easier for him to find work.

By the early sixties, Van Ronk had a loyal following who regularly attended his village performances. He played primarily at the Gaslight and Gerde's Folk City. His audiences were attracted to his rough voice, and as he said, his choices of songs were most often sung by people who did not possess a pretty voice. Some of the other performers at these clubs included Bob Dylan, Phil Ochs, Noel Stookey, Bill Cosby, Tom Paxton, and Hugh Romney, best known as Wavy Gravy.

Van Ronk met Dylan after watching him perform at the Cafe Wha. As he recalled it, Dylan was new in town with an abrasive voice, and it was tough for him to find work. According to Van Ronk, the only time the Gaslight's owner would use Dylan was when he wanted to clear the place out. Van Ronk recalled the young Dylan frequently crashing on his couch.

Albert Grossman, who managed Van Ronk for a short time, considered making him part of the group that became Peter, Paul, and Mary. While that didn't happen, the trio did record a Van Rock song on their first album. The album sold well, and Van Rock made more money on that song titled "Bamboo" than any he had written.

In 1962, Van Ronk signed a two-album contract with Prestige records. The first album was to be called *Dave Van Ronk, New York's Finest*, but Van Ronk objected because it made him sound like a cop. It was released as *Dave Van Ronk Folksinger*, and the album included what many people regard as his signature song "Cocaine Blues." As he tells it in his memoir, he was so closely associated with the song many thought he wrote it. He tells about running into Jackson Browne in the mid-seventies and

Van Ronk album cover.

Browne telling him he had recorded one of his songs. Hearing this was welcome news to Van Ronk since he would receive royalties from the sale of the record, so he asked Browne, "Which one?" The response he got was "Cocaine Blues." He informed Browne that that was a Gary Davis song.

As the folk wave rolled in the sixties, so did Van Ronk. He was recording an album a year and continued performing and doing some touring. The 1964 reader's poll in a Boston folk magazine named Van Ronk as the favorite visiting performer ahead of Bob Dylan and Phil Ochs. He had also signed a recording contract with a major label Mercury. Dylan stated that he thought the best he could do was to be as big as Dave Van Ronk.

Van Ronk's and Dylan's paths crossed again in the seventies, thanks to Phil Ochs. Ochs organized a benefit concert called "The Friends of Chile—An Evening with Salvador Allende" in 1974. Dylan joined a bill that included Ochs, Van Ronk, Pete Seeger, and Arlo Guthrie in a sing out against the right-wing Chilean general Augusto Pinochet.

The simple plaque marks the final resting place of the Greenwich Village musician.

Unfortunately for Dylan, he got falling-down drunk before his performance. He performed what has been described as an incomprehensible version of "Blowin' in the Wind" while Van Ronk held onto him to keep Dylan from falling over.

When Ochs committed suicide in 1976, Van Ronk was among those who performed at his memorial concert playing his bluesy version of the folk song "He Was A Friend of Mine."

Van Ronk continued to perform and record for the rest of his life. Many believe that he is underestimated as a musician and a blues guitarist. *New York Times* music critic Robert Shelton described Van Ronk as "the musical mayor of MacDougal Street." He added that Van Ronk was Bob Dylan's first New York guru and described his manner as rough and testy, disguising a warm, sensitive core.

Van Ronk died on February 10, 2002, in a New York hospital from cardiopulmonary failure while undergoing postoperative treatment for colon cancer. He was laid to rest in the First Presbyterian Church Cemetery in Manhattan.

If You Go:

See Chapter 8 on **Alexander Hamilton**.

Bibliography

BOOKS

Angelou, Maya. *The Heart of a Woman*. New York: Random House Trade Paperbacks, 2009.

Bowen, Catherine Drinker. *Miracle at Philadelphia: The Story of the Constitutional Convention, May to September 1787*. New York: Little, Brown, 2010.

Bowles, Jerry G. *A Thousand Sundays: The Story of the Ed Sullivan Show*. New York: G.P. Putnam's Sons, 1980.

Caro, Robert. *The Power Broker: Robert Moses and the Fall of New York*. New York: Vintage Books, 1975.

Coffey, David. *Sheridan's Lieutenants: Phil Sheridan, His Generals, and the Final Year of the Civil War*. Wilmington, DE: Rowman & Littlefield Publishers, 2005.

Farley, James A. *Jim Farley's Story: The Roosevelt Years*. Whitefish, Mont.: Kessinger Publishing, 2007.

Farrell, Joe and Joe Farley. *Keystone Tombstones Volume One*. Mechanicsburg, PA: Sunbury Press, 2020.

———. *Keystone Tombstones Volume Two*. Mechanicsburg, PA: Sunbury Press, 2020.

———. *Keystone Tombstones Volume Three*. Mechanicsburg, PA: Sunbury Press, 2020.

Fountain, Charles. *Sportswriter: The Life and Times of Grantland Rice*. Bridgewater, NJ: Replica Books, 2000.

Grant, Ulysses S. *Personal Memoirs of Ulysses S. Grant*. 1886.

Hamilton, Alexander, James Madison, and John Jay. *The Federalist Papers*. New York: Mentor Books, 1961.

Holiday, Billie, and Iris Menéndez. *Lady Sings the Blues*. Barcelona: Tusquets, 2015.

Houdini, Harry. *Houdini: A Magician Among the Spirits*. Amsterdam, The Netherlands: Fredonia Books, 2002.

Kahn, Roger. *The Boys of Summer*. New York: HarperCollins e-Books, 2014.

Kane, Larry. *Lennon Revealed*. England: Running Press (PA), 2005.

King, Alan, and Chris Chase. *Name Dropping: The Life and Lies of Alan King*. New York: Simon & Schuster, 1997.

MacPherson, James M. *Battle Cry of Freedom: The Civil War Era*. London: Penguin, 1990.

Robinson, Jackie, and Alfred Duckett. *I Never Had It Made: An Autobiography*. Hopewell, N.J.: Ecco Press, 1995.

Sales, Soupy. *Soupy Sez!: My Zany Life and Times*. M. Evans & Company, 2003.

Scroop, Daniel Mark. *Mr. Democrat: Jim Farley, the New Deal and the Making of Modern American Politics*. University of Michigan Press, 2009.

Slayton, Robert A. *Empire Statesman: The Rise and Redemption of Al Smith*. New York, NY: Free Press, 2001.

Smith, Jean Edward. *Grant: A Biography.* Newtown, Conn. : American Political Biography Press, 2014.

Stanton, Elizabeth Cady, Ellen Carol DuBois, and Ann D. Gordon. *Eighty Years and More: Reminiscences, 1815-1897.* New York: Simon & Schuster Paperbacks, 2020.

Van Ronk, Dave, and Elijah Wald. *The Mayor of MacDougal Street: A Memoir.* Da Capo Press, 2013.

Weisberger, Bernard A. *America Afire: Jefferson, Adams, and the First Contested Election.* New York, NY: Perennial, 2001.

FILMS

42. Directed by Brian Helgeland. Burbank: Legendary Pictures, 2016.

Baseball. Directed by Ken Burns. Alexandria, Va.: PBS Home Video, 2010.

Lady Sings the Blues. Directed by Sidney J. Furie. Hollywood: Paramount Pictures, 1972.

The Black Hand. Directed by Antonio Racioppi. Rome: Roma Film, 1973.

The Graduate. Directed by Mike Nichols. Hollywood: Embassy Pictures, 1967.

The Jackie Robinson Story. Directed by Alfred E. Green. Hollywood: Eagle-Lion Films, 1950.

ONLINE RESOURCES

Ancestry.com – Family tree information and vital records.

Archive.nytimes.com – for access to *New York Times* articles.

FamousAmericans.net – for information on many individuals.

FindaGrave.com – for burial information, vital statistics, and obituaries.

IMDb.com – for information about movies, television series, actors, and actresses.

Newspapers.com – Hundreds of newspaper articles were accessed—too numerous to mention here.

TeachingAmericanHistory.com – for information on many individuals.

TheHistoryJunkie.com – for information on many individuals.

USHistory.org – for information on many individuals.

Wikipedia.com – for general historical information.

Index

Index

www.ingramcontent.com/pod-product-compliance
Lightning Source LLC
LaVergne TN
LVHW091027080826
845145LV00002B/386

* 9 7 8 1 6 2 0 0 6 4 7 5 7 *